Studies in Writing & Rhetoric

Other Books in the Studies in Writing & Rhetoric Series

Embodied Literacies

Embodied Literacies

Imageword and a Poetics of Teaching

Kristie S. Fleckenstein

SOUTHERN ILLINOIS UNIVERSITY PRESS

Carbondale

Publication partially funded by a subvention grant from The Conference on College
Composition and Communication of the National Council of Teachers of English.

Library of Congress Cataloging-in-Publication Data

Fleckenstein, Kristie S.
  Embodied literacies : imageword and a poetics of teaching / Kristie S.
Fleckenstein.
      p. cm. — (Studies in writing & rhetoric)
  Includes bibliographical references (p.) and index.
    1. English language—Rhetoric—Study and teaching. 2. English language—
  Rhetoric—Study and teaching—Moral and ethical aspects. 3. English language—
  Style—Study and teaching (Higher) 4. Meaning (Philosophy)—Study and teaching
  (Higher) 5. Figures of speech—Study and teaching (Higher) 6. Report writing—
  Study and teaching (Higher) 7. Poetics—Study and teaching (Higher) I. Title.
  II. Series.
  PE1404 .F58 2003
  808'.042'071—dc21   2002152738
  ISBN 0-8093-2526-8 (alk. paper)

Printed on recycled paper. ♻

To my daughters, Anna Lauren and Lindsey Marie

Contents

Acknowledgments

Without a doubt, writing is about invention, the furious exaltation of new ideas being born. But it is also about staying the course. I thank the many people key to both exaltation and endurance: my writing partners Nancy Myers and Sue Hum, who tag teamed throughout this entire process, reading innumerable drafts and demanding stylistic as well as intellectual rigor; my longtime friend Linda Calendrillo, who shared with me twenty-five hundred years of imagistic and rhetorical history; Robert Brooke and his editorial assistants, Maria Montaperto and Virginia Crisco, who saw the promise in this work and whose faith in its completion never flagged; Janice Walker and Bruce Ballenger, who gently and firmly guided this book to its current form.

I also thank my many students for their contribution and for their endurance. They include former students from the mid nineties who generously responded to my requests for permission to refer to their work and our classroom interactions with signed consent forms and, more important, with e-mails, letters, and photographs of their children that updated their lives and demonstrated gratifying enthusiasm for the book. Special thanks to Jessica Bowman and James Copp, whom I first enlisted in this project and who, in response, forwarded e-mails, picture albums, drafts, and peer commentary on their work. I regret that I was unable to tap the richness of their writing and their learning for this book. Stay with me for the next one, guys. I thank as well the graduate students who assisted with the various incarnations of this book: Suocai Su, Xiaolin Li, and Amy McCauley, all of whom read drafts, tracked down sources, and saved me from my own extravagances. I especially appreciate the work of Carmen Siering, who carefully and thoughtfully created the index. Included in my thanks is undergraduate editorial intern Deb Smolsky, who freely contributed her organization skills and indefatigable energy.

I acknowledge the professional support I received during this project: Ball State University, whose faculty grant provided time to write, money to travel, and faith in my ability to bring this project to fruition; Monica Bauer, who walked me through the grant process; Sharon Pinkerton, officer manager extraordinaire, whose wry sense of humor kept me tethered to the ridiculous; Jamie Miles, graphic artist and scholar, who always had time to create something new for me.

I also thank those at Southern Illinois University Press who nursed this book through production. I particularly thank Wayne Larsen for his meticulous copyediting and for his ability to turn an awkward phrase into a graceful one. I also thank Barb Martin for her work on the illustrations.

I thank my family: my older sister Darlene, who inspires me to stay the course by her step-by-step determination to finish a college degree before she reaches retirement; my younger sister Teri, who reminds me that a life in a book is only as rich as a life outside a book (cuckoo, Teri!); my parents, John Sealy and Ila Martin Sealy, and my mother-in-law Anna Morland Fleckenstein, all of whom have taught me that a work of love and a love of work are the same thing.

Finally, I come to my children, Anna Lauren and Lindsey Marie, who weave implicitly and explicitly throughout this book. I thank them for their fascination with this process, their frustration with my mental abstraction, and their patience when I co-opted the computer. You have enriched my life, my teaching, and my writing.

The strengths of this book belong to these and to the many others who contributed in various ways to this project. The weaknesses remain mine.

Embodied Literacies

Introduction

When Words Take Form

> Nothing happens in the "real" world unless it first happens in the images in our heads.
>
> —Gloria Anzaldúa, *Borderlands/La Frontera*

> It [portfolio] all started with a picture of a heart being separated by bold lines.
>
> —Janey, portfolio narrative

"I can't write."

"I'm sorry?" I ask in confusion. It is early afternoon, the end of my second session with my spring semester composition class, and Gloria,[1] one of my students, waylays me in the hall.

She repeats. "I can't write." A pause. "I just wanted you to know—because this is a writing class." We stand together outside our classroom, buffeted by the students streaming past us.

"What makes you think you can't write?" I respond, puzzled.

"I had to take one-oh-two," she offers baldly. A quick glance, immediately lowered. She confesses to the floor her matriculation in our year-long composition sequence designed for underprepared students as if she were a felon coming clean. "I didn't get it then. I won't get it now." An unhappy sigh. "I just wanted to warn you."

"Well, perhaps we could change that?" I ask, tentative and uncertain in the face of such conviction.

"No. I just can't write."

Teacher-scholars have wisely analyzed self-perceptions and beliefs similar to Gloria's from the angle of discourse communities, cognitive blocks, and institutional-cum-societal conditioning. The value of such analyses has been established and validated. While not discounting the importance of reading literacy through a web of textuality, this book focuses on a different dimension of students' literate behaviors. What happens to literacy, to our narratives of its possibilities, its limits, its joys, and its pains, when we picture writing-reading through what art historian Barbara Maria Stafford calls a rival imaginary, one guided by the logic of the image?[2] Stafford argues that "we need to disestablish the view of cognition as dominantly and aggressively linguistic," labeling such linguistic supremacy as "a narcissistic tribal compulsion to overemphasize the agency of *logos* and annihilate rival imaginaries" (7). W. J. T. Mitchell concurs, pointing out that, in the midst of our current linguistic turn, we read the world as a text, which includes reading imagery according to the logic of language. What is needed is a "pictorial turn" in which we picture the world through the logic of the image, a turn that is already taking place (*Picture* 11). Besides picturing the world, we need to picture literacy, to disestablish our definitions of literacy as dominantly and aggressively linguistic. We need to seek an alternative imaginary that enables us to conceive of writing-reading as something more than words, more than language.

Embodied Literacies: Imageword and a Poetics of Teaching explores literacy through a rival imaginary. It places the language arts classroom and teacher at the juncture of image and word to examine the ways in which imagery does and undoes, enables and disables not only the teaching of writing-reading but also the act of writing-reading, for we cannot set the act apart from the teaching. *Embodied Literacies* is predicated on the belief that imagery, the incarnation of meaning in various modes and modalities, is inextricable from the linguistic manifestation of meaning and thus inextricable from the ways in which linguistic meaning is taught. It offers a double vision of writing-reading based on that fusion of image and word, a double vision of literacy as imageword, mutually constitutive, mutually infused. This double vision is then shifted to the classroom, reconfiguring what we teach, how we teach, and how we teach ethically.

Such a multifaceted endeavor—one that imbues both meaning and pedagogy with imagery—comes at a critical time in our cultural history. According to visual critic Nicholas Mirzoeff, our current postmodern crisis is not a product of our textuality. Rather, it is a product of our imagery. "[I]t is the visual crisis of culture that creates postmodernity," he asserts, "not its textuality" (3). Our students, our children, and we ourselves are immersed in a culture that lives its life on-screen and in front of a screen (Mirzoeff 1). We not only endure surveillance from cameras in malls, at ATMs, and in computerized classrooms but also turn the camera on ourselves and others, displaying our lives through web cams, digital videos, and photographs that flicker on the computer screen or are glued in more traditional scrapbooks. Nor is our on-screen life strictly visual. Visual imagery is tangled with images of sound, movement, taste, touch, and smell. From our immersion in surround-sound technology to our positions on theater chairs that gyrate wildly in concert with pictures on the screen or screens around us, we are living at a time when reality and image dissolve on multiple fronts; we create (and market) technology to ensure that dissolution. "With Vega," one Sony advertisement points out, "you don't watch TV, you feel it—in a place called Sony."

We are subject to an overwhelming barrage of images from an overwhelming number of outlets to the extent that we begin to visualize—to conceptualize in imagistic terms—that which is not even an image (Mirzoeff 5).[3] Because of the ubiquity of images within our culture, Stafford wonders "who is still capable of saying what information 'uncontaminated' by instruments and graphics might look like?" (44). As teachers of writing-reading, we are confronted with a similar question: who is still capable of saying what *literacy* "uncontaminated" by instruments and graphics might look like? Living in a culture saturated with images, we evolve literacies marked by those images. Janey, a student in my first-semester composition course, discovers this connection in the course of writing a difficult but rewarding paper. She notes in her portfolio narrative that "[i]t all started with a picture of a heart being separated by bold lines."

Rhetoric and composition scholars with a variety of theoretical perspectives have also recognized the mutuality of visuality and literacy, having explored the nexus of image and word from myriad aspects.[4] Anne Haas Dyson's work highlights especially the influence of images on the literacy acquisition of first-graders. Dyson's two-year ethnographic study of first-graders learning to write and read reveals the importance of what she calls the "performative enactment of an imagined context," a context derived to a large degree from the popular media (368). A goal of her study, Dyson explains, is to help "illuminate a quality of contemporary childhood ignored in most literacy learning research—its media-saturated nature" (369). In his work on the influence of media and literacy in the new millennium, Peter Smagorinsky argues for an expanded definition of literacy, one that encompasses the multiple meanings embedded within his preferred term: *composing*. Language does not have "exclusive properties for enabling people to construct and represent meaning," he points out, and our literacy practices and pedagogy will have to account for our expanded means of representation ("Snippets" 278).

Because imagery is an inescapable part of our psychological, social, and textual lives, it needs to be an integral part of our epistemologies and of our literacy teaching. By failing to attend to imagery, or doing so only elliptically, we cannot adequately address how our images imprison and free us, how they hurt and heal us, and how they oppress and transform us. We cannot address how meaning is aesthetic, embodied, and spiritual at the same time that it is intellectual, communal, and secular. What is necessary for our meanings and our classrooms is a double dialectic, a double vision of literacy as image and word, as *imageword*.

Embodied Literacies: Imageword and a Poetics of Teaching is permeated with and organized by that dialectical doubling on multiple layers: the doubling of embodiment as both incarnation and unification, the doubling of image and word, of writing-reading, and of a poetics of meaning and of teaching. I have chosen to use *imageword* as my core term to highlight these mutually constitutive partnerships, emphasizing especially the inextricability of language and imagery in any literate act. Image and word are always melded in meaning. A word on a page is an image, as is the space within which it is ensconced. Physically shaped according to the dictates of such professional organizations as the Modern Language Association and the American Psychological Association, an academic essay itself is an image, a kind of textual art. In the thrall of the printed page, we might forget or ignore the imagistic aspect of textuality, but the evolution of digital technologies forces this realization upon us. From visual poetics in which the verbal form of a poem morphs into different shapes at the twitch of a mouse to MOOs and chat rooms where we watch our words scroll across a screen, the digital realm emphasizes repeatedly the quality of text as art, as image.[5] The rise of "netsex," language-mediated erotic interaction in the absence of physical contact, relies on the inseparability of image and word (McRae).[6] The term *imageword* reminds us of this inevitable linkage of image and word in meaning.

Finally, by blending image and word, I resist the inclination to configure imagery as a verbal or cultural artifact, one that can be "read" like a text. In the rhetorical history of the West, imagery has been included in the canons of memory and style; the former has virtually disappeared from our pedagogical consideration and the latter has been co-opted by poetics at least since the Renaissance. Since the seventeenth century especially, imagery has been valued predominantly for its role in literature and reading.[7] A central goal of *Embodied Literacies* is to destabilize the divisions and the implicit linear cause-effect sequencing between image and word, writing and reading, meaning and teaching by reconstituting these categories and their relationships as imageword. This book reframes imagery not as an artifact, although it can be that, but more important, as a process by which we create and respond to that artifact. Simultaneously, it reframes text as image. Within this frame, asking which comes first—image or word, writing or reading, meaning or teaching—is tantamount to asking whether the chicken precedes the egg. The term *imageword* highlights these twisting loops and circular cause-effect relationships, affording us a double vision. Thus, a literacy and a literacy praxis framed through imageword do not require that we denigrate language and instead glorify the formative and transformative power of imagery. They require that we focus neither on imagery nor on language but on the necessary melding of imageword in meaning. They require that we move beyond the binary of word and image into a poetics of meaning from which we can then move into a poetics of teaching.

A systematic examination of a fundamentally aesthetic experience, a poetics teases out the "laws" that structure such experiences. A poetics is necessary when the phenomenon under investigation is primarily composed of and by imagination, aided by both thought and reality. Rather than seeking to identify causal relationships, a poetics focuses on resonance, the "threshold of being" where we experience the "reverberation" of imagination, where we are those reverberations (Bachelard xvi). A writing-reading pedagogy that creates itself out of the play of imagery and language demands a poetics, for as Michèle Le Dœuff explains, interpretation cannot be understood outside poetics: "Playing on a calculus of pain, a distribution of affective values, it [imagery] works a seduction, produces and structures a fantasy. At this point interpretation cannot do without poetics" (12). At this point, neither can teaching.

Learning is not primarily linguistic; it is not primarily imagistic. Rather, it results from the double play of language and image in myriad forms. As such, we need to position ourselves within the fusion of image and word, within imageword so that we write-read from the center of a poetics. *Embodied Literacies* details such repositioning, offering an alternative imaginary, one based on a theory of imageword and an ecological system of meaning. The theory of imageword is predicated on double logics: the logic of imagery that unmarks boundaries and the logic of discourse that marks boundaries. The transaction among discursive and imagistic logics results in a fluid, dynamic, ecological meaning. Central to that ecological meaning is the quality of dissolving and resolving boundaries, a quality that also serves as the organizing principle of the book, moving us from a theory of imageword to praxis of imageword.

Chapter 1 opens with a brief polemic for a poetics of meaning, offering four reasons for the embodiment of literacy through imagery. I then provide a rival imaginary based on the double logics of imageword, describing the shape and function of those logics as well as their necessary transaction. I define *meaning* as an ecology in which the mutually constitutive logics of imagery and language complement and clash in a writhing network of reciprocal loops. As a statement about imageword, meaning exists only as long as the pathways that constitute image and word exist.

I turn to literacy in chapter 2, plotting the implications of imageword's double logics for our students' writing-reading. An imageword ecology is configured within four permeable parameters: bodies, cultures, places, and times. As imageword slips across the porous boundaries of bodies, cultures, places, and times, it mutates, metamorphosing into different shapes: body imagery, cultural imagery, and so forth. Literacy evolves at these sites of change, in these moments of permutation, acting out of and acting out this movement. I describe the embodied literacies that materialize at these four sites, underscoring the value that each transformation holds for us as teachers, moving us beyond a poetics of imageword into a poetics of teaching.

By defining literacy as that which emerges from the dissolution and resolution of boundaries as imageword moves across four permeable planes, I open the door to a different literacy praxis. In chapters 3, 4, and 5 and the conclusion, I walk through that open door, exploring the answer to four crucial questions: what do we teach, what do we teach with, how do we teach, and how do we teach ethically? In chapter 3, I describe the shape and the dynamic of a poetics of teaching. Extending my discussion of literacy in chapter 2, I identify the three embodied literacies—somatic, polyscopic, and lateral—that serve as the subject of our writing-reading classrooms and organize these literacies via a dynamic of immersion, emergence, and transformation.

In chapter 4, I address the subject matter—the slippery texts— necessary for a poetics of teaching. The texts with which we choose to teach embodied literacies slip across three boundaries—topics, genres, and media—blurring the traditional demarcations. I describe each area of slippage, then provide three illustrations of the specific deployments of literacies and texts through body biographies, spatial geographies, and autobiographical diffraction.

What we teach, however, is only a part of a poetics of teaching. The essence of a poetics is that it eschews linear, causal relationships with their reifying implications, attending instead to reverberations of imageword's double logics. Therefore, in chapter 5, I address how we organize our instruction and our learning environments so that we maintain the openness and dynamism so characteristic of imageword. Drawing on imageword's double logics, I argue for the value of double mapping, the process of juxtaposing the complementary and conflicting logics of imageword. I define double mapping, describe how to double map our instructional environment, and then offer three double-mapped writing-reading units aimed at fostering somatic, polyscopic, and lateral literacies.

Finally, in my conclusion, I explore the ethical resonances of an imageword ecology, suggesting that it requires us to situate ourselves in two places at once: within the weave of community and within the demands of civic space. I illustrate the possibilities and responsibilities of this double positioning by turning to a troublesome moment in a graduate class, tracing how a teaching stance might grow out of the resonance across somatic, polyscopic, and lateral literacies.

By conceiving of literacy and of literacy teaching through the double logics of imageword, we position our classrooms and ourselves on the uncertain cusp of a dynamic and embodied meaning. We balance on the unstable ground where realities materialize and dematerialize in response to our own literate moves. The gift that we derive from our balancing act is that we have the means to change our dreams even as we dream them. As imageword, we are both image and word simultaneously; we are poised always at the sites of changing borders. Thus, we need not be trapped within the tentacles of an image or a word. Rather, an imageword holds for us the seeds of its own dissolution and resolution into something different, perhaps even something better. And so I end with my beginning.

Gloria sits in my office, clinging to her book bag, a material anchor in a sea of words.

"Think about your paper as a conversation with your reader," I urge. "Think, 'okay, what is my reader going to say in response to that sentence? What is she going to think?' Then write a response to that."

Her arms tighten against the despair, against the painful, trapped words.

"But I don't know what my reader will say. I don't know my reader."

Silence.

"Well," I offer tentatively, "you could draw your reader first. Tape the picture in front of you. Write to the picture—write with the picture."

She looks up, jolted, if only momentarily, out of her desolation.

"Write to a picture? Writers do that?"

"Yes," I confess. "Writers do that."

1 / Imageword: An Alternative Imaginary for a Poetics of Meaning

> There are times in life when the question of knowing if one can think differently than one thinks, and perceive differently than one perceives, is absolutely necessary if one is to go on looking and reflecting at all.
>
> —Michel Foucault, *The Use of Pleasure*

> One of my main focuses [for images that belittle women] was Brittany [*sic*] Spears, because she is an example of using her body for power. I just wanted to prove that women still have a long way to go to be looked at as equal[. . .]. Because if they were equal to men, then they wouldn't have to use sex and their body to get attention, they could just be themselves.
>
> —Katherine, portfolio narrative

Anna stands patiently by my bed, a darker shadow in the shadows of a four A.M. rainy predawn. "Can I come into bed with you?" she whispers urgently. "The birds are coming through my window." Hearing the rain peck on the house, I lift the covers, and she quickly climbs over my body to lie curled against me, warmed and protected by a body that loves her. For the next ninety minutes, until the five-thirty alarm, she will drowse but not sleep, fearing that her nightmare birds will chip successfully through screen and glass if she sleeps too securely.

My elder daughter's night terrors began when she was a toddler and continue unabated. Giant green grasshoppers invade her dreams, grasshoppers whose headless forms open to reveal her struggling body, as well as mine, consumed in the body of the monster. A jack-in-the-box, tinkling "All Around the Mulberry Bush," pops open and drags her down into the dark box with him. Huge, wiggling silverfish drop on her bed from the attic, holding her down

with their weight, smothering her with their feathery forms, absorb-
ing her into their mass. When the lights are out and the dark-
ness eats at her courage, Anna becomes frequent prey to the creep-
ing terrors her dreams conjure for her. For Anna, images are not
ephemeral fancies. For Anna, images have weight, power, and tenacity. She is not alone in this belief.

"I am 21 years old and I am not blind," Aletha writes, and what
she sees is her culture's

> subliminal message: the white dolls, namely Barbie, reflect
> how revered and wanted the American white girls are,
> whereas, the black, shelved, underproduced dolls are sec-
> ond and unchosen; a direct reflection on black females in
> our society. Because I am one of these black females, I can-
> not help but notice these subtleties.

Trapped in a complex web of cultural images that systematically
erode her body and her self-esteem, Aletha sees herself through
those dominant images: "I am a black doll sitting on the shelf and I
cannot change that." Fully grown, past the age of night terrors,
Aletha understands, like Anna, that images can wield a bruising
force, that monsters still leap from the closet.

The prevalence of imagery in our lives indicates the extent to
which imagery needs to transform our theories of meaning. Locked
within the word, we cannot understand how images hurt or heal us.
We cannot understand how images embody meaning at the same
time that they render it communal. We cannot understand how images free the spirit while they simultaneously imprison it within a
frame of social strictures. We require a poetics of meaning, a necessary prelude to a poetics of teaching, for, to reconfigure our teaching, we must first reconfigure the sense of meaning that permeates
that teaching. In this chapter, I propose an alternative imaginary for
a poetics of meaning. I begin with a polemic, offering four reasons
for lodging meaning on a "threshold of being," vibrating to the "reverberation of imagination" (Bachelard xvi). Then I delineate a poetics of meaning, proposing as my rival imaginary the theory of

imageword offered in three parts. I describe in turn the corporeal logic of image and the discursive logic of word, the circular play of those logics in imageword, and the ecological system of meaning produced by that circular dynamic. Within this imaginary, meaning is conceived as a product of the mutually constitutive imageword. It is a statement about imageword. Such a poetics of meaning expands the parameters of literacy and literacy teaching to embrace the dreams that haunt us and the images that craft us, enabling us to address not only the linguistic and the imagistic aspects of meaning but, more important, the nexus between the two. When we reposition our meanings here on the threshold of being, resonating to the reverberations of the imagination, we can also reposition our teaching.

A Polemic for a Poetics of Meaning

There are four important reasons for transforming meaning and teaching into a poetics. First, and perhaps most pressing, is the extent to which imagery permeates our lives. Thought, meaning, and texts are all infused with imagery. Like Anna and Aletha, we are all awash internally and externally in a continuous onslaught of imagery. Our waking and our sleeping lives, our social and private lives are punctuated by the chaotic flow of images, those that we see, smell, hear, feel, and taste. We carry those images with us, consciously and unconsciously seeking their guidance, submitting to their coercion, as we compose grocery lists, remember our students' names, and respond to *X-Files*. In fact, in *De Anima*, a work that sets forth his philosophy of mind, Aristotle tells us that images are the precursors, the necessary ground for deliberative thought. Without images, there is no possibility of thought. Twenty-five centuries later, neuroscientist Antonio Damasio calls imagery the basis of our core and autobiographical identities, echoing Oliver Sacks, who links imagery with the coherence of the human soul.

In addition, without imagery, we would also be unable to create textual meaning for ourselves and for others. Ann E. Berthoff implicitly advocates a poetics of meaning when she defines composing as an act of the imagination, grounding any act of meaning making within the process of seeing. Berthoff asserts that meaning making is a product of the "prime agent of human perception," inextricable from perception and from metaphor (Coleridge qtd. in *Sense* 20). She identifies perception—the act of seeing—and concept formation as "radically alike": "When we see, we compose" (31). Like image formation, composing "is a matter of seeing relationships" (36), the essential premise for Berthoff's composition text *Forming/ Thinking/Writing:* "Seeing relationships is the book's working concept of thinking" (5). The act of composing with writing cannot be severed from the act of composing with our senses.

This realization that thought, meaning, and texts are crafted out of images weaves throughout much of Western intellectual history and surfaces as a consistent strategy in education.[1] Developmentally, the decisive moment in the evolutionary history of humanity occurred not when homo sapiens uttered the first word but when imagery shaped the need and desire to utter that word as a means to share an image (Langer, *Philosophical* 42). Lev Vygotsky, famed for choosing the word as the smallest unit of psychological meaning and for transforming Piaget's egocentric speech into internalized social speech, acknowledges the same weft and weave of imagery as the matrix of all thought:

> When I wish to communicate the thought that today I saw a barefoot boy in a blue shirt running down the street, I do not see every item separately. I conceive of all this in one thought [. . .]. In his [a speaker's] mind the whole thought is present at once [. . .]. A thought may be compared to a cloud shedding a shower of words. (150)

Slipping through our everyday discourse, imagery configures community by connecting us to one another as members of that community, a phenomenon crucial to Robert Hariman and John Louis Lucaites' approach to photojournalism. In addition, sociolinguist Deborah Tannen in *Talking Voices* describes how the mental creation of an imagistic scene functions as an engagement strategy in our daily verbal discourse, as well as in our literary discourse. Finally, Michèle Le Dœuff claims that all discourse, even that of philosophy, the most abstract of disciplines, cannot exist without imagery. Textual imagery enables a system to say what cannot be said with words, what cannot be uttered within the constraints of the discourse itself, but what must be said for that discourse to survive. To mean, to communicate, and to connect requires that we situate ourselves at the point where imagery and language meet, confirming the need for a poetics of meaning to frame our literacy teaching.

Our students' evolving literacies, perhaps more than our own literacies, reflect the extent to which imagery and language blur and thus the extent to which we require a poetics of meaning. As a child of the 1950s, I did not experience television or attend my first film until I was eight years old. I did not own a computer until I returned to graduate school for a doctorate in 1985, and I traversed the Internet for the first time, entering through a gateway of icons and navigating through the same iconography, in 1994 when a student young enough to be my son walked me through the process of setting up a modem and accessing the university server. Thus, my literacy acquisition was tightly tied to print media. My children, however, born in the 1990s, were raised on *Sesame Street,* treated to Disney films, and immersed in the computer world of Jump Start Preschool before I first dipped my toe into the surf of the Internet. Balancing themselves on the cusp between word and image, our children and our students inhabit a transgressive world where Pokémon—Japanese pocket monsters who began their existence as video game characters—morph from the narrow world of the arcade to the textual world of trading cards, to television cartoons, to the print of novels, to the action of summer films. They have eaten so fully of the fruit of the image that the habits of imagery are at the marrow of their intellectual, social, and textual existence. Immersed in a life replete with images, our students already locate themselves and their writing-reading at the suture points of image and word. Raised with Nintendo 64, Game Boy, television, videos, and the hypermedia of Digimon.com, they automatically juggle the frequently conflicting constraints of word and image. Here, in this generation's developing literacy, the neat demarcations between image and word explode, and my children and my students swim with the currents of an image-saturated culture (Mirzoeff). The second reason we need a poetics of meaning lies with the paradox that imagery evokes. Why does the pictorial turn seem to be happening now? W. J. T. Mitchell asks in *Picture Theory*. Because imagery is a paradox specific to our moment, he replies. The enthusiasm for imagery, reflected in its overwhelming influx through electronic reproduction, is simultaneously coupled with anxiety evoked by that imagery's power (15). As imagery proliferates, so increases our resistance to it. Thus, we are drawn to imagery at the same time that we are repelled by it. The same paradox structures our lives as teachers. We are both encouraged and discouraged from exploring imagery. On the one hand, we are urged to theorize about "visual literacy" and incorporate such literacy into our classroom praxis. The recent *Standards for the English Language Arts,* composed jointly by the National Council of Teachers of English (NCTE) and the International Reading Association (IRA), includes an explicit focus on visual literacy: "We must therefore challenge students to analyze critically the texts they view and to integrate their visual knowledge with their knowledge of other forms of language," *Standards* states (7). Such edicts reflect NCTE and IRA's acknowledgement of the highly saturated visual culture within which our students grow to citizenship and to literacy. The collection *Images in Language, Media, and Mind* edited by Roy F. Fox is predicated on the belief that imagery is as important as language in the creation of meaning. As Fox points out in his introduction,

> Today our inner and outer worlds are dominated by images
> —whether we receive them, send them, or think them;
> whether they happen inside our heads or outside our skin;
> whether we find them in proposals or poems, in casual conversations or environmental impact statements, in dreams
> or in ads for Dodge trucks or on computer screens, in films
> or scientific reports or Pepsi commercials [. . .]. The image, in whatever form, is the primary underlying structure

in language, media, and mind—our most basic element in
communicating and creating. (x)

Similarly, the collection *Language and Image in the Reading-Writing
Classroom* highlights the reciprocity of language and image, offering
specific strategies for integrating mental, graphic, and verbal imagery into our writing-reading classrooms (Fleckenstein, Calendrillo, and Worley). The explicit acknowledgement of the imagistic
nature of our culture and our meaning, particularly with the proliferation of the image-laden World Wide Web, leads scholars such as
Kathleen E. Welch and Jay David Bolter to emphasize the shifts in
literacy that imagery evokes and the demands it makes on us to re-
conceptualize our meaning making. In *Art on My Mind,* bell hooks
calls our attention to the necessity of a visual politics—an examination of "the way that race, gender, and class shape art practices
(who makes art, how it sells, who values it, who writes about it)"
(xii)—particularly in regards to art but applicable to ways of seeing
that we internalize and enforce, at times to our own detriment.
Thus, we are, on the one hand, encouraged to investigate imagery,
especially visual imagery, and integrate it into our classroom practices.

    The paradox of imagery is that while we are encouraged to pur-
sue it, we are also discouraged from pursuing it by two contradictory positions that arise from two different disciplines, both of
which influence writing-reading studies. We are discouraged from
integrating imagery by the status of imagery in cognitive psychology,
a discipline that manifests itself in various guises throughout writing-
reading. Regardless of the groundbreaking work of Stephen Kosslyn
in *Ghosts in the Mind's Machine,* in which he provides a rationale for
the existence and study of mental images as significant elements of
humanity's inner life, mental imagery is still regarded by the majority of cognitive psychologists as inconsequential. Like the light-
emitting diodes on a computer, they argue, imagery does not contribute to or influence human intellect (Pylyshyn). Images might
be flashy and colorful, but these mental LEDs have nothing to do
with the mind's creation of knowledge because all knowledge is

propositionally based in amodal, linguistically coded structures. Therefore, imagery is just a "surface" ripple, a byproduct of these amodal relationships, letting us know that the mind-machine is working. Like a computer's LEDS, mental imagery is epiphenomenal and, thus, of no real interest to psychologists seeking to understand human cognition. This position hits closest to home in writing-reading studies where schema theory, an explanatory construct based on amodal relationships, remains a formidable influence (Adams and Collins; Pearson and Stephens). Current conceptualizations of schema theory eschew imagery in spite of the fact that Sir Frederic Bartlett, the father of schema theory, bucked the behaviorist tide in the 1930s to posit a critical role for imagery in the construction and reconstruction of perception, memory, and knowledge. Mark Sadoski and Allan Paivio have critiqued the limitations of schema theory's amodal bias. Jointly and with Ernest Goetz, they argue that schema theory's recent manifestation (as opposed to Bartlett's initial construction) cannot account for either the evocation or the function of imagery and emotion in literacy activities. They offer Paivio's dual coding theory (DCT) as an alternative, one that provides greater explanatory power and flexibility.[2] However, regardless of Sadoski and Paivio's cogent criticisms and their application of DCT to pedagogy (*Imagery and Text*), schema theory remains the dominant framework for work in writing-reading. Thus, the cognitive paradigm by which many of us conceptualize the creation and the teaching of meaning automatically denigrates imagery as nonessential, trapping us in the paradox of encouragement and discouragement.

We are also discouraged from integrating imagery in our teaching by the status of imagery, especially visual imagery, in French continental philosophy. Influential in American postsecondary theorizing, French continental philosophy ascribes so much power to the visual system that it explicitly and systematically demands an erasure of the visual because of its formidable role in tyranny and colonization (Jay, *Downcast*). This is the anxiety to which Mitchell refers, an anxiety that increases proportionately in relation to the prevalence of imagery. Historian Martin Jay labels this denigration of imagery *antiocularcentrism*. He traces this attitude to an erroneous association of vision with logocentrism, the belief that "seeing" provides unmediated access to a foundational and verifiable reality.[3] Jay connects ocularcentrism to the seventeenth-century perspectivalism of Cartesian philosophy and Descartes's work with optics, which positions the observer as disembodied and nonparticipatory, like the photographer behind the camera who records reality without interpreting it. This unmediated view from nowhere (or everywhere) frames the subject within a certain place but frees the observer from any connection to the subject (or to the place). Within the context of Cartesian perspectivalism, the observer is never a part of that which is observed, just as the photographer can never be a part of the photograph.[4] Antiocularcentrism is a rejection of Cartesian perspectivalism, a move that simultaneously rejects all vision and all visual imagery.[5]

Proliferating yet threatening, imagery pulls us into a paradox, and our confusion ensuing from these mixed messages—encouragement and discouragement—tends to dissuade many of us from exploring imagery at all. Such dissuasion prevents us from understanding imagery's necessary presence in the creation of our own meaning or our students' reliance on it. But we cannot resolve the paradox by simply dismissing imagery or returning it "to naïve mimesis, copy or correspondence theories of representation, or a renewed metaphysics of pictorial presence" (Mitchell, *Picture* 16). Rather, we must embrace the paradox without resolving it. To do so requires a poetics of meaning, one that offers a "postlinguistic, postsemiotic rediscovery of the picture as a complex interplay between visuality, apparatus, institutions, discourse, bodies, and figurality" (16).

In addition to proliferation and paradox, the third reason we need a poetics of meaning grows out of the complexity of imagery. We can neither categorize imagery neatly nor limit it to a single modality. If we could simply reduce imagery to a copy, a representation, empty of meaning except that which is endowed by language, we would not require a poetics. But the nature of imagery is both protean and amorphous. Imagery just does not lend itself to a neat, easy, or stable definition. Rather, imagery is messy and tends to make teaching messy as well. It is, as French philosopher Gaston Bachelard notes, more a case of resonance and reverberation than of sharply delineated categories. For instance, it is difficult to demarcate the line that separates imagery and language, as illustrated in verbal imagery.[6] Then, it is also difficult to separate different categories of images—perceptual, graphic, mental, verbal—from one another, a process that cannot be pursued without language, further blurring the line between image and word. In *Iconology* Mitchell claims that the separations (and confluences) among perceptual image, graphic image, mental image, and verbal image are all matters of language, specifically matters of the disciplinary language by means of which a particular kind of image is defined. He resolves this dilemma by offering a definition of imagery as a family of resemblances. Here, resemblances among images can be traced with a genealogical family tree. All members are connected, but not all members are connected by means of the same characteristics. Such a means of defining imagery, however, leaves teacher-scholars in an uneasy territory where neither map—the definitions—nor the territory—the image itself—is stable. We cannot determine with any facility where perception ends and mental imagery begins. Nor can we determine where mental imagery ends and verbal imagery begins, if, in fact, a verbal image can even exist within a mental image. Furthermore, we run aground on the relationship between graphic imagery—which exists "out there" as a phenomenon accessible on its own terms to everyone—and perception and memory. These issues, lacking definitive responses, contribute to the need for a poetics, one that enables teachers to tackle imagery as a product of resonance.

In addition to these conundrums of categorization, the problem with the modality—the sensory arena—of imagery underscores the need for a poetics. While most of us tend to associate imagery with the visual but static realm—one of "snapshot" memories or "albums" of mental images that we shuffle through to find the "right" one—imagery encompasses a range of modalities that nest within one another. We live within and construct our worlds out of an array of different sensory images: "[A]s most of our awareness of the world is a continual play of impressions, our primitive intellectual equipment is largely a fund of images, not necessarily visual, but often gestic, kinesthetic, verbal or what I can only call 'situational'" (Langer, *Mind* 59). It is a fragment of sound, not a scrap of visual memory, that pulls Nancy Sòmmers back into her childhood: "I cannot think of my childhood without hearing voices, deep, heavily accented, instructive German voices" (23). For Proust, it is the taste of madeleine dipped into tea that tumbles him into the past. And, for me, it is the smell of sizzling bacon that resurrects the ghosts of Christmas. We are all subject to the tug of imagery in all its sensory richness. Snatches of music replay themselves internally, many times to our intense irritation. The remembered taste, perhaps the guilty taste, of last night's chocolate mousse makes us salivate for more. We choose a silk blouse (or scorn a tie) because of the sensation against skin (and throat). We rely on body images to get us up the stairs in the dark, to hit a twelve-inch softball out of the infield, to play "Heart and Soul" on the piano.[7]

Imagery comes in an unending stream and a range of individual modalities. Rarely do these modalities remain neatly demarcated. Images tend to nest a range of senses, resulting in meanings that are collaborative products of sound, sight, and touch, providing full and resonant (what Sandra Harding would call robust) significance to meaning. "Seeing" doesn't occur alone or in isolation but is accompanied by feeling. After all, the physiological system of visualization includes the apparatus to detect texture. Furthermore, touching frequently evokes colors; sounds carry with them visions and visceral twinges, each suggesting the nesting of imagery. It is this nested quality that makes imagery such a powerful strategy in desensitization therapy, during which a patient learns to defang a phobia by imagining the very thing he or she fears. It is this nested quality that Lamaze training offers to expectant mothers as a shield against labor pains. And it is this nested quality that poets exploit in synesthesia, the combination of senses from different domains, such as in "blue taste" or "silvered sound." Rather than reducing imagery to a single dimension, a poetics of meaning highlights an image's multidimensionality and by doing so renders our work as literacy teachers multidimensional.

Finally, the fourth and last reason we need a poetics of meaning is the imperative to push beyond visual literacy. Because of the overwhelming barrage of senses associated with imagery, what happens too frequently when imagery does become a subject of study (or a pedagogical strategy) is that it is simplified to a single visual dimension, a result of this visually saturated age in which display is the dominant mode of validation. A visual image is isolated from— that is, treated as isolatable from—other modalities and serves as the sole focus of imagistic literacy. Visual literacy reduces the confusion inherent in imagery by limiting what constitutes imagistic literacy to that which is visually palpable (and, thus, can be ostensibly "shared" as a common text-phenomenon between teacher and student, scholar and scholar). While visual imagery is important, such a reductive mapping of imagery is based on two errors: it replicates an ocularcentric view that removes the constructive influence of seer, and it denigrates or ignores other equally important aspects of imagery.[8]

A poetics of meaning enables us to attend to these myriad facets of imagery. For example, Aristotle claims that the realm of touch, including kinesthetic imagery—that is, experiencing the feel of an action without actually performing it—is second only to visualization in its cognitive power. Aristotle places *orexis* at the heart of all change—intellectual, emotional, physical. *Orexis,* which Martha Craven Nussbaum in her translation of Aristotle's *De Motu Animalium* defines as a desire that requires a reaching out to one's environment, is kinesthetically based; therefore, change is kinesthetic. Muscles bunching during an exam, fingers twitching when we stumble on a good idea, the inclination of the body during intense listening all testify to the physiological image necessary for any movement: that of the mind, the heart, and the body. Bartlett's schema theory suggests that we construct (and reconstruct) knowledge on the basis of a feeling; thus, we all evolve mental and physical proprioception. Elizabeth Bates in the *Emergence of Symbols* accords kinesthetic imagery a foundational role in language acquisition, pointing out that a child learns the definition of *spoon* by using a spoon to stir imaginary cake batter. The word is the movement. Cognitive psychologist Rand Spiro, a scholar who works predominantly in reading theory, claims that "ideas" have a visceral feel. Although Spiro traces the connections between knowledge and kinesthetic imagery back to Bartlett, he could as well have quoted psychologist Eugene Gendlin. Gendlin's concept of felt sense underscores the kinesthetic foundation of thought, the necessary "underbelly of thought." A poetics of meaning undercuts the tendency to conceive of imagery in terms of visual literacy and reconnects us to the entire range of the human sensorium.

We need a poetics of meaning where imagery is more than just another text, more than a separate mental system that interfaces with language, more than a one-dimensional strategy. To understand and teach while sensitive to the images that haunt Anna's dreams and circumscribe Aletha's body image, we need an alternative imaginary that enables us to theorize the inextricable play of image and word in meaning.

An Alternative Imaginary for a Poetics of Meaning

The alternative imaginary I propose is based on the dynamics of imageword in which the logic of image and the logic of word are joined in a mutually constitutive system. This rival imaginary embraces the fluid, recursive movement of image into word and back again, casting meaning as neither image nor word but as a statement about the dance of both, infused with both. There are three key aspects of imageword. First is the idea of double logics: imagery's corporeal *is* logic and word's discursive *as-if* logic. Second is the circular, looping movement of these logics, a movement that underscores the inseparability of imageword. Third is the ecological system that results from the dance of imageword crisscrossing its own permeable borders.

First, imageword is a product of double logics. An image, regardless of modality or form, evolves from and coheres by means of a special kind of logic: the logic of *is*, a logic that unmarks rather than marks boundaries. Troping Blaise Pascal, who muses in the *Pensées* that the heart has its reasons that reason knows not of, Gregory Bateson calls imagery an "algorithm of the heart," one possessing its own grammar and organization. An image is marked by its ana-logic, or *is* logic, which operates according to the grammar of metaphor.[9] As Bateson explains, imagery functions via the logic underlying "syllogism in grass": Grass dies. Men die. Men are grass. Considered bad logic by logicians because it affirms the consequent and considered bad grammar by linguists because it lacks digital systematism, *is* logic resonates to the union of subjects, to the unmarking of boundaries separating classes. Tied to the primary processes, *is* logic contains no "not," no linguistic markers indicating modality (indicative, imperative, subjunctive), no tenses (except the present), no means to divide elements into classes. As a result, it cannot discriminate between the image it creates and the random reality it orders. Through *is* logic, the line separating order and disorder, pattern and chaos, disappears. Thus, when we dream, we are unable to separate the reality from the dream, the sound of the raindrops from the sounds of birds pecking through the window. The dream is the reality. While we may assign symbolic value to dream elements after the fact, the moment of experience, the moment of performance is the reality. Primary attention is focused not on subjects but on relationships: Men are grass. Raindrops are birds. In a narrow sense, the relationships within corporeal logic are those between self and other, self and environment. As a result, the subject matter of imagery is feeling, what Le Dœuff identifies as a calculus of pain.

As Bateson and others have argued, *is* logic serves as the grammar by which the reality, the materiality, of our natural world is created. *Is* logic is corporeal logic. Imagery and materiality are inextricable. For example, our neurophysiology operates via imagery's *is* logic (Damasio; Greenfield). All biological life is infused with this corporeal logic (Bateson and Bateson 26–30). In the preverbal realm of biology, Bateson reminds us, there is nothing except imagery. Life existed for millions of years before the first word was ever spoken and will continue to exist after the last voice is silenced. "It becomes evident that metaphor is not just pretty poetry, it is not either good or bad logic, but is in fact the logic upon which the biological world has been built," Gregory Bateson explains (Bateson and Bateson 30). Imagistic communication is not optional; it is required. Without it our material reality would not exist. The bodies and the environments we inhabit are inseparable from imagistic communication, from corporeal *is* logic.

The corporeal logic of imagery renders all images fluid and constructed. An image is not something that we perceive; it is a process that we enact. A common error, Bartlett wrote in *Remembering* more than seventy years ago, is the belief that imagery is lifeless and fixed, either in memory or in reality. Instead, he argues, "[I]images are mobile, living, constantly undergoing change, under the persistent influence of our feelings and ideas" (15).[10] As a process, imaging is a verb, an action that parses the chaos of reality into specific patterns. As a product, an image is one of the patterns of its own selection process, subject to continual alteration, for images shift "to form structures which do not correspond with anything that has ever been present, in a concrete sensory fashion, to the observer" (Bartlett 14–15). The verb *imaging* is transitive, and its direct object is always itself, the noun *image*. Solipsistic though it may sound, imaging—the process of creating patterns—creates an image that turns around to create the very process from which it was created. Process and product come to be simultaneously. Neither precedes the other. Thus, image is action, agent, and object jumbled together within its own tangled hierarchy because it is inextricably immersed in the relationships that create it as it creates those relationships. Regardless of modality (touch, sight, sound, etc.) or manifestation (graphic, verbal, mental), an image exists by means of the relationships it creates; yet those relationships are at the same time a product of its existence.

It is difficult to wrap our minds around the fact that an image is something that we construct as it constructs us, not something stable that we perceive. Everything that we know subjectively about an image contradicts the idea that an image exists both as a constellation of relationships and a creator of that constellation. Beyond

the realm of dreams and hallucinations, what we imagine is that
which exists (or once existed) outside us, whether we are feeling it,
seeing it, hearing it, or remembering it. But as Bateson points out,

> [W]hen I aim my eyes at what I think is a tree, I receive an
> image of something green. But that image is not 'out there.'
> To believe that is itself a form of superstition, for the image
> is a creation of my own, shaped and colored by many cir-
> cumstances, including my preconceptions. (Bateson and
> Bateson 53)

He further explains that an image cannot be totally divorced from
the chaos of reality because it is a part of that reality, but the connection between imagery and reality must be approached cautiously:

> I do believe—really I do—that there is some connection
> between my 'experience' and what is happening 'out there'
> to affect my sense organs. But I treat that connection [. . .]
> as very mysterious and requiring much investigation. (Bate-
> son and Bateson 53)

Counterintuitive though it may seem, an image exists as a fluid pattern of mutually creating elements that relies on those pathways for
existence.[11]

Two examples illustrate this complex concept of imagery's mutually creating elements. The first involves Anna and her night terrors. Confused by the dark and the mists of sleep, Anna all too
easily shuttles between paradoxical realities, inhabiting both simultaneously: the world in which birds peck through her window and
the world in which raindrops ping on the windowpane. The gift
as well as the curse of imagery is the ability to dwell in paradox,
to entertain two (or more) contradictory ideas at the same time.
Crucial to the logic of imagery is that *both* worlds—the world of
birds and the world of raindrops—are mutually constructed and
both, even though contradictory, are believed simultaneously. On
one level, Anna knows that it is rain tapping on her window. For

instance, turning on the light and opening the window, I once let the rain-soaked wind wash over Anna, enabling her to experience the sounds by feeling them as rain, not as birds. In the light, with my arms around her, Anna even enjoyed the experience. Thus, I disrupted the pathways on which the images are dependent. But eventually the lights went off, the arms evanesced, and she was once again alone with the sound of rain morphing into the sound of birds. Even as she enacts one reality (rain), she enacts another contradictory reality (birds). Both realities are inseparable, for they grow out of each other. To contend with the *is* logic by which these imagistic realities cohere, Anna had to develop an array of strategies that allowed her to deal with both birds and raindrops—both realities—at the same time: additional night-lights, a butterfly net (to catch the birds if they get through the window), vigilance (to stop the birds from getting to her sister's room), stories (vigorous retellings in the light of day of what she will do with those birds if they try to get through her window), and explorations of the physics of rainstorms. Rather than ignore or dismiss the seemingly ephemeral imagery in Anna's dream world, she incorporated that imagery into her daytime meaning making, an essential move because her dreams could not be divorced from the realities of her waking life. To address the terrors of one world, she had to grapple with them in the context of the other world.

The second example to illustrate the layers of imagery and the persuasive *is* logic involves a young woman struggling with the memory of a sexual assault. A student in my first-semester composition class, Katherine chose as the topic of her first paper an attempted rape she experienced at the end of her sophomore year in high school while visiting a resort in Puerto Rico. As she explains in her portfolio narrative, she chooses this subject because "I believe that it [sexual assault] needs to be talked about more, so girls won't be so naïve and the ones who have experienced it won't feel so ashamed." At the core of these memories is the paradox of responsibility: she is both agent and victim of the attack. In her memories, Katherine shuttles between a reality in which she is solely responsible for the assault—she chose to drink excessively, she chose to leave the party without her brother, she chose to enter an elevator that held only two unfamiliar men and herself—and a reality in which the men who attacked her are responsible for the assault. In her narrative, she describes that they initiated the contact, they ignored her verbal efforts to dissuade them, they attempted to overcome her physical struggles and to silence her cries with violence. The corporeal *is* logic by which she constructs her realities and her memories unmarks the boundaries between these contradictory realities, these identities of agent and victim. Part of her difficulty in confronting the painful memories results from the paradoxical realities that she enacts simultaneously. As she explained in a writing conference, she felt caught in a web of conflicting emotions: rage directed at herself and at her assailants. The devastating aftermath—her failed romantic relationships, her fear of sexual contact with another, her self-hatred—derived in part from the inevitable but diffused rage that could find no definitive target. Coming to temporary peace with this experience involved disrupting through drawing and journal writing the agent-victim paradox, the dynamic that hurls her along these contradictory pathways, by attempting to align the paradoxes. By recalling her experience in pictures and word, Katherine grapples with the realization that both realities, both interpretations of her experience, are true. She concedes that "I realize now this wasn't my fault and this unfortunately could happen to any girl" at the same time that she simultaneously urges young women to "take precautions," to assume responsibility for their actions, aware that "[r]apists come in all shapes and sizes." She is agent and victim, imager and imaged, and by means of this paradox, Katherine discovers that her memories are not fixed, not lifeless. Rather, they are fluid and constructed, allowing her a measure of control over the reciprocity of her experiences and her identity, over her actions and her reactions.

The second strand to imageword's double logics is its discursive *as if* logic. In contrast to the unmarking of imagery's *is* logic, language's *as if* logic marks boundaries by separating reality into categories and subjects. In human culture, language is the dominant ordering system that parses and arranges the chaos of reality into distinctive units. It is what Peter Smagorinsky, quoting Michael Cole, calls the "tool of tools" in our mediation toolbox ("Snippets" 277; "Social"). Unlike the patterning of imagery, however, the patterning of language is based on discursive *as if* logic that operates via the "syllogism in Barbara": All men die. Socrates is a man. Socrates will die. This syllogistic logic functions by means of classification or categorization: Men is a category; Socrates is a member of that category; therefore, Socrates shares the conditions of membership in that category, one of which is death. But categories are a linguistic invention; they do not exist in nature (Burke, *Grammar*, ch. 2). We are able to generalize because of language's unique ability to make distinctions, to set up boundaries. As Kenneth Burke reminds us, "there are no negatives in nature, and [. . .] this ingenious addition to the universe is solely a product of human symbol systems" (*Language* 9). Like a digital code, discourse enables us to parse our reality into an infinite number of facets that we can then substitute for reality. It gives us a portable reality. For example, *tree* is not. When we think of *tree*, we do not have trees in our heads with branches protruding from our ears and leaves tickling our noses. Instead, we have the word-concept—the *as if* reality—in our minds (Fleckenstein, "Writing Bodies"). Discursive *as if* logic punctuates chaos in such a way that we can conceptualize trees even as we systematically destroy them. With an image, we are tied to the experience, a participant carried along on and by the stream flowing through our heads and around us. But, with language, we can be the observer of our own participation, dipping into that stream of experience at will and reflecting on that stream.

If we accept that the logic undergirding language is the logic of *as if*, the logic of substitution, then we must accept that language, like image, is paradoxical: it creates a reality while simultaneously negating that reality. Marked by its sequential linearity, its interior manifestation as telegraphese, and its ability to organize reality into superordinate-subordinate categories, language enables us to create a map of reality and know that it is a map. Through language, we can focus on the typical (what is similar among items), thus creating a category. But we can also focus on the atypical (what is different among items), thus discriminating between categories, as with the concept of opposite (Aylwin). It is because of language that we have a category called "imagery" and a phenomenon called "meaning." Furthermore, language offers us the possibility of reality testing. Functioning as an operation of the ego and girded with the reality principle, language weaves a tapestry that we call reality (and identity) against which we judge the falsity of all other representations (Freud). Thus, if the gift of imagery is the gift of *is,* then the gift of language is the gift of *is not.*

Through language and its gift of *not,* Katherine disrupts the pathways of her destructive self-recrimination—she is *not* responsible for her attack—and carves out some rhetorical value in her experience. Through discursive logic's power to test reality, Katherine uses writing about her hotel elevator assault to remark the boundaries and address the paradoxical logic that has so haunted her. She sifts through those memories, parceling out what she did, what the men did, testing the scope and strength of the realities she finds through the process of classification. As a function of the ego, discursive *as if* logic offers Katherine an element of control over the progression and the sequence of those memories, juxtaposing one frame against another, measuring the degree of reality immanent in each. Without the gift of language, not only would she be unable to sort through and separate her memories to discover that agency and victimization can exist simultaneously, but she would also be unable to find within this paradoxical moment a message worth communicating to an audience of young women: that, while women can and must take precautions to protect themselves from sexual attack, they must also insist on the assailants' responsibility and accountability for their own violent actions. As she writes to her audience of young women, brutally depicting for them what could happen and what they can do to reduce the opportunities for assault, she exercises discursive *as if* logic to reshape her realities.

In addition to imageword's double logics, the second important quality of this alternative imaginary is the movement of these double logics. *Is* and *as if* logics join in recursive feedback and feed forward loops so complex that we cannot determine where one stops and another begins. The transactional dynamic by which double logics function resembles a Möbius strip, a strange loop in which we can start on one side and traverse the loops until we are opposite our starting point but still on a single side (fig. 1.1). Although it has been necessary to separate image and word in order to understand the logics that constitute them, doing so also implies that imagery is somehow separable from language. Neither image nor word exists without the other. Imagery and language are inseparable in meaning. "By naming the world," Berthoff reminds us, "we hold images in mind; we remember" (*Sense* 21). Infused with double logics and double being, image and word are mutually constitutive, mutually creative, hence, imageword.

Nowhere is the movement of imageword better illustrated than in the illusion that words are names of things and not the things themselves. The reason that Alfred Korzybski kept asserting that

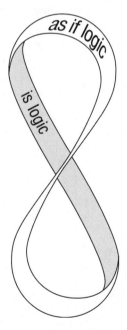

Fig. 1.1. Transacting double logics

the map is not the territory is the frequency with which the map is (mis)taken as the territory. Names do not exist in the isolated splendor of their own logic. If they did, we would have no problem differentiating between the name and thing. But words are always snarled within the logic of the image, a mutuality that permeates meaning on various levels. Vygotsky's experiments with children and concept formation in *Thought and Language* illustrate one level of this tangle. Vygotsky suggests that children (as opposed to adults) confuse word and object. For instance, when directed to call a goat a dog, the children could not do so without importing the physical characteristics of a goat to a dog (e.g., We can call the dog a goat if it has horns). Such a conflation, however, is understandable if we consider the imagistic logic at work in both the concept of dog and goat. What children rely on is the twist of word and image. Adults are subject to the same knot of relationships, manifested on a more subtle level. We may carry the word-concept in our minds, the sign *tree* rather than the maple in the front yard. But we also carry with that word-concept a visceral, physiological reaction (Peirce).

Language serves as an effective means to punctuate the chaos of reality because it is immersed in its own system of networked rules: syntactic rules, such as Chomsky's transformation grammar; semantic rules, such as Fillmore's case grammars; pragmatic rules, such as Grice's conversational maxims; and so on. But those rules rely on imagistic logic. The differences that dictate what should become *tree* are determined by the rules established within a system and by the reality out of which the system constructs itself. As C. S. Peirce points out, every sign possesses its own material dimension that functions as a constraint on what it can and cannot mean, undercutting Saussure's argument that the only connection between signifier and signified is arbitrary.[12] Language might divide and conquer reality by naming it, but language is a part and a result of that chaos in the first place. It, too, has material weight and substance. Language and its *as if* logic are inseparable from reality's chaos and imagery's corporeal *is* logic.

The intertwined movement of imageword's double logics are also exemplified in DNA, whose own double helix structure mimics that of imageword. Although contemporary scientific communities treat DNA as a language or a code so that its grammar can be mapped systematically by the human genome project, DNA is composed of both image and word, both *is* and *as if* logics. DNA does exist as a two-dimensional code, but that code is incapable of initiating anything unless it is embedded within the materiality of an egg. Only when lodged within the chemical matrix of a cell can DNA enact the physiological development of an embryo. At the same time, the egg and its ambient chemicals are themselves products of the DNA sequencing they initiate. Without DNA somewhere within its looping existence, the egg would not exist to interpret and thus initiate its own growth. And without the egg, the DNA would not exist. It is the conjunction of egg and DNA that calls life into existence. Life is the meaning evoked by the dance of DNA and chemicals within a cellular context. "The tissues of a plant could not 'read' the genotypic instructions carried in chromosomes of every cell unless cell and tissue exist, at that given moment, in a contextual structure," Bateson reminds us (*Steps* 153–56).

So it is with imageword. While corporeal logic may exist, it cannot be known without language. We might disconnect image from language. We do this every night in our dreams. But without language, we cannot do anything with those dreams except experience them. Imagistic *is* logic lodges us in the moment. To be tugged out of the present, to be known as anything other than life as it is lived, we need the *as if* logic of language. Similarly, language can exist outside the logic of the image but with no meaning. The process of naming, the meaningfulness of language, is predicated on the existence of imagery. In life and in meaning, imagery and language enfold each other, creating each other. We can no more separate imagery from language, corporeal *is* logic from discursive *as if* logic, than we can create life by splicing DNA outside the biological matrix of a cell. Similarly, we might use language to define imagery, as I do here, but that language is born in imagery, catching us in a round robin of image and word creating each other as they enfold each other. We cannot point to a beginning or end to one particular level—to either image or word—because imageword exists as a dialectical, circular, messy, and contradictory process. We cannot name the world without imagining the world, but we cannot imagine the world within naming it.

Such a circular, contradictory dynamic is at play in Katherine's first essay. Strictly confessional writing, writing which recreates in painful detail an emotional upheaval, cohering and organizing itself along the pathways of corporeal logic, continually reenacts the moment of trauma. To linger over that is to trap the writer in a painful corporeal moment, offering no strategy for either testing or disrupting the pathways of that reality. The reciprocity of corporeal and discursive logics provides a vantage point for addressing the thorny issue of trauma writing, of students choosing to address sensitive, emotional issues within the context of a writing class, just as Katherine chose to do. After Katherine reenacts through imagistic logic the assault in journal writing and drawing, she must also draw on discursive logic, the movement into the power of *not,* of classification, of agency. James Pennebaker's landmark studies of writing and healing suggest as much, for a crucial axis along which he plots the course of health is the shifts in pronouns from "I" to "you" to "we" and the movement among those stances. The rival imaginary of imageword highlights the necessary reciprocity among logics in meaning, from individual to others and back again, enabling us to enact shifts in perspective, important for coping not only with personal trauma but also with national and international trauma.

The third quality of this alternative imaginary extends imageword's double logics into an ecology. The strange looping of double logics in imageword results in an ecological system of meaning, an interlocking array of mutually impinging relationships composed of the flow of double logics through the networked pathways. Bateson describes meaning as a "complicated, living, struggling, cooperating tangle" in which ideas live and die "because they don't fit with [each] other" (*Sacred* 265). We cannot point to any one part of the system and say here lies meaning because it is a property emerging from the entire configuration, traceable to no single causal force but only to the resonance of its transient pathways. Nor is Bateson's sense of an ecological meaning limited to language. It encompasses biological, cultural, and psychological realms. In his introduction to *Steps to an Ecology of Mind*, Bateson announces,

> [H]ere at the beginning let me state my belief that such matters as the bilateral symmetry of an animal, the patterned arrangement of leaves in a plant, the escalation of an armaments race, the processes of courtship, the nature of play, the grammar of a sentence, the mystery of biological evolution, and the contemporary crisis in man's [sic] relationship to his environment can only be understood in terms of such an ecology of ideas as I propose. (xvii)

Covering the spectrum of meaningfulness from evolution to poetry to epigenesis, ecological meaning is a "stochastic process," a process in which "a stream of events that is random in certain aspects" connects with "a nonrandom selective process which causes certain of the random components to 'survive' longer than others" (*Mind* 159). Bateson points out that we can never know reality. Instead, we can only know "differences": relationships *between* stimuli significant in some way to a perceiver. Bateson defines the smallest unit of meaning as "the differences that make a difference" (*Steps* 459). No living creature, from petunias to homo sapiens, has any sort of direct or unmediated access to the chaotic flow of the stimuli that constitutes existence. Rather, we engage in highly sophisticated filtering processes crafted out of two logics: that dictated by imagery and that dictated by word. What slips through the "filters" are not stimuli; what slips through are transforms of stimuli (Langer, *Philosophy*). We do not perceive stimulus A, for instance, a stone on the path. Instead, we perceive the difference between stimulus A— the stone—and stimulus B—the path, or between the stone at one time and the stone at another time. Furthermore, we perceive the stone only if it is significant in some way to us: for example, if we stub a toe. Three factors are necessary to transform stimuli into meaning: the objects (path and stone), the differences, and a perceiver (person who stubs her toe) that fuses objects-differences into a meaningful system.[13] What we call meaning is not any one element of this array. It is a name for the entire array of relationships that function as an ecology.

To illustrate, "we" do not "see" the stone in isolation. Instead, a set of fluid relationships (the "we") constructs the stone as a set of relationships between leaf, ground, foot, resonating to Peirce's triadic meaning in which to know a sign requires a sign (140–42).

"We" construct only relationships that yield the perception of stone important to us in some way, and by so doing "we" construct ourselves because "we" exist as an extension of the differences "we" assign to the stone. Thus, a stone becomes something that "we" avoid (because we do not want the pain of a stone bruise), something to pick up (because we want to add it to a collection), something to use (because we want to anchor the corner of a picnic blanket), and something that "we" can see (because we are physiologically able to perceive objects at rest), all processes that define us as well as the stone and yield a configuration of a particular mind. Neither meaning nor a meaning maker is in itself a direct "bit" of some sort of ontic reality that exists "out there," prior to perception. Rather, both consist of transacting webs of relationships within which both are weaver and woven.

We have countless examples of this complex ecological transaction. Bronislaw Malinowski tells us that the Trobriand Islanders in New Guinea do not see resemblances between mother and child or between siblings. Children resemble fathers, and two brothers can resemble the father but not each other. Similarities between mother and children, perceived by outsiders, do not constitute differences that make a difference in the Islanders' system (Bolles 107). But these resemblances (significant aspects of an unknowable reality) do not exist prior to the kinship system within which they are significant. Nor does the kinship system exist outside the resemblances. The two—kinship system and resemblances—create each other. Any idea comes to be, becomes a something, by means of the valuation of differences because an idea is an array of relationships that exists through those differences. It is therefore impossible to define "kinship system" before defining "difference"; but "difference" cannot be defined outside "kinship system." It is in and through difference that an idea evolves, and that idea continues as long as the valuation of difference remains desirable.

The shifting movement of double logics marking and unmarking differences in an ecological system is also central to our perceptions of beauty and justice. Elaine Scarry in *On Beauty* captures the necessary mutuality of objects, differences, and perceiver. Errors in beauty, Scarry argues, occur when we discover that something once perceived as beautiful is not and when we discover that something previously unseen, in her case a palm tree, is suddenly beautiful. The differences that matter are changed, as well as the array of constituting relationships. The entire means of perception, the "rules" by which we see, are altered. We can commit errors of beauty—both gaining and losing beauty—because of the interdependence of difference and relationships. "How one walks through the world, the endless small adjustments of balance, is affected by the *shifting* weights of beautiful things," she explains (15, my emphasis), and the weights shift because of how we walk through the world.

Two implications of ecological meaning require careful emphasis. First, what becomes meaning is the difference that is significant to a particular perceiver within a particular context. But meaning is not a product of the perceiver. The perceiver is herself constituted from those relationships, never outside the dance of relationships. Meaning is the name that we assign to the tangle of objects, differences, and perceiver. Shift any element of that equation, and the boundaries constituting meaning shift. Second, perceiver and perception are looped in a kind of circular causality. We cannot point to perceiver or perception (meaning maker and meaning) and say that one comes before the other, produces the other. Each is part of the same constellation of meaning, a constellation that Bateson calls an ecology of mind or an ecology of ideas, deliberately choosing not to assign the appellation of mind to any single relationship or element, even to that of the perceiver (meaning maker) herself.

The act of writing-reading itself—of transforming marks into meaning—offers a final illustration of the confusing twists of an ecology of meaning. Meaning is found in neither the black marks of ink on a white page nor on the page itself. Instead, meaning is the result of the differences between the black ink and the white page that matter—that are perceived as significant in some way—to a writer-reader. In the act of creating those differences, however, the writer-reader also constitutes herself—is evoked—by the information she creates between the gaps of ink, page, and self. She becomes a writer-reader as defined by the system within which she both immerses herself and creates. Writer-reader, ink, and page materialize by means of that recognition, a theory of "reading" the world analogous to Louise Rosenblatt's transaction reading in which text and reader are mutually evoked within the constraints of a specific environment.[14] To exist, a difference requires a system to identify (or mark) it as a difference that matters, but the system requires that "difference" to exist in the first place. Marking or punctuating the flow of reality so that some "things" become significant while other "things" remain unperceived is an act of the entire system of relationships. And these differences exist only as long as the relationships—the double logics—constituting the system exist. As Bateson explains, "The messages and guidelines for order exist only, as it were, in sand or are written on the surface of waters. Almost any disturbance [. . .] will destroy them" (*Steps* 482).

Katherine and her work in my first-semester composition class provide a final illustration of ecological meaning. Throughout her semester's work, Katherine wove a complex, tangled web of mind, body, and texts. From her first essay to her last, Katherine integrated her life, the places of her life, and the cultural discourses within which she was immersed. She began the semester with images of a physical assault and ended the semester with images of a media assault, highlighting the web of meaning within which her personal trauma was replicated in frightening ways on a cultural level. As the topic of her final paper, in which she was required to integrate secondary sources, Katherine chose to explore sexually charged media images aimed at young girls, images implicitly persuading them that they are their bodies and only their bodies, a topic that was foreshadowed in, if not a direct outgrowth of, her first paper. She explains in her portfolio narrative that she "just wanted to prove that women still have a long way to go to be looked at as equal[. . .]. Because if they were equal to men, then they wouldn't have to use sex and their body to get attention, they could just be themselves." She opens a preliminary draft of this final assignment with an anecdote involving her preteen cousin, who announces at a family get-together that she is too fat: "'I can't eat, I'm on a diet so I can get a boyfriend.' This is the phrase that came out of my ten-year-old cousin a couple [of] weeks ago." Katherine then proceeds to explore the extent to which women shape their bodies according to an array of visual and textual messages, from the lyrics in songs to the kaleidoscopic images ranging from rock videos to children's toys, all of which connect a woman's self-worth to her body. Katherine's work highlights the ecological quality of meaning in that, even while it unites in complex ways images and words, it also emphasizes the multiple, interlocking levels within which the linkage between images and words exists: bodies, families, communities, cultures. "How vain of a society do we have when a woman's worth is based upon her looks instead of her character and intelligence?" Katherine concludes. This is a national problem, she notes, and one that will not change until "these unrealistic messages and images are changed." An ecological dynamic that embraces confessional writing and simultaneously moves our students into persuasive discourse is how we make writing-reading meaningful to our students.

Literacy and Imageword

This alternative imaginary radically reorders how we look at our students' efforts to become literate members of a particular community. Let me illustrate three kinds of reordering by returning to Gloria, a student in my first-year composition course whom I presented briefly in my introduction. Throughout her sixteen weeks with me, Gloria struggled unceasingly with her conviction that she was not a writer, would never be a writer. If we think about Gloria as an ecology, as an identity crafted out of the weave of double logics, we can begin to identify ways that we might help her reenvision herself as a writer. Gloria's image of herself as a "not-writer" is a coconstruction, a joint production of corporeal and discursive logics, within which I am implicated. To undermine Gloria's image of herself as a not-writer, we must jointly reweave her ecology. One means of egress into that ecology lies with the variability of Gloria's image of herself as not-writer, an image that shifts from situation to situation, disappearing in some literate performances, dominating in others. Thus, Gloria's belief in her failure as a writer, which is so strong in an academic classroom, is less dominant when she writes to her son's teacher excusing his absenteeism. Working together, we teased out the double logics that cohere as "writer" in one scene and use that coherence to reconfigure another scene so that it might yield an ecology called "writer."

Second, the dissolution and resolution of boundaries central to an alternative imaginary based on imageword emphasizes the inextricability of corporeality and meaning, and that dynamic is also at play in Gloria's vision of herself as a not-writer. Words and bodies can join in healing (Anderson and MacCurdy; Baumlin and Baumlin), but they can also join in harming, for instance, the injury resulting from the institutional policy of labeling some students "underprepared" writer-readers. This naming, subject to corporeal logic, sinks all the way to the bone, providing a tacit rationale for any student's continued belief in her own failed literacy despite repeated evidence of academic success. Thus, Gloria carries into my class her belief in her failure as a proficient writer rather than her successes in her previous class. Nor does the physical experience of writing-reading counteract this conviction. Like most of us, Gloria frequently found writing-reading a physical and psychological struggle. Academic writing is a laborious and many times unrewarding process, and Gloria relied on those physical sensations to code her self-perceptions. The reasoning at the heart of such coding is seductive, a seduction we are all subject to: If writing-reading is difficult, then it must be because I am not a writer-reader. If I were a writer-reader, I wouldn't have to struggle. We return to syllogism in grass: Writing hurts. Failure hurts. Writing is failure. In spite of writing-reading success on a variety of levels—either ours or Gloria's—what remains relevant is the visceral experience, the anxiety, the procrastination, the pounding pulse, and the sweaty palms that accompany writing efforts.

Third, the double logics of imageword emphasize the inextricability of meaning and place in writing-reading. Meaning is literally ecological. Because it is both a place and within a place, it cannot be abstracted from the physical environment within which it is created nor the physical environment that it creates. Thus, Mike Rose begins the literacy narrative of his life with a house in South Los Angeles: "Let me tell you about our house," he says, guiding us through the front door into the small living room of the one-bedroom home where he grew to adulthood. Rose leads us on a tour of the sparse rooms and of the surrounding block of buildings on South Vermont, marking them in adulthood as they marked him in his youth. Emplaced within the parameters of Vermont Avenue, he says, "I developed a picture of human existence that rendered it short and brutish or sad and aimless or long and quiet with rewards like afternoon naps, the evening newspaper, walks around the block, occasional letters from children in other states" (18). It is this image of existence that overshadows Rose's entire narrative, his research agenda, and the pedagogy-curriculum he advocates.

To define meaning as an ecology of mutually transacting relationships is to construct meaning via the double logics of imageword. The central characteristic of these double logics is the marking and unmarking of boundaries. Imageword blurs the distinctions between perceiver and perception, perceiver and context. It is here in this collapse of boundaries even as boundaries are erected that we can envision a different literacy and a different classroom. It is here that we might reconfigure a student's adamant belief in her failure as a writer-reader. It is here that we might reshape injurious racialized images promulgated by our immersion in a particular body, culture, place, and time. It is here that we might find a reprieve from and meaning in personal trauma. Finally, it is here that we might dream anew, transforming our nightmares in and out of the classroom. "A dream book?" Anna asks me in puzzlement. "Aunt Sheri sent me a dream book? What do I do with a dream book?"

"You write about your dreams, you describe your dreams," I tell her. She slowly traces an empty line on a pale blue page. "Well, can I draw them, too?"

"You can do both."

2 / From a Poetics of Meaning to a Poetics of Teaching

The image method [of thinking] remains the method of
brilliant discovery, whereby realms organized by interests
usually kept apart are brought together.
—Frederic C. Bartlett, *Remembering*

This chapter is an argument for pleasure in the confusion of
boundaries and for responsibility in their construction.
—Donna J. Haraway, *Simians, Cyborgs, and Women*

I drew my picture and put it up on the board and we discussed
possible ways my paper could go and different audiences I
could have.
—Meaghan, portfolio narrative

Mrs. Bullock, Anna's second grade teacher, called me one Friday
afternoon. "Mrs. Fleckenstein, this is Kay Bullock. Would you be
able to come by this afternoon? I think we might have a problem
with Anna." Nightmare visions materialized: blood, spitting, tantrums; bloody spitting tantrums. "What's the problem?" I choked
out. The voice hesitated. "Well, I've just finished grading her spelling test, and she wrote all of her words backwards." Spelling backwards? I was hyperventilating over a spelling problem? My fight-
flight responses eased immediately. A spelling problem I could deal
with. Not that it was, as I soon discovered, really a spelling problem. It was, in fact, a problem of spelling all of her words correctly
—but backwards. Anna had reversed the order of her spelling
words, putting her numbers in the middle of the page and writing
the letters of her spelling word from right to left. Thus, *library*
started with *y* on the left-hand margin, ending with *l* in the middle
of the page, disrupting the accepted mode of reading left to right.

Although Anna manifested no overt signs of any visual or neurological hiccups—she explained that she was taking some poetic license, writing the words backwards out of boredom—she and her sister did experience a consistent and typical problem with reversing *b*s, *d*s, 7s, 9s, and 3s. The solution, however, was neither panic nor a regimen of remedial drills. Instead, inspired by research in early language development and supported by my pediatrician, I enrolled my daughters in dance, a process that trained their bodies to orient themselves in space. To address a potential problem of writing-reading, a problem that had its roots in their spatial orientation, my daughters needed something in addition to traditional instruction in writing-reading. They needed to dance into literacy. Imageword's corporeal and discursive logics fused, and my daughters honed their writing-reading by tapping their way through the choreography of "I'm a Dancing Star."[1]

I begin this chapter with a story about one aspect of my daughter's developing literacy because it illustrates a question we must address to move from a poetics of meaning to a poetics of teaching: how does literacy evolve out of and within imageword's alternative imaginary? Answering this question requires exploring the connections between imageword's double logics and specific enactments of writing-reading, including everything from composing grocery lists to designing Web sites to shaping letters of the alphabet. Central to that exploration is the liquidity of imageword. Immersed within an ecological system of meaning, imageword continually erodes not only the separation between image and word but also divisions among the myriad aspects—bodies, cultures, places, and times—comprising any system of meaning. Word and image, cell and organ, bodies and places, places and cultures, cultures and times—each flows into one another through borders rendered permeable and osmotic by imageword. From mitochondria to community, from neurons to neon lights, imageword marks and unmarks boundaries only artificially separating bodies, cultures, places, and times, reconfiguring itself as it reconfigures the loops within an ecology of meaning (fig. 2.1). The fluid transaction of double logics ensures that imageword mutates, metamorphoses into different shapes as its

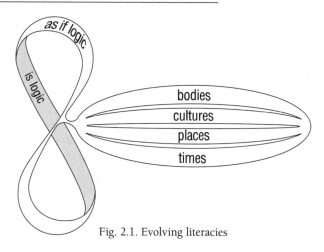

Fig. 2.1. Evolving literacies

slips across the porous edges of its own system. Thus, Meaghan, a student in my first-semester composition class, discovers myriad audiences and arguments in the confluence of a sketch and a class discussion of that sketch. Her literacy, her essay, evolves at these sites of change, in these moments of permutation, acting out of and acting out these shifts. For Anna, at this moment of her life, literacy shapes itself where her body and her language come together. The borders between corporeality and discourse dissolve, and literacy evolves as she positions herself in space, learning through the conjunction of movement, classroom instruction, and at-home reading the directionality of letters, the embodiment of writing. Twirling in shiny tap shoes, Anna crafts and is crafted by that literacy. It is this very dynamic of dissolving boundaries and evolving literacy that provides egress into a poetics of teaching.

In this chapter, I trace the materialization of literacy at four permeable sites—bodies, cultures, places, and times—using that liquid movement to shape a literacy of border crossings.[2] Within each section I begin by tracing the osmotic dynamic of imageword within and across a particular porous arena. I then tie this movement to the specific configuration of literacy that evolves out of that fusion. Finally, I describe how this newly shaped literacy enriches teaching.

Imagewords, Bodies, and Literacy

In August 1993, a close friend of mine, midterm in her second pregnancy, suffered a rupture of the uterine membrane, losing precious amniotic fluid. Rushed to Michael Reese Hospital in downtown Chicago, Jean was confined to complete bed rest in an effort to save her pregnancy. Housed in the wing of the maternity ward devoted to women with endangered pregnancies, Jean was surrounded by and participated in the tragedies of mothers struggling to save unborn children. In the midst of this site of emotional turmoil, she was told to remain serene, to reduce the stress levels that contributed to the onset of premature labor. Positioned within an environment that reminded her on a daily basis of her worst fears, Jean was told not to fear.

Jean's response to this impossible situation was to immerse herself in an alternate universe, one that operated according to different rules. A science-fiction writer, Jean ignored her own writing projects and her three personal journals. Instead, she entered the fantasy world of the planet Pern, where dragons and their telepathic riders save Pern from destruction. Focusing on these Anne McCaffrey novels, Jean lived in a realm removed from the wrenching drama played out around her of women losing unborn babies, allaying the panic that opened the door to her own unwelcome labor pains. Against one-in-one-hundred odds, Jean spent ten weeks reading her way to the thirty-first week of pregnancy, successfully delivering her daughter Molly.

Jean anchored her daughter to her unruly body through an umbilicus constructed of words, a process that highlights the fusion of corporeal and discursive logics in imageword.[3] "Books don't happen in my mind," novelist Isabel Allende says; "they happen somewhere in my belly" (8). Like Allende's "elephant pregnancy," Jean's books also materialized somewhere in her belly, reshaping her body in the process. I begin my exploration of literacy with this osmotic boundary between bodies and imageword because it is breached most frequently and maintained most rigidly within our educational systems, especially situated as we are in the West, where the separation between body and mind is reified in our intellectual, social, and spiritual practices. Regardless of the many and varied ways in which bodies are banned from our contemplative, intellectual lives, our personal and professional experiences indicate that bodies are not easily ousted, not easily subdued. The tenacity of our bodies and their continual eruption through the tissue of words are the result of the corporeal *is* logic of imagery.

Imagery's corporeal *is* logic powers the construction of the biological world. Imagery's logic creates not only pretty pictures but also the living world. Without imagery's *is* logic, we could not function mentally. Recent work in neurology has indicated that neurons communicate analogically, by means of "is" relationships in which neural receptors match chemical codes, sending messages by a complex and only partially understood weaving of imagistic messages (Damasio; Greenfield). Just like our mental existence, our physiological existence—our flesh, bones, and blood—is similarly a product of corporeal *is* logic, as medical semiotics demonstrates. For example, our epigenetic development is guided by *is* logic, as is our immune system; lymphocytes "match" the composition of invaders via the iconic structuring of corporeal logic (Bateson, *Steps*; Hoffmeyer). Imbued with corporeal *is* logic, thus imbued with bodies, imageword highlights the inescapability of our multifaceted physical realities in meaning. Any use of language implicates a use of corporeality, blurring the distinctions between flesh and word, bodies and texts.

What emerges from this permeable site is a literacy of bodysigns, a literacy in which we are neither writers nor bodies, but writing bodies (Fleckenstein, "Writing Bodies"; "Bodysigns"). A corporeal literacy points us to the material dimension of writing-reading, to meaning's reliance on our physical participation in the world. And this physiological dimension is evident on myriad levels. Our acquisition of oral language evolves through our actions in the world, from babies lying in cribs vocalizing a litany of nonsense syllables to toddlers learning to say *spoon* as they pretend to mix cake batter in an imaginary bowl with an imaginary spoon (Bates; Britton). Our acquisition of print literacy is taught and learned physically, from children manipulating wooden puzzle pieces to children writing letters in bath bubbles on the sides of bathtubs.

Historian of science Morris Berman writes that, in the late nineteenth century, his grandfather began his literacy training in Belorussia by eating the letters of the Hebrew alphabet drenched in honey, tying literacy to a literal consumption of words (*Reenchantment* 267–68).[4] Even our physical experiences with writing-reading, from immersion in literacy-rich environments to early memories of reading on a loved one's lap, are implicated in our enactments of literacy. Deborah Brandt points out that understanding literacy requires understanding these material dimensions:

> the complexities involved when a preschooler takes up writing to displace her mother's reading, or when a daughter decodes her father's burdens along with the nightly news, or when a child's first attempt at *imitatio* begins with the guilt of theft. ("Remembering" 460)

Through imageword's dissolving-evolving dynamic, we gain a literacy that is inextricable from its corporeal matrix, its formation within the context of bodies. As teachers we gain a poetics of teaching that is equally grounded in material contexts. The first value that a literacy of bodysigns offers us as teachers is that we can teach to the health of the individual and the health of the community. Teaching (or not teaching) literacy directly implicates the spiritual, psychological, and physical health of the citizenry and of the community as a whole. From the classical times, the spiritual health of the city-state was integrated with the spiritual health of rhetoric, the soul of the *politikos* inextricable from the soul of the city-state (Reeve). An essential purpose for the evolution of rhetoric was to protect the well-being of the city-state and its complement of citizens. Likewise, the political founders of this country conceived of the health of the nation in terms of a literate citizenry, a citizenry capable of obtaining information and, on the basis of that information, making the right decisions. Much of what we currently practice in our writing-reading classrooms is predicated on crafting responsible citizens who can actively participate in maintaining the health of democracy (Farrell; M. Rose).

In addition, as Jean's experiences with her endangered pregnancy reveal, writing-reading goes well beyond the spiritual health of a nation. Writing-reading is intimately involved in the physiological and psychological health of the individual. Like Jean, many have found writing-reading therapeutic (Rinaldi; Tyler; Waddell). In their groundbreaking collection *Writing and Healing,* editors Charles Anderson and Marian MacCurdy commend the curative powers deployed by a web of words. The multifaceted aspects of health can all be affected by writing, they argue. Whether of mind, body, or spirit, health is not a phenomenon separate and distinct from the operation of language. Instead, "[a]s we manipulate the words on the page, as we articulate to ourselves and to others the emotional truth of our pasts, we become agents for our own healing" (7).[5] James Pennebaker's work highlights even further the dissolving boundaries between bodies and imagewords. His experimental projects over the past decade have consistently pointed to the role of therapeutic writing in physiological and psychological wellness, especially in fostering the development of an individual's T cells, which fight off infections. Literacy as an agent of health thus becomes a valid part of our classroom teaching. The commitment to each child's right to literacy, motivated for laudable social and political reasons, is accompanied by a parallel commitment to each child's right to health through that literacy. Denying a child literacy, then, is tantamount to denying that child a means of ensuring his or her personal and communal welfare.

The second value teachers gain from a literacy of bodysigns is a new insight into student resistance and accommodation to academic writing-reading. From the perspective of a corporeal literacy, learning writing-reading means learning a particular physical orientation, crafting a particular body. Consider, again, Anna's situation with her nagging reversal of letters, admittedly only a low-level literacy snag but an important level nonetheless. Altering her uncertainty about the direction in which 3s, *b*s, *d*s, and *p*s orient themselves required, in part, altering her way of orienting herself physically in the world. An even more radical reorganization is required as students are trained in academic literacy. Successful academic writing reflects what Lynn Z. Bloom wryly terms the eleven virtues of writing, ranging from self-reliance to cleanliness and punctuality, qualities derived from living a middle-class life in a middle-class space (Bloom; Brodkey, "Writing on" and "Writing Permitted"). Becoming a successful writer-reader requires crafting a middle-class physiological orientation. It is for this reason that Linda Brodkey can castigate first-year composition classes as a "middle-class" holding pen ("Writing Permitted").

Furthermore, "good" writing also imposes on students the bodies of white, heterosexual, middle-class males (Battersby, *Gender and Phenomenal*; Fleckenstein, "Resistance"). Early Renaissance scholar Christine de Pisan, one of Western Europe's first professional writers, describes just that process. To become an author, she reconfigures herself male:

> Formerly, I was a woman; now
> I am a man, I do not lie;
> My stride demonstrates it well enough.
> (qtd. in Battersby, *Gender* 68)

Out of the early Renaissance and into the twentieth century, Jane Flax argues that women can succeed in the academy only to the extent that they can remake their bodies male. Woe to the gravid academic.[6] Is it any surprise, then, that students who bring into our classrooms marginalized literacies and marginalized bodies struggle with the imposition of a dominant literacy, a dominant body?

By plotting the historical arcs of his identity and his participation in school on the basis of his body image, Roderick obliquely explores this crucial conjunction of corporeality and literacy (fig. 2.2). A highly successful student in my first-semester composition class, Roderick was a powerful presence physically and intellectually. Standing well over six feet tall and with the highly toned, clearly articulated physique of a disciplined athlete, he towered over his classmates, guiding classroom discussion and providing thoughtful peer commentary throughout the semester. His performance in class, as well as his writing quality, earned him an invitation to become a peer tutor in the university writing center, an

Fig. 2.2. Roderick's essay portfolio cover page

unheard-of honor for a first-year student. Gentle, courageous, and intellectually incisive, Roderick traced in his first paper the evolution of his identity and of his body, beginning with a troubled youth in which he experienced social rejection and academic alienation because of his chubby form: "I was called names like fatso, big butt, four-eyes, fat boy, and Rod-a-dick. I was tripped, abused, picked on, and chastised by my peers all because of my appearance." To gain both social acceptance and academic success, Roderick changed his body—literally. During his middle school years, by systematically adhering to a healthy diet and rigid exercise regimen, Roderick honed for himself the kind of body that brought him favorable attention, socially and academically. "By the time I reached my senior

year of high school [...] everyone in school either knew me or
knew of me," he writes, an acceptance that culminated in his elec-
tion as homecoming king, a moment of happiness in which he felt
"finally accepted for who I was." But, with his new body and new
social success, Roderick also discovered new accountability.
Although he accrued previously elusive social capital, he was
simultaneously dismayed by aspects of his behavior and the behavior of his friends who solidified their sense of self-importance by
ridiculing classmates who failed to adhere to the right "look." "I
started to notice my friends treating others the way I had been
treated," he reports, "and it made me sick to my stomach." Something more was needed, he decided, something that embraced both
the body he now possessed and the child who lingered within: behavior that reflected an attitude of hope and acceptance. "So I began
to use my position in school society for things I believed in. I organized Toy Drives for homeless children. I traveled to D.C. again to
take part in the writing of the Teen Anti-Violence Resolution. I got
back to what was really important to me." As a result of his evolution from marginalized body and marginalized student citizenship
to class president, Roderick shaped a corporeal, intellectual, and
social position from which he could offer hope to young people.
Rather than join the forces that had earlier in his life rejected him
because of his body, he created a space in which he could invite different bodies, less accepted bodies, into academic and social circles:
"I went to middle schools and elementary schools and spoke about
what I had gone through. [...] They saw hope in me, and I saw
myself in them." Weaving a narrative that highlights the inextricability of language, school, and bodies, Roderick takes responsibility
for constructing new boundaries and new lives out of words and
corporeality.

   A poetics of teaching grounded in a literacy of bodies develops
a praxis that underscores more than just teaching writing-reading
as an intellectual change. In addition to the acquisition of new discourse rules and protocols, a poetics of teaching foregrounds physiological change. It requires an understanding of students' embodiment,

incorporating the corporeal dimension of resistance, accommodation, and enculturation into what has been too long conceived as a predominantly linguistic phenomenon.

Imagewords, Cultures, and Literacy

The second porous boundary across which imageword shape-shifts is that separating bodysigns and cultures. A corporeal literacy encompasses only a single facet of a poetics of meaning, a single loop in an ecology of meaning. Imageword also morphs across the porous plane of culture, configuring literacy at that site as well. From one perspective, bodies constitute what Kenneth Burke calls the universal situation; however, from another perspective, bodies themselves are a product of the culture within which they are immersed. As Paul Schilder points out, "the body is a social phenomenon," as well as a corporeal one (127), a truth reflected in Roderick's efforts to shape a body that garnered him greater social success. Humans, Burke says, are separated from their natural condition by instruments of their own making (*Language* 13), instruments that craft for them a different "natural" condition.[7] We do not live in nature; we live in culture, which frequently one-ups nature. Burke calls this the process of second naturing. Using the tools we construct, humans "make a set of habits that become a kind of 'second nature,'" become "a special set of expectations, shaped by custom, [that] [. . .] seem 'natural'" (*Language* 13). Imagery is the means, perhaps even the dominant means, by which a culture second natures its members, and one way it does so is by inculcating a particular way of seeing.

Imageword serves as a central process by which cultural membership is effected, and it does that by privileging a way of seeing. Every culture is marked by a habitual way of organizing image and word. Our social participation is predicated on mastering this dominant way of seeing, on joining what Norman Bryson calls a vision, as well as a discourse, community. For instance, the Middle Ages were organized according to a way of seeing that denigrated human vision and valorized God's word. Bryson characterizes the

Middle Ages as a culture in which image is systematically subordinated to the word. He points to the composition of stained glass windows in medieval cathedrals, highlighting the fact that this visual art is controlled by the language surrounding and infusing the picture. Because human sight must not supplant spiritual sight, the word of God is valued over the deceiving vision of human kind. To avoid excommunication—disbarment from the European religious community—citizens learned and practiced this way of seeing, one that diminishes the value of its own vision.

Our students participate in the academy by fashioning ways of seeing that organize the knowledge of specific disciplines, and they experience a similar "casting out"—or excommunication—when ways of seeing collide. Dana, one of my graduate students specializing in linguistics, had to contend with conflicting ways of seeing to succeed in modern rhetorical theory. Dana unenthusiastically entered my required seminar in modern rhetorical theory, pointing out quietly on the first day that rhetoric had little relevance for her work in linguistics. Throughout the semester, she struggled to control her distaste for a subject area so totally foreign to her linguistic orientation while continuing to produce work that would allow her to maintain her exemplary GPA. First, the panoramic scope of rhetoric bothered her, the effort on the part of the theorists we studied to ferret out the rules, the patterns governing meaning on a social and cultural scale that seemed to embrace everything. Accustomed to focusing on narrowly construed phenomena—sounds, functions of single words in discourse, sentence level relationships—Dana found the idea of addressing questions such as the relationship between language and the nature of reality frustrating and distracting because they required her to alter her visual and mental orientation; they required her to alter her ways of perceiving language and reality, reorganizing their conjunction. Second, the participatory nature of seeing in modern rhetorical theory—the inability to detach the user of language from the language used, the seer from the seen—contradicted the detached, empirically oriented Baconian vision that characterizes linguistics. Uneasy, withdrawn, and reluctant, Dana became a quiet, resisting presence in the seminar—until we read Gloria Anzaldúa, a writer who attends so explicitly to the collision of ways of seeing and ways of being.

Raised in a missionary community in Papua New Guinea, Dana herself negotiated oppositional ways of being and seeing in her private life, at home neither in Papua New Guinea nor in America. She reveals in a journal:

> I am an American and have no way to escape that fact, but I am also not an American. I was born in Papua New Guinea and lived there until I was 18, aside from year-long furloughs in the us every four years. I am not a Papua New Guinean, but I am also a Papua New Guinean. I have been included and marginalized in both cultures, and have never truly belonged in either one.

Guided by Anzaldúa's own efforts to hone multiple ways of seeing, Dana found an entry point into a different vision necessary for modern rhetorical theory. She continues in the same journal entry:

> When I read this assignment, I was delighted not only because of her use of language and the fact that she is from a different culture, but because I could identify with living on the borders. For me the borders have been related to language, culture, identity, and home.

On the basis of what Dana calls her "visceral" response to Anzaldúa, she finds a point of identification with modern rhetorical theory, a way into the panoramic and participatory vision so characteristic of modern rhetoric theory. She concludes her essay: "I have not yet figured out who I am, where I belong, or where I am going. This is why I like Anzaldúa. She has a strong sense of who she is, where she belongs, and where she is going, despite the borders on which she lives. I want to be that sort of bridge."

This aspect of literacy enables us as teachers to attend to the habituated ways of seeing that dominate a particular culture and to explore their impact on our classrooms. By attending to the intersections between ways of seeing and ways of speaking, we discover new dimensions to our students' struggles with writing-reading. Three such ways of seeing—spectacle, surveillance, and antinomy—influence our literacy teaching in the West.

As a result of the barrage of imagery that community members consume but seldom produce, we are shaped according to the habit of spectacle. Guy Debord claims that by living enmeshed within the sticky strands of an imagery produced always by others, we are reconfigured as *Homo Spectator*. Debord defines spectacle as a "social relationship between people that is mediated by images" (*Society* 12, his emphasis). According to Debord, the constant and intense onslaught of imagery throughout modern Western culture establishes a one-way process of communication (*Society* 19) in which we are transformed into passive consumers without a history, trapped in the immediacy of the moment, and stripped of independent expertise (*Comments* 12, 15, 17). Debord claims that spectacle steals from us our memories, eternally binding us to the present.

The habit of spectacle—restricting us to a decontextualized and ahistorical immediacy—offers us important insights into writer's block and identity block. Traditionally characterized as an outgrowth of a cognitive bottleneck, a too rigid application of rules that were designed to be heuristics rather than algorithms, or an absence of appropriate discourse protocols, writer's block has been tied tightly to the ways in which a culture uses language. Through spectacle, we witness an entirely different dimension of writer's block: the ways in which an image-saturated culture can habituate writer-readers into believing that they have nothing significant to say, no history to guide them, and no pool of expertise from which to draw. As consumers rather than producers of images, student writer-readers can easily grow into the belief that, in addition to having nothing to say, they have no reason to write, no authority to write. In effect, citizens of a society of spectacle are acclimated in their own passivity, their own conviction in the impossibility of an alternative reality.

Furthermore, spectacle enables us to connect writer's block with the larger issue of identity block, especially in terms of the passivity that the habit of spectacle fosters. For instance, Maya Angelou's narrator in *I Know Why the Caged Bird Sings* reveals the tyranny of a way of seeing that configures the seer as submissive, as a subject only when seen as a desirable object, a desirability determined by the imagery of the moment. For example, Angelou's narrator resolves to "look like one of the sweet little white girls who were everybody's dream of what was right with the world" (1), finding in that resolution an egress into social and self agency. Claudia, Toni Morrison's ten-year-old narrator in *The Bluest Eye* identifies this process of colonization by spectacle, listing the images that mediate social relationships and identities: "Adults, older girls, shops, magazines, newspapers, window-signs—all the world had agreed that a blue-eyed, yellow-haired, pink-skinned doll was what every girl child treasured" (20). Immersed within a scopic regime that inculcates passivity and that shapes an identity whose reality is predicated on being seen as a desirable object, Angelou's narrator and Morrison's Claudia contend with the tyranny of a socially validated way of seeing, one that configures them as objects of the gaze (J. Berger).

Our students struggle with the same confluence of spectacle and gender identity. For instance, Aletha's compulsion to conceive of herself in terms of a doll and her resultant conceptualization of herself as both unwanted and undervalued are joint products of a way of seeing, *as a way of being seen as desirable.* Endowed with generous physical beauty as well as incisive intelligence, Aletha struggled with her position as a black woman in a culture dominated by images of white beauty. She characterized herself—she saw herself—in terms of the images she views: as a black doll left on a dusty shelf, unchosen, unwanted, bereft of any power to change the status quo. Trapped in the present, helpless in the face of her own powerlessness, she was quiescent. She writes that she can neither say nor do anything that will alter her situation. Instead, she can only wait until someone outside her control chooses her and removes her from the shelf. At play here is the phenomenon of spectacle, a way of seeing that traps us in passivity and an eternal present, eroding discourse by negotiating social reality through images alone, and an array of imagewords that impose on women the identity of the seen, the characteristics of what Laura Mulvey calls "to be looked-at-ness" (11). Conceived of in these terms, personal and rhetorical identities operate under visual as well as discursive constraints, indicating the need to evolve pedagogical approaches that address the confluence of ways of seeing and ways of saying.

Another way of seeing taught by immersion in an image-rich culture is that of surveillance. Michel Foucault has argued persuasively that we live not in an age of spectacle but in an age of surveillance (*Discipline* 217).[8] Visual ordering is the predominant means by which bodies are disciplined and second natured into docility (170–71). Via spatial arrangements and visual technologies, a person is reduced to that which is seen but does not see; a person becomes an object of information but never the subject in communication (200). Central to Foucault's argument about surveillance, though, is the degree to which individuals internalize the habit of surveillance so that it becomes the tool by which we establish our presence in the world. We monitor our own integration into a social group and into a life by means of the tenets of surveillance. And these tenets influence the ways students establish literate identities for themselves, constraining how, when, where, and to what extent they can configure themselves as literate. The cost of surveillance is painfully illustrated in the effort of Viviana, a Latina student at the University of California Berkeley, to retain a sense of herself as literate after the onset of carpal tunnel syndrome (CTS) during her final year at Berkeley. Resulting from an acute irritation of the tendons in the wrist, an irritation that causes debilitating pain whenever the sufferer attempts to use her hand (416), CTS prevented Viviana from performing literate acts in the socially prescribed manner and precipitated doubts concerning her identity as a literate individual.[9] Because of this physical infirmity, Viviana could no longer hold a pencil or type at a keyboard. And because she could no longer perform physically and publicly the actions of a literate person, Viviana came to question her right to be called literate. "[A]lmost every time we interviewed her," researchers Jabari Mahiri and Amanda J. Godley note, "she recounted stories of how she was feeling less educated and even less intelligent because she couldn't write" (419; 425–26). Viviana explains: "I would say that I don't see myself as a complete student, maybe just like half a student, if that makes sense" (426). Through numerous examples, Viviana pointed to the frequency with which she had once demonstrated her literacy ability and literate identity: through her volunteer work in various Latino organizations, her role as mediator in her culture, and her duties as translator in her family. When she could no longer perform her literacy, when she, on the contrary, had to depend on another performing for her, her identity as literate and her faith in her own literacy began to erode. If one cannot be seen, be witnessed as a writer-reader, then the conviction in one's identity as a writer-reader dissipates. Internalizing the tenets of surveillance—the need to be seen as literate by performing literate acts in the culturally prescribed manner—Viviana struggled to finish her college education and retain her dream of graduate school.

The habit of surveillance offers teachers a different insight into the privileging of public performance in literacy pedagogy. For example, the habit of surveillance persuades us that literacy must be enacted on a social stage; it must manifest itself in a visual display that can be monitored. The literacy our students and we practice in private—whether revisions of writing-reading or personal journals—or outside the classroom does not constitute "literate behavior." Rather, literacy only includes those acts that are acknowledged within a particular public sphere. Furthermore, to be validated as literate, that performance must be witnessed by others. It is the reactions of others to our literate performances that determine whether in fact we are literate. We depend on their judgments to confirm our literate identities, to evaluate us. Finally, because of the force of the habit of surveillance, we discipline ourselves and our performances to the accepted communal norms of literate behavior. The degree to which we deviate from these criteria is the degree to which we judge ourselves as illiterate. Considering our students' struggles through the habit of surveillance enables us to understand not only the power of literacy but also the continued dominance within a culture of a single form of literacy, replicated in a cycle of public performances.

The final habit fostered by our immersion within an image-saturated culture is of antinomy, a term Burke uses to highlight the antinomian or the disintegrating thrust of his philosophy (*Grammar,* ch. 2). The habits of spectacle and surveillance establish and promulgate a particular order in society, reflecting the power of imageword to function as a nomos, a structuring agent. Because we live awash in a tsunami of fragmentary, decontextualized, morphed, and contradictory imagewords, we are also, and paradoxically, trained in the habit of antinomy, of breaking and reshaping patterns of order. As visual critic Nicholas Mirzoeff points out, the fragmentation, disorder, and confusion of postmodernity are the result of a visual rather than a textual crisis in our culture. The habit of antinomy is marked by two seemingly opposite characteristics: participation and contradiction. The fragmentation of imagery invites the perceiver into an active partnership with perception. Mirzoeff characterizes the visual event as "an interaction of the visual sign, the technology that enables and sustains the sign, and the viewer" (13). The second element of antinomy is contradiction. Contradiction is implicit within order because we craft order, including imagistic order, out of bits and pieces, keeping some while discarding others. Burke reminds us continually that a way of seeing is a way of not seeing (*Permanence* 48–49). As a result, order is always scarred by suture marks, and all those bits and pieces we leave out press against those sutures, agitating for attention. Because imageword can exist in an oppositional relationship to itself, contradiction is a crucial component of meaning. Images and words, engaged in what Donna J. Haraway calls ricocheting mimesis, possess no automatic one-to-one correlation; thus, even as they can in one instance complement themselves, in a double action they can also compete, offering radically different takes on meaning (*Modest* 179).

The habit of antimony helps us reconfigure our literacy classrooms by endowing them with the gift of change. Through antinomy we can better understand how new kinds of meanings, new kinds of literate identities are crafted even in the midst of a dominant order. A question with which many of us struggle is how we might through literacy transform our students' lives for the better (Bridwell-Bowles). If we all swim in the sea of symbols and if those symbols configure our identities, where do we find a position outside that symbolic sea to recognize the need for change, let alone effect that change (Fleckenstein "Bodysigns")? The habit of antinomy answers that question, for us and for our students, because it underscores the contradictions inherent in that symbolic sea. Even as we participate—swim in that sea—we are simultaneously bombarded by the contradictions within that milieu. Gillian Rose refers to this paradoxical position as the outsider-insider stance, in which we inhabit a symbolic, are shaped by that symbolic, and yet exist outside that symbolic.

It is through antinomy that we effect change. For instance, antinomy enables Morrison's narrator Claudia, subject to the tyranny of both spectacle and the Shirley Temple doll, to smash the doll, to eviscerate it in an effort to discover what makes it so desirable. Claudia protests that it is with her that the celluloid Bo Jangles should be dancing, not with Shirley Temple. It is through antinomy as well that Aletha breaks out of the confines of spectacle, of passivity, reaching a point in her thinking and writing where she can conclude that her struggles with identity and self-esteem stem not just from questions of race but also from questions of gender. At a crucial juncture in her writing, she notes a contradiction in her situation as an unchosen. Her brother did not experience the same rejection that she remembers from her high school years. Instead, he was popular, highly sought after, and an active seeker himself. This contradiction shifts her perspectives so that she confronts not only the tyranny of racialized images—she is a *black* doll—but also the tyranny of gendered images—she is a black *doll,* a designation derived from the power that men wield in a culture as seers, not as the seen.[10] Antinomy enables her to recognize that she is subject to the intertwined imageword loops of both race and gender, providing her with a rhetorical position of agency, a position from which she can reconceive of her identity. Haraway urges us to take pleasure in the dissolution of boundaries and responsibility for their resolution. The movement of imageword across the permeable plane of culture serves as a site within which a literacy evolves, for which we must be accountable and for which our pedagogy must be answerable. Central to that accountability, though, is the movement across additional borders, for culture, like bodies, is a permeable plane, shaped by the reciprocal influences of places and times, which Edward Soja calls the vertical and the horizontal dimensions of social being and consciousness. I turn next to the vertical axis—that of place—to explore the literacy that evolves there.

Imagewords, Places, and Literacy

"The present epoch will perhaps be above all the epoch of space," Foucault notes, highlighting a widening of his interests in history to encompass concerns of geography ("Of Other" 22). He continues, "We are at a moment, I believe, when our experience of the world is less that of a long life developing through time than that of a network that connects points and intersects with its own skein" (22). The networked space Foucault configures is infused with the double logics of imageword. In many ways, place, like bodies and cultures, is an imageword, existing simultaneously in three realms—internal, external, and social—each of which holds a special value for a poetics of teaching.

First, place is an internal geography, and it exists as an interior landscape because of imageword. Nowhere is this more clearly illustrated than in the work of Gaston Bachelard, who in his lyrical *Poetics of Space* explores the nature and the power of images of home.[11] He investigates specifically the confluence of our images of this intimate, private space with our meanings. The house or houses where we are born and grow to maturity, he argues, are inextricable from the images in and of our souls: "Our soul is an abode," he writes. "And by remembering 'house' and 'rooms,' we learn to 'abide within ourselves," for "not only our memories, but the things we have forgotten are 'housed'" (xxxvii).[12] The places within which we live and grow to maturity sink within our bodies and our psyches, shaping themselves as internal images. Bachelard then proceeds to unlock his inner house and walk us through its rooms from the basement to the attic, highlighting the "passionate liaison of our bodies, which do not forget, with an unforgettable house" (15).

A spatial literacy underscores the convergence of external reality dissolving into (evolving out of) internal geography and the outgrowth of writing-reading at this site of convergence. Essential to any literate performance is feeling sufficiently at home in a place so that we will speak and write. When we enter the classroom, we carry a map—an interior image and internal geography—of our comfort zone in the world. If we are lucky, the academic place corresponds in essential ways to that inner geography, ensuring that the classroom is integrated into the intimate images of our safe areas. But not all of us are so lucky. Quite simply, not all of our students have crafted comfortable interior geographies of the academy and our classrooms; place remains for them an unfamiliar terrain. Janet Zandy recounts a "memory rupture" of this alien and alienating academic place. It is Parents' Weekend, and she arrives with her mother, both overdressed for the occasion and experiencing "a discomfort we do not voice.[. . .] Neither of us feels welcomed. I see in my mother's face a hidden sadness; I feel a shame I try to deny" (*Liberating* 65). Despite Zandy's matriculation, neither student nor parent feels at home in that place. Zandy's academic success results in spite of this alienation, which continues to plague her well into her professional life. Adding to the pain of displacement is the inability to articulate that sense of alienation: "The discrepancy between what my mother and I felt and the scene that was played out could not be acknowledged. We had intense feelings but we didn't have the language to identify and affirm them" (65). Similarly, such experiences testify to the limits of Mike Rose's dream, envisioned within the walls of his Vermont Avenue home: "I wanted to be released from the despair that surrounded me on South Vermont and from my own troubled sense of exclusion" (46). Thus, the value of a spatial literacy is that it emphasizes the necessity of rooting our students within the academy, of developing strategies that ensure that schoolrooms become a part of their internal geography without displacing that geography.

Such a spatial literacy figured in my efforts to address Gloria's belief in herself as a failed writer. Negotiating the writing tasks that were extensions of her home environment—notes to her son's teachers, grocery lists, short notes to me—posed little problem for Gloria. She was comfortable in that geography. But the academic environment with its array of tasks was the alien land. One of the strategies we tried was aligning the two interior geographies so that the academy gradually became a home site. We overlapped elements of the home environment, where some kinds of writing proceeded unimpeded, with the academic environment. I encouraged her to try writing her class papers at her kitchen table, the site of warmth and safety, instead of at the library computer lab. Whenever possible, I tried to meet her outside my office to discuss that writing. We would sit over coffee, amidst the remains of food, with papers around us, confusing the interior maps of academic and domestic terrains.

Place exists as more than an intimate, interior map crafted out of imagery's corporeal *is* logic, powerful although that logic might be. The second way that imageword dissolves the boundaries of place, shape-shifting as it does so, is through the external imagery of place, the geography and architecture of public spaces. Sign and design, rhetoric and architecture are inextricable (Goldhill; Sennett). As various scholars have pointed out, our language— our social and political rhetorics—is shaped by the design of public spaces, including the electronic agora of the World Wide Web (William J. Mitchell; Stafford), and that design is imagistically based.[13] Sociologist Richard Sennett notes that the city plan and architectural design of classical Athens resonated to the desire for "naked speaking" dominant during that era in that place. The city spaces were shaped to facilitate public speaking, emphasizing the necessary role of both imagery and language in the crafting of "real" places. Debord similarly argues that the rise of spectacle in our culture is facilitated by the disappearance of specific places, those of the coffee houses, cafés, and other meeting places where people gathered to exchange news and views.[14] Where we are directly impinges on what we can imagine and what we can say. Such a truth holds for intimate spaces, external spaces, and writing spaces. Thus, Nedra Reynolds can remind us that "[p]lace does matter; surroundings do have an effect on learning or attitudes toward learning, and material spaces have a political edge. In short, where writing instruction takes place has everything to do with how" (20).

The second value of a spatial literacy is its recognition that we carry the place within which we grow to literacy into the classroom with us. The work of Shirley Brice Heath draws clear connections between language socialization and designed space in her follow-up study of two children, grown to adulthood, from the original Trackton family: Zinnia Mae and Sissy. Zinnia Mae, single mother of a daughter and twin boys, lives in an isolated, small, three-room apartment on the sixth floor of an Atlanta housing development. Because the elevator is broken, Zinnia Mae must carry all three children down (and subsequently up) six flights of stairs in order to go outside, which she does only rarely. She and the children spend the majority of their time alone within the small apartment walls. Based on transcripts of tape-recorded interactions and the mother's notes, Heath describes the children's language socialization within this environment. Conversation is characterized by limited two-way (dyadic) talk dealing with specifics of the moment; multiparty talk is rare and the stimulation of outside contact even rarer. Heath concludes that the "climate of despair about American inner cites" makes it easy to see Zinnia Mae's "cultural membership as created (or obliterated) by her particular location and exacerbated by her own physical condition" (222). By contrast, the second case study of Sissy and her son Denny emphasizes the influences an extended family holds for literacy. In a small rental house, Denny participated in multiparty talk and enjoyed the stimulation of the outside world.

Eventually the family moved into a three-bedroom, two-story public housing apartment. In this place,

> [t]he full range of challenging language that surrounded toddlers on the plaza of Trackton in Sissy's childhood reappeared for Denny in a housing situation that kept the extended family together and provided numerous spaces for out-of-doors play under the watchful eye of family and neighbors. (228)

Heath's study demonstrates in dramatic ways how literacy evolves out of place, reinforcing the importance of remembering not only where we and our students come from but also how place impinges on our teaching and learning. A spatial literacy helps us to recognize that any disparagement of a student's use of language, however unconscious, automatically disparages that student's home, the student's physical community.

Finally, the third way that imageword unmarks and marks the borders of place is its constitution as a coproduction, as a socially constructed realm. Place does not exist in isolation, as some sort of ontic reality that can imprint us and our words without being affected by those words. Rather, place is a meeting point among actors, yielding what Haraway, citing Susanna Heckht and Alexander Cockburn, calls social nature: an ecology coconstituted by humans, land, and other organisms ("Promise" 309–10). A scene comes into existence within and because of a particular social system, one that is itself supported by these imagewords of place. For example, Christina Haas highlights the social nature of place in her exploration of the space created around an abortion clinic by a legal document, a Permanent Injunction, specifying what constitutes public space, where protesters can gather, and what constitutes private space, which protesters are barred from entering. The Permanent Injunction, a verbal articulation of a particular social system, dictates the geography—the visual parameters and design—of a space. Yet that legal document depends on, even requires, beliefs about the nature of public-private places. Environment and observer are locked in a complex network of mutually validating presuppositions and suppositions (Bateson, *Mind* 154). Any sort of change—within environment or observer—requires "various sorts of relaxation or contradictions within the system of presuppositions" (154). Understanding the constraints of place requires understanding how presuppositions and physical configuration—imageword—interlock to craft for us a mutable place.

As a coproduction, a spatial literacy requires that we consider the extent to which our classrooms, shaped by institutional mandates that exclude some students while including others, have material implications. Place results from the double logics of materiality and discourse converging and replicating. Obstacles to academic success evolve in part because of institutional edicts that ignore those material constraints. Mary Soliday highlights how rules and restrictions that bracket out the life situations of students, especially working-class students—commitments to families, jobs, commuting distances—transform those lives into impediments to education. For example, the lack of quality child care in universities increases the difficulties a single mother faces when she returns to school. Through inflexible scheduling, inadequate satellite classrooms, not to mention increasing tuition costs, institutions prevent working-class students from matriculating into and graduating from a university. The growing commitment to and eventual requirement of technological literacy merely exacerbates the obstacles a working-class student faces. Not only do many lack frequent and regular access to technology at their homes, but they also may be unable to spend time in on-campus labs because of their familial responsibilities. While institutional edicts may not create the students' material conditions, those edicts make the students' material conditions matter. Enlightened by a spatial literacy, we are called to craft different environments, different places, where we enact compassionate policies and teaching practices that root our students in a place called school without severing their roots to other places, other literacies.

Imagewords, Times, and Literacy

"All right, folks," I begin even before I unlock the door to the computer classroom, "we have a lot to do today, so we need to get started now." As my students file around chairs and light up screens, I talk nonstop. "I want you to take about five minutes and describe a bit of Case's conflict in *Neuromancer*." As keyboards click, I circulate behind my students, engaging in a bit of visual eavesdropping. One student glances up uneasily. "I need more time," he whispers. "Five minutes isn't enough." I regretfully shake my head. "We don't have more time," I whisper back. Throughout the seventy-five-minute class, I keep the pace going, speeding up as the clock ticks closer to 3:15. Milling outside the computer room doors, students congregate for the next class. "No," I warn my class, "don't start putting your books away yet. You're mine until 3:15, and I plan to use all the time I have." At 3:20 we empty the room, two students walking with me as we continue discussing Case's relationship with the artificial intelligence, Neuromancer. Too soon, I have to break off even that conversation. I need to get home so that I can gather my daughters and chauffeur them to a 5:30 soccer practice, grabbing them off the field fifteen minutes before the end of practice so that we can reach gymnastics and dance only ten minutes late.

Time is not a lazy, meandering stream I fish in; it is more like a wild, white-water ride. Many literacy scholars assert that time, not space, has been given short shrift in literacy studies, exiled as it is from the spatial parameters of the printed page. Linda Brodkey implies as much when she says that "[t]he pleasures of writing are unlike the other pleasures of my life. It's not that others are any more or less pleasurable, but that the unexpected moments in writing when time becomes space literally and figuratively move me" ("Writing Permitted" 5). Walter Ong in *Orality and Literacy* specifically associates print text with the ontology of space rather than the ontology of time. As he argues, "the shift from oral to written speech is essentially a shift from sound to visual space" (117), making visual space a central focus of attention when we should be attending as well to the temporal aspect of orality. Without discounting the importance of textual place, Steven B. Katz argues for renewed attention to the temporal dimension of writing-reading, especially as manifested in the musical quality of oral language.[15] Both Ong, whom physicist Paul Davies calls a master of temporal symbolism, and Katz claim that too little attention has been paid to time in literacy studies. Meaning can be only artificially abstracted from time. Imageword morphing across the borders of time repositions meaning within time. The corporeal *is* logic of imagery yields for us the importance of felt time, and the discursive *as if* logic of word imposes on us the weight of metronomic time. Let me describe each, highlighting the temporal literacy that evolves at their points of convergence and the value that that literacy holds for our teaching.

Felt time is a product of the corporeality of image's *is* logic impinging on time. Felt time refers to the various manifestations of time experienced by anyone performing some task, for example, writing-reading. We get at felt time by looking at literacy from the inside out rather than from the outside in, as most research examining literacy as a process has done.[16] For example, Isaac Newton's seventeenth-century experiments with optics established central truths about the nature and behavior of light. However, bending light through a prism tells only half the story. What is absent from Newton's account of light is any consideration of the phenomenological experience, the felt truth or truths that the sense of light has for people.[17] A similar argument can be made for explanations of performative time—the time involved in a literacy performance; they, too, are bereft of the experience of time. A commonly accepted temporal truth about performative time is Ann Berthoff's concept of allatonceness, the idea that for meaning to occur we must "speak and seek for meaning at one and the same time," a process that simultaneously involves "naming, inferring, referring, recognizing, remembering, marking time, wondering, wandering, envisaging, matching, discarding, checking, inventing" (*Sense* 86).

Although Berthoff describes how allatonceness is experienced by writers, the specific visceral and phenomenological responses to allatonceness remain underexplored. Consider the range of felt times experienced in a single act of writing-reading. For example, when we are "jammed" against a writer's block, an intellectually and physically painful place to inhabit, time expands. Under this duress, our perception of time shifts so that it seems to lengthen, widen, deepen, until it becomes so all-encompassing that we fear we will never escape, never get over, under, or around that block. Trapped within these "long" hours, we are tempted to quit: to stop writing, stop reading, stop school itself. Note the number of former graduate students who end their academic careers ABD or the number of students who drop our classes midway through the semester. On the other hand, when we are torn by multiple and competing deadlines, time contracts; we become preternaturally sensitive to the ticks on the clock. Pressured by the need to complete assignments and honor commitments, we struggle against the frightening constriction of time, its force compressing chests and throats. The ensuing panic as time flies leads us to intellectual and rhetorical shortcuts, to simplifying tasks and reducing complexity. Finally, to compensate for the perils of both expanding and constricting time, there is what I call magic time, the moments, far too rare, in writing-reading when time quite simply disappears. It ceases to exist as a significant factor, either as a parameter for the literacy act or as an inhibitor for shifting levels. Mihaly Csikszentmihalyi calls these moments *flow*, "the holistic experience that people feel when they act with total involvement" (36). In a flow state, we become so absorbed by an activity that we lose conscious awareness of external factors: "there is little distinction between self and environment, between stimulus and response, or between past, present, and future" (36). Our experience of time as parsed and parsable disappears. If we were followers of Zen, we would call these precious experiences outside time as living fully in time, living in the fullness of the moment when we are wrapped so totally in the experience of writing-reading that meaning evolves free from the sticky fingers of time. For many of us, the memory of and the hope for magic time is the only thing that keeps us writing-reading through the more painful moments.

These paradoxical felt times in writing-reading illustrate the fragmentation of time, the impossibility of assigning a single sense of time to writing-reading. But a second reorganization effected by imageword crisscrossing the borders of time contravenes this fragmentation by imposing measured time on our experiences and performances. In felt time, imageword's corporeal logic morphs across time's boundaries to split literacy into many different times. But imageword's discursive logic also morphs across time's edges. It shape-shifts into metronomic time, what John Lofty defines in his ethnography of time and literacy as any time that is parsed into neatly allocated segments, characteristic of controlled environments, from work places to prisons to schools. Metronomic time contradicts, denies, and controls felt time through a careful orchestration of any and all performances. It holds felt time to the rigid dictates of linear time, attempting to tame and contain the potential chaos of felt time.

A temporal literacy evolves from these sites of change, one tangled in its own contradictions. We are always subject to the doubleness of felt time with its fragmentation and metronomic time with its strict control. Each conspires to undermine and contradict the other, a phenomenon we experience when we do some of our best work in response to deadline pressure or when our students' academic success is linked integrally to their acquisition of time management skills. The value of a temporal literacy is this doubleness. First, such a literacy prevents us from assigning a single time line to literacy. Instead, it fractures the temporal linearity of writing-reading, a consideration that demands of us flexibility in our approaches to our students' experiences of their own performances of literacy, a flexibility that we badly need. As teachers functioning within the confines of metronomic time, we tend to strategize everything: we assign so much time for teaching techniques of invention, drafting, and revision, in the process reducing the complexity and recursiveness of each and treating writing-reading as problems to

be solved logically and clearly. Within the pressure of a single semester, we allow little time for error, little time for waiting for a kai-
rotic moment, either in our teaching or in our students' writing-
reading, because we march to the beat of clock and calendar. We
have no opportunity to teach for the richness of what W. Keith
Duffy calls imperfection. Writing-reading must be done and done
now so that it can be assessed. But a temporal literacy, with the in-
fusion of felt times and metronomic time, requires us to open up
the linear progression of the syllabus to the play of felt times. It
provides a rationale for teaching writing-reading in such a way, and
in such a time frame, that we can invite experiences of "magic
time," those moments in writing-reading when we are in the "flow"
and literacy runs apace, towing us delightedly in its wake.[18]

The second value that a temporal literacy holds for our teaching is that it allows us to assess the degree to which metronomic
time has reduced effective teaching to effective timekeeping and to
effective classroom control. Foucault perceptively notes that time-
tables serve as a central means of discipline. They control activities in schools, workshops, and hospitals by establishing rhythms,
imposing specific occupations, and regulating cycles of repetition
(*Discipline* 149). Foucault offers examples of school time, divided
into minutes, that dictate what would happen when: "8.45 entrance
of the monitor, 8.52 the monitor's summons" and so forth (150),
reminding me in frightening ways of my own rough outline for
a day's class: freewrite on *Case* and *Neuromancer* (five minutes),
share freewrite (ten minutes), and so forth, slicing up my seventy-
five minutes into discrete activities. Lofty refers to this use of time-
tables to control activity as time that clicks away with the regularity
of a metronome, its rhythm set by the institution, not by the individual.

This metronomic time not only controls behavior but also determines what is important, functioning as an intellectual gate-
keeper. If we allocate "time" within our instructional day for a specific activity, then we have implicitly validated the importance of
that activity. If we delete an activity from the day's (semester's)
schedule, because we just do not have enough time, then we send

the message that that activity (or material) is extraneous. To illustrate, when my daughters attended elementary school in Kansas, the school system privileged recreational reading to the extent that it provided time within the curriculum for what was called DEAR time: drop everything and read. However, when the children moved from Kansas to an Indiana school, DEAR time disappeared from a curriculum heavily influenced by the state's mandated assessment instrument: the Indiana Standard Test of Educational Progress (ISTEP). Rather than budgeting time for recreational reading, or even allowing students to read during the lull between the completion of one activity and the beginning of another, students in my daughters' fourth and second grade classes were expected to complete booklets consisting of fill-in-the-blank questions on Indiana history or worksheets on phonics. The message implicit within this policy is that recreational reading is not important enough to warrant school time.

Perhaps an even more serious act of control that a temporal literacy reveals is the use of metronomic time within the educational curriculum to inculcate a particular system of values. As Lofty notes, "Despite the apparent absence of human signature to our clock culture, people shape time to embody and to represent the values currently most important to their social, economic, and political life" (4). Children enter our classrooms with diverse experiences of time, their temporal orientation marked by their geography, gender, race, class, and ethnicity. However, the imposition of a metronomic time set by the institution sends the unspoken message that all other times are of lesser value. Lofty describes the conflict engendered when metronomic time collides with island time—a time established by the rhythm of tides, daylight, and seasons. In a Maine fishing community, the site of Lofty's ethnographic study, time is measured by means other than clocks. As Lofty points out, "A local storekeeper tells me that he sells clocks only to summer visitors" (16). This is not to suggest that time is unimportant to island life; it is, in fact, essential to daily decisions. But that time is measured differently. Within the community of professional fishermen, worth is measured by the amount of time spent on the water

(17). And that time can be broken down into what Mike, one of Lofty's former junior high students who left school in ninth grade to begin his career as a lobsterman, refers to the as "big time" (when everything is important and "you measure it down to the smallest unit") and "small time" ("when it's nothin' at all") (27). Fishermen determine the length of their day by the pace of their activities; they are free to work as quickly or as slowly as they wish. The rate doesn't affect the size of the day's catch, but it does affect the length of their workday. This fluidity and the element of personal control over the pace of one's day as a lobsterman are violated by the regimented tempo of school activities, Lofty points out. And that violation serves as the source of Mike's frustration with his academic experiences, including those in his English class. His ability to determine his personal tempo, to decide when to switch from activity to activity, when to leave the lunchroom, when to hand in a paper is undermined by the metronomic time the teachers use to establish and maintain a particular pace of instruction (36). As Lofty notes, "School not only institutionalises clock time and socialises students into its values but minimises the need for students to be responsible for their own management of time" (92). Through a temporal literacy, we better understand the constructed nature of time, as well as its forms of control. We are better able to detect the power of metronomic time and counter it with experiences that allow for a fuller play of students' felt times. A temporal literacy renders the time of literacy teaching just as fluid as the nature of the literacy itself.

Anna no longer writes her spelling words backwards, she no longer bobbles her *d*s and *b*s, she no longer taps on stage in feathers and sequins. Roderick proceeds through his freshman year with success and confidence. Aletha keeps pace with her medical internship, Dana fuses rhetoric and linguistics in a dissertation that explores the discourse of chat rooms, and Meaghan transforms drawings into essays. Each continues to weave his or her literacy out of the unstable movement of imagewords shape-shifting across bodies, cultures, places, and times. By focusing our attention on these sites, we reclaim for our students, our children, and ourselves not literacy but embodied literacies and move closer to a poetics of teaching. Understanding how literacies evolve out of and are enacted within these porous sites enables us to reconfigure literacy instruction. Because meaning is choreographed among the transacting planes of bodies, cultures, places, and times, we are called to choreograph similarly our literacy praxis, moving to imageword's rhythm and pulsing to its dynamic.

3 / The Shape and the Dynamic of a Poetics of Teaching

[. . .] cut loose from my words
[. . . . .]
remember: the body's pain and the pain on the street
are not the same   but you can learn
from the edges that blur   O you who love clear edges
more than anything   watch the edges that blur
          —Adrienne Rich, "29" of "Contradictions: Tracking Poems"

Last May, an unusually hot, muggy morning in central Indiana, my younger daughter staged a tantrum when I refused to let her wear sweatpants (a good three inches too short) and a heavy matching T-shirt (also three inches too short) to school. Lindsey is neither rebellious nor masochistic; she merely wanted to wear clothes emblazoned with Pikachu's image. Pikachu is a small, yellow, lop-eared, electrically charged Pokémon, and Lindsey is obsessed with Pokémon. These Japanese pocket monsters that began life as a video game, then morphed to trading cards, cartoons and movies, and related paraphernalia, then back again to the arcades via Game Boy form the center of her conscious and probably unconscious existence. Dressed in Pokémon clothes, speaking a Pokémon language of hit points, badges, and gym masters, and enacting a Pokémon life, Lindsey constructs a fluid identity that enables her to navigate the rigors of school, playground, and home.

Lindsey's fascination with and incorporation of Pokémon in her waking and sleeping lives reflect the myriad ways in which the literacies of bodies and of place, of culture and of time evolve out of the shifting borders of an imageword ecology. Adrienne Rich urges us to cut loose from words, to watch the edges that blur. "[R]emember," she tells us, "the body's pain and the pain on the street / are not the same but you can learn / from the edges that blur O you who love clear edges / more than anything else watch the edges that blur" (111). Chapter 3 focuses on those blurred edges, the confluence of literacies that constitute the health of all human beings. The structure of any meaning emerges from the connections our minds and bodies make as we live within a specific place and time, subject to the social habits we evolve. Foucault notes that "our experience of the world is less that of a long life developing through time than that of a network that connects points and intersects with its own skein" ("Of Other" 22). To teach literacy, then, is to forge somatic, cultural, and environmental health as we live within historical and experiential time.[1] By focusing on the edges that blur—that amorphous realm wherein Lindsey shapes for herself a multifaceted identity out of an ecology of imagewords—chapter 3 extends the work of chapters 1 and 2 by describing the shape and the dynamic of a poetics of teaching.

I begin with the mercurial shape of literacy instruction. The four permeable sites within which and out of which literacy evolves resolve into three embodied literacies—somatic, polyscopic, and lateral literacies—and these embodied literacies structure a poetics of teaching. I describe the organization and enactment of each in our students' lives. I then turn to the dynamic permeating a poetics of teaching. The continual movement of imageword crisscrossing physical-social-spatial-temporal borders, a movement that generates embodied literacies, is also the movement, the rhythm, by which a poetics of teaching organizes itself. Positioned where the edges blur, our literacy classrooms become a site of and opportunities for a provocative dynamic. A poetics of teaching pulses to immersion, the experience of our deep connectiveness across the loops of an imageword ecology; to emergence, a recognition of the structure and rules governing that ecology; to transformation, the evolution of imagistic and rhetorical practices enabling us to evoke new connections, new ecologies; and to reimmersion, a new positioning in a different ecology, a different matrix of connections. The culmination of embodied literacies organized as a provocative dynamic is a multifaceted healthfulness, the well-being of the physical, textual, and spiritual worlds within which we live, a healthfulness permeated with and constituted by the constant weave of imageword's double logics.

Embodied Literacies

Over the past two years, Lindsey has been systematically creating herself and her world by means of embodied literacies. She sleeps on Pokémon sheets surrounded by walls covered with Pokémon posters. She carries to school in her Pokémon backpack (along with her Pokémon lunch box) four or five Pokémon novels, accompanied by at least one stuffed Pokémon toy (negotiated down from three) and various small plastic Pokémon figures. When she is angry with me, she will crawl into her dark closet, close the door, and curl up under the hanging clothes, claiming that she is returning to her Pokéball to recharge. She records both anger and recharging in the daily entries of the multiple notebooks she keeps, all of which, for the past year, have been addressed to Pikachu (and have included Pokémon poems, Pokémon songs, and Pokémon stories). With her sister's help, she has created an elaborate Pokémon world in the playroom where they and the neighborhood children stage Pokémon plays they have written (based on Pokémon short stories Lindsey wrote for school). She rehearses Pokémon narratives in the bathtub, lining up small, colorful plastic figures around the entire rim of the tub, whispering dialogue to herself. She plays a Pokémon board game with anyone she can enlist and, when she cannot find any willing victims, pores over her collection of Pokémon cards and Pokémon manuals, memorizing hit points, evolutionary progressions, and powers.

Nor is she happy just to play with or write about Pokémon. Lindsey has gradually attempted to remake herself physically into Ash Ketchum, the human character in the Pokémon pantheon who is seeking to become a Pokémon master. She dresses like Ash, in jeans and T-shirt (preferably one of her Pokémon T-shirts). She refuses to wear shorts (because Ash does not). She sleeps in her Ash Ketchum hat and attempts to gobble up her dinner because "Mom, that's how Ash does it." She demands that her hair be cut above her ears like Ash's, and, if she could manage it, I am sure she would try to cry in a fountain of light—just as Ash does in the cartoons and movies.

To craft for herself such an intricately constructed world and identity, Lindsey draws on myriad literacies, slipping and sliding gaily across the borders of an imageword ecology. A single literacy cannot account for the range of meanings and experiences she creates. Nor can that which is performed within the confines of a schoolroom and assessed by means of standardized tests be privileged as the sole manifestation of literacy. Instead, Lindsey's literacy exists as a hybrid of many literacies, a realization that allows us to extend the scope of literacy to embrace a multiplicity of media (New London Group; Stroupe) and a multiplicity of contexts (Street).[2] Who she is and how she navigates the world are imbricated with, dependent on, and manifested in imagewords negotiated through cartoons, drawings, illustrated novels, physical movements, transitional objects, dreams, and diary entries. What is at play in Lindsey's efforts to weave a meaningful life is her conscious and unconscious reliance on embodied literacies. Embodied literacies focus attention on the specific organization and deployment of shared ways of knowing that organize our experiences across media and across life. Regardless of whether we make meaning through print, iconography, or both, our enactments possess three common literacies: somatic, polyscopic, and lateral literacies.

These three specific literacies are the culmination of ways of knowing and meaning derived from imagewords moving across bodies, cultures, places, and times. They represent the fusion of these planes and these ways of knowing (fig. 3.1). Thus, somatic literacy encompasses the reciprocity of places and bodies; polyscopic literacy captures the juncture of culture, bodies, and places; finally, lateral literacy ties together temporal literacy and spatial literacy. Embodied literacies highlight the reciprocity, the mutual constitution of the entire array of loops in an ecology of meaning. The shape of a poetics of teaching is derived from these three literacies feeding into each other. Thus, if teachers are concerned with the acquisition and enactment of a specific literacy practice—for

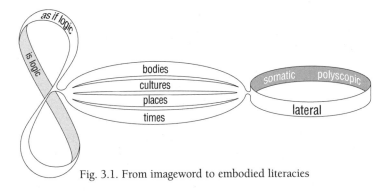

Fig. 3.1. From imageword to embodied literacies

example, digital literacy, defined as a way of knowing the symbol-system and conventions of the digital realm and a way of using that knowledge to facilitate our participation in that realm—then they would teach digital literacy via the embodied literacies that give rise to those literacy performances. They would structure their instruction and their environments to foster the somatic, polyscopic, and lateral literacies that unite to create digital literacy or print literacy or visual literacy. These ways of knowing—not a specific literacy practice—shape a poetics of teaching.

Somatic Literacy

A combination of corporeal and spatial literacies, somatic literacy concerns how we construct and participate in the world through our bodies and how we know the world as bodies positioned in specific sites. It embraces the level of kinesthetic learning, from the proprioception that allows us to orient ourselves spatially in the world to the twitch of our fingers on an imaginary keyboard when we think of writing. It embraces emotions issuing from our limbic system and circulating through the higher cortical regions, which Antonio Damasio in a flight of poetry calls the body murmuring to the mind. And it embraces what Ernest G. Schachtel calls allocentric perception, a "full turning toward [an] object that makes possible [a] direct encounter with it and not merely a quick registration of its familiar features according to ready labels" (221).

Through somatic literacy, students conceptualize meanings as multi-sensual and as sited, incorporating into writing-reading the sensuality and positionality necessary for our physical existence within the world.

Somatic literacy weaves throughout Lindsey's immersion in Pokémon. Her creation and inhabitation of a Pokémon world is an overwhelmingly corporeal act operating on myriad levels. The most visible is the restructuring of her physical environment—her bedroom—so that she is saturated in a Pokémon mythos. Even when sleeping, Lindsey surrounds herself with and embraces several stuffed Pikachus of various sizes. She redefines her physical presence to correspond to the dictates of her Pokémon world. This redefinition is reflected in her efforts to emulate Ash Ketchum, from choosing similar clothes to imitating body language and social habits. It is also manifested in Lindsey's complementary and conflicting desire to be Pikachu. Thus, she curls up in her closet when driven by indignation; she pursues karate instead of gymnastics because karate will allow her to be a more proficient Pokémon; and she threatens her sister with a shock attack. Finally, in a delightfully revealing and delightfully typical move, Lindsey consumes Pikachu, in the form of decorated birthday cakes and sugar cookies.

Somatic literacy is evident as well in her writing-reading. Here Lindsey relies to a large degree on her role-playing, where she moves fluidly and confidently from one physical stance to another. To illustrate, Lindsey asked me recently to keyboard one of her short stories, something I do frequently. As I typed the story that she read aloud from her handwritten page, she discovered gaps and omissions in her short story. To rectify the flaws she identified, Lindsey moved around the room, morphing various Pokémon guises, shifting her body and voice, using that physical role-playing as a heuristic to expand and elaborate her text. By embodying her Pokémon world, she was better able to create that world through words. It was a magical merging of herself, her toys, and her words. The richness of her experiences with the Pokémon novels and her own creative writing derives from her deep somatic connection with her fantasy world.

Somatic literacy also manifests itself in our students' and our own textual practices: through the rituals we enact as an egress into writing-reading, through our resistance to particular modes or prescribed ways of writing-reading, and through the act of memory itself. Marion Joan Francoz presents a "model of memory that embodies an infinitely complex neurological network, activated, constituted, and reconstituted by interactions with the environment," offering "a nexus between biological and cultural, between presence and process" (26).[3] Because memory—rhetoric's fourth canon —is embodied, rhetorical practices are inevitably embodied.

Somatic literacy also functions as the organizing principle for particular kinds of literacies, for example, working-class literacy. Janet Zandy argues that working-class language traces its antecedents to material existence (rather than canonized literature) and historic events (rather than abstract theory). Elastic, defying easy genre or historical classification, working-class language is a tool for survival in which intellect and emotion merge in an "ongoing dialogue between private pain and public speech" (Introduction 11). Working-class language use shares physical language because "working-class people practice a language of the body that eludes theoretical textual studies" (Zandy, *Liberating* 5), a point underscored by Karyn Hollis's study of the poetry of working-class women enrolled at Bryn Mawr during the 1920s and 1930s. Hollis argues that the working-class women involved in summer school at Bryn Mawr manifested a "cultural logic or 'grammar'" that was "largely corporeal, based on their physical exploitation for the benefit of a 'lady' of another class" (98). Their poetry, Hollis explains, reveals a "bodily motif" and "reveals how a pedagogical project can progress from textual to physical context" (99). Almost seven decades later, working-class students lack the same quiet hands and neutral faces, Zandy points out, because their bodies are not separated from their discourse. "The physicality of class difference, the use of the body for expression, communication, and as a substitute for abstract language, is evident in the literature produced by working-class writers, but is rarely recognized, never mind theorized, as a language system" (*Liberating* 5).

Somatic literacy involves the development and the deployment of what Schachtel calls an allocentric perception and an allocentric attitude, especially evident in responses to art and poetry. Because somatic literacy operates by means of imagery's corporeal *is* logic, it unmarks boundaries and dissolves subject-object duality. Allocentric perception and attitude reflect this same dissolution of boundaries. In allocentric perception the perceiver, actively participating in the perception, opens herself "toward it [the percept] receptively, or, figuratively or literally, takes hold of it, tries to 'grasp it'" (83). Successful perception is predicated on a kind of mutual assimilation in which ego identity and utilitarian needs are subordinated to openness. For example, Schachtel describes an allocentric attitude as

> one of profound interest in the object, and complete openness and receptivity toward it, a full turning toward the object which makes possible the direct encounter with it and not merely a quick registration of its familiar features according to ready labels. (220–21)

Historian of science Morris Berman calls this means of perception "participating consciousness," in which we are not alienated observers of but direct participants in a human destiny indivisible from that of the cosmos (*Reenchantment* 23).[4] Knowledge results from a process "of visceral/poetic/erotic identification" (139).[5] To know, one must submerge oneself in an experience, not detach oneself from it to view it from afar. Knowledge comes about "through identification, or collapse of subject/object distinction" (181), and "[r]ationality, as it turns out, begins to play a role only after the knowledge has been obtained viscerally" (139). Because we permeate the world, we must "literally eat the other, take it into our guts, and as a result we are changed by it" (268). We "know a thing precisely in the act of identification, and this identification is as much sensual as it is intellectual. It is a *totality* of experience: the 'sensuous intellect'" (Berman, *Coming* 75).

This sensuous intellect or allocentric attitude is the aim and the essence of somatic literacy. When students exercise their somatic literacy, they conceptualize meanings as multisensual and as sited, incorporating into writing-reading the sensuality and positionality implicit in all human existence and validating the legitimacy of those experiences. They evolve and deploy corporeal means to participate physically in the world. Literate citizenship is also somatic citizenship.[6]

Polyscopic Literacy
Produced through the fusion of culture, bodies, and places, polyscopic literacy concerns how we evolve and deploy specific ways of seeing and how we organize our realities, including our textual realities, according to specific networks of reinforcing images. First, to construct meaning in the world, we tacitly rely on a dominant imageword dynamic permeating a culture during an historical moment, an identifiable yoking and relative valuing of imagery and language. Donna J. Haraway reminds us that "all eyes, including our own organic ones, are active perceptual systems building in translation and specific ways of seeing, that is, ways of life," and I would add ways of literacy (*Simians* 190). Thus, Foucault can write in visual terms of the historical fault line that exists between the Middle Ages and the Enlightenment. He points to the differences between a participatory way of seeing in which word, image, and world were mutually reinforcing and a detached way of seeing in which word, image, and world were amputated from one another, severing the connection between perceiver and perception (*Order* 17–42). Learning how to mean and learning how to participate in a culture cannot be excised from learning how to see in a particular way because a culture—its infrastructure and its exoskeleton—is organized around this dynamic.

A way of seeing is intrinsic to Lindsey's literacy, to her construction and inhabitation of her Pokémon world. For Lindsey, her Pokémon way of life is predicated on the mutuality of image and word and on her active participation in the creation of each. Every diary entry and story she creates reveals this dynamic, for words are accompanied by pictures; words frequently are pictures.[7] While this process is subtle, it is not passive. Rather, her negotiation of the imageword dynamic is a constructive act, in which she is an integral agent. She generates those imagewords by physically enacting her stories, which exposes her to different spatial perspectives.

Our students are not immune to the influence of a way of seeing. Our students' and our own textual practices reflect the development and deployment of ways of seeing the world, including those that differ from ways of seeing promulgated by the academic system or by the culture at large. For example, Christine Bennett has argued for the importance of teaching what she calls "multicultural competence," defined as "competence in multiple ways of perceiving, evaluating, and doing" (191). Multicultural competence acknowledges that individuals possess a "view of the world that is not universally shared and that differs profoundly from that held by many members of different nations and ethnic groups" (191). Crucial to this enterprise is the recognition that one's cultural membership and construction of the world is predicated on the development of a way of seeing that world. "Vision," Haraway reminds us, "is *always* a question of the power to see" (*Simians* 192).

In addition to an imageword dynamic, polyscopic literacy also involves the construction of and adherence to networks of reinforcing imagewords validated within a culture. Developing proficiency in a way of seeing, and thereby developing one's cultural membership, is interwoven with constructing and adhering to an array of imagewords. We cannot separate what we see from how we see. Lindsey's literacy again offers insight into this aspect of polyscopism. The configurations of reinforcing imagewords serve as raw materials Lindsey molds and reshapes to conform to the angles of her life. The Pokémon commercial mythos serves only as the starting point for her creativity; she has no compunction about evolving alternative storylines or entirely new storylines, each of which challenges the commercial Pokémon. She and her sister have even created new Pokémon. Lindsey takes the imagewords produced through posters, novels, cartoons, and games, negotiating their constraints and her desires. This is a reciprocal process, however, in that the reinforcing imagewords also mold and reshape

Lindsey's life, dictating wardrobe choices, sibling behavior, and acceptable responses to anger. Lindsey finds her array of Pokémon imagewords enabling. She uses them to explore the possibilities of agency in her world, and she uses them as portals into different worlds in which she is an active participant and a creative force. But such configurations can be disabling as well. Mike Rose achingly illustrates this possibility in *Lives on the Boundary*. Turning to his classmates' responses to both their vocational educational curriculum and to their configuration by the administration as voc ed students, Rose reveals how imagewords can be disabling. In the midst of a discussion in religion class on talent and achievement, one of Rose's classmates announces that he just wants to be "average" (28). This is a typical reaction to voc ed placement, Rose says, one in which students sees themselves according to the imagewords constructed by the school administration, protecting themselves "from such suffocating madness by taking on with a vengeance the identity implied in the vocational track" (29). Assignment to the voc ed track carried with it a particular organization of imagewords dictating identity, dictating what is real and truth: One is, at best, average. Students can use this configuration as a point of resistance or as a goal, Rose says, but it always serves as the students' starting point for self-definition.

Feminist struggles with metaphor highlight the troubling reciprocity of enablement and disablement in reinforcing imagewords, evident in both Lindsey's and Rose's experiences. As Meryl Altman points out, "[f]eminist criticism, and feminism more generally, have both feared and loved metaphor," resisting, on the one hand, uses of metaphor to restrict and reduce Woman to a trope, and, on the other hand, drawn to the transformative potential of metaphor to reconfigure reality (495–96). Patricia Yaeger in *Honey-Mad Women* addresses this problem specifically in regard to women writing. Feminists argue that women have been silenced by a male-dominated language in which women have no avenue to speak their desires, their pleasures. They are trapped in a disabling array of images that stress a woman's "alienation from her own powers of metaphor" (4). But women can access the power of language by evolving a new matrix of enabling images. Yaeger turns to the "honey-mad woman," the archetypal image liberated by poet Mary Oliver, a woman "mad for the honey of speech" (4). These new images of women seizing words and aiming them with their own purposes redefine women's marginality, reverse their alienation, and enable their speaking. The metaphor of the honey-mad woman "gives us a map for defining a countertradition within women's writing, a tradition in which the woman writer appropriates language 'racked up' in her body and starts to sing" (28).

A third characteristic also marks polyscopic literacy, and that is the multiplicity of visions and networked imagewords. A culture is marked by more than one way of seeing, more than a single network of imageword. We constantly shift among perspectives, a process clearly manifested in Lindsey's literacy. Lindsey inhabits more than one position, sees through more than one set of eyes: through the culturally mandated vision of her Pokémon world; through the fracturing vision of her home, influenced by a mother less than thrilled with the Pokémon craze; through the collaborative sight of sister and playmates; through literal shifts in vision as she moves herself physically, crouching and crawling to see the world as Pikachu, as a gym master, as Ash. These same multiple perspectives are reflected in our students' survival (or extinction) in the academy. Part of becoming a successful student, one who not only moves between disciplinary boundaries demanded by an undergraduate education but also one who navigates the competing demands of a single discipline characteristic of graduate studies, is predicated on juggling different ways of seeing. Thus, as students learn the discourse of the biology lab report, they are simultaneously learning the way of seeing privileged within biology, that which Martin Jay identifies as Baconian empiricism ("Scopic"). Then, when these same students shift to an English class, one in which they are required to read and respond to literature, they are invited into a different way of seeing, one more reflective of Schachtel's allocentric perception.

Polyscopic literacy involves the development and deployment of multiple ways of seeing and multiple networked images. Through polyscopic literacy, we learn to shape and to recognize the partiality of our visions of and in the world, as well as the limitations and possibilities of the configuration of imagewords reigning in a culture at a particular time and place. The aim of polyscopic literacy is to reinforce the partiality of perspective, the sitedness of sight. Polyscopic literacy enhances our awareness of the limits of our way of knowing and our knowledge and invites us to evolve alternative ways of seeing, a process that Haraway warns is marked by considerable angst but one that is also necessary for our social and psychological health (*Modest* 182).[8]

Lateral Literacy

Resulting from the fusion of spatial and temporal literacies, lateral literacy concerns how we evolve and organize narratives faceted by time and space.[9] Few deny the necessity of stories for crafting our epistemology, our morality, and individual and cultural identities (Bruner; Fisher). A lateral narrative is a story or, perhaps more accurate, stories that fuse space and time so that the sequential flow of chronology is disrupted to take into account simultaneities that are not simultaneous. As physicist Paul Davies reminds us, place disrupts what can be conceived as coincident, for an action in one place at one time will not occur in concert with an act in another place. There will always be minute (or vast) differences in time lines, depending on the distances between events. This is not just a case of different perspectives on the same events. The interpenetration of space and time calls into question the sameness of time lines and challenges the linearity of narratives.

Because we are stretched along the horizontal and vertical dimensions of social being and consciousness, we are subject to what postmodern geographer Edward Soja refers to as lateral narratives, stories whose chronological linearity is disrupted by the presence of places, by events that are and are not simultaneous. The stories that we live are the product of both time and space, constituting a "spatial hermeneutic" that makes it possible "to enter the narration at almost any point without losing track of the general objective: to create more critically revealing ways of looking at the combination

of time and space, history and geography, period and region, sequence and simultaneity" (Soja 2). Essayist Nancy Mairs points
out that

> [t]he search for lost time necessitates spatial, not merely
> temporal recall. [. . .] We can impose a grid of time onto
> our memories, much as we sketch lines of latitude and lon-
> gitude on a globe, a useful device for knowing when or
> where we are in relation to some other event or spot used
> as a reference point. But the memories won't yield up their
> freight in response. For that we have to let go of lifelines
> and plunge into the multiple modalities—sensory, emo-
> tional, cognitive—which have encoded the past and will
> realize it, transformed, into the present. (*Remembering* 9)

Lateral literacy is the multimodal process we have developed
to fashion a meaning from the many conflicting spatial-temporal
planes we live within by composing stories that weave together
time and space.[10] To paraphrase Emily Dickinson, it is the process
by which we tell the truth slant, by which we keep that truth fluid.
Lindsey's Pokémon stories manifest her reliance on lateral literacies,
shifting as they constantly do in response to place and time overlapping in myriad combinations. Perhaps the most obvious enactment
of lateral literacies results from Lindsey's continual movement between media, a movement that requires her to evolve and negotiate different imagistic and narrative practices. Shifting between media results in a kind of narrative refraction. Refraction refers to
the visual phenomenon that occurs as light travels through different media and changes speed, resulting in visual disjunctures. For
instance, when light travels through the water of a crystal vase,
it produces the illusion that the stem of a flower is broken even as
it stands upright. The temporal integrity or backbone of narratives is also broken as the narratives morph through different media. My daughter's Pokémon stories demonstrate this break. Lindsey
is a connoisseur of Paint, using this computer program to draw
elaborate, ongoing stories with multiple levels and intricate spatial

relationships. When she transforms these spatial narratives into a textual story, she transforms the nature of the story, juggling the constraints of verbal description and action, highlighting elements absent from her picture. However, this shift in narrative elicited by the constraints of writing draws her back to her Paint figure, which she had stored on the computer desktop, so that she continually revises the image, working by turns on Paint narrative and textual narratives.

A second and more subtle way that Lindsey manifests (and relies on) lateral literacy is through the process of diffracting narratives. In optics, diffraction results from the interference of light waves as they pass an opaque body. The interference produces a fuzzy region between the shadowy area and the lighted area that, upon examination, resolves itself into light and dark lines. Diffraction grids filter light through thin slits, a process that diffuses light into its multiple colors. This is the method of critique, of "critical consciousness" advocated by Haraway in opposition to reflection (*Modest* 34, 272; "Promise"). Diffraction patterns record the history of an interaction, she writes, unlike reflection, which merely replicates an interaction. Lindsey's narratives are subject to this subtle process in two ways. For Lindsey, Pokémon is both a solitary and collaborative activity. When she is engaged with her sister and the neighborhood children in the Pokémon playroom that they have jointly created, a single narrative fails to satisfy the group's desire. Instead, they demand that Lindsey relate the history of the story— where it came from, how she wrote it—so that they can proceed to rewrite the narrative collaboratively, splitting it into lateral lines. Finally, Lindsey has gradually begun altering the shape of her private Pokémon narratives as a result of my repeated interference, my efforts to critique the Pokémon mythos. Troubled by the ethical system that infuses the Pokémon world, I have frequently asked Lindsey to tell me stories about Pikachu's capture, about Charizard's incarceration for disobedience in his Pokéball, about Pokémon who do not want to fight for their masters, and about Pokémon mothers whose children have been enslaved by an evil master. Such interference has gradually resulted in subtle shifts in her narratives, in plotlines where Pokémon masters, including Ash Ketchum, her hero, are conspicuously absent. Instead, Pokémon have their own adventures, freed from the confines of Pokéballs and the human drive to use them to become gym masters. Through diffraction, Lindsey splits story lines into their multiple histories, undermining her conviction in one story, one meaning, one identity.

Our students' and our own textual practices also involve the development and deployment of lateral literacies, especially evident in the navigation of cyberspace. A term coined by William Gibson for his 1984 novel *Neuromancer, cyberspace* refers to the felt sense of connectivity that comes into being when individuals communicate through a complex network of computer nodes. Cyberspace disrupts traditional narrative linearity, providing a fertile environment for our students' development and practice of lateral literacies. This is evident not only in the poetics of cyberspace, that is, in the fiction and poetry created for and distributed through the World Wide Web (www), but also in the nonnarrative Web sites that proliferate throughout the Internet. The habits we acquire as a result of our immersion in what Craig Stroupe calls the hybrid environment of hypermediated cyberspace encourage us to think in terms of lateral narratives whether we are navigating a story or not.[11] The separations between Web sites, images, and words are subject to constant erosions that reconfigure their boundaries. At the click of a mouse, a hotlink in a text can open a word into a graph; a hotlinked point on the graph can morph into a new text or a new image, one fluid with movement and sound. Clear-cut divisions between space-time and imageword can no longer be maintained. Nor can the divisions between primary or central text be maintained. As George Landow notes, within the hypermediated realm of cyberspace, the marginal and the central are complementary; the definition of what constitutes central or primary text is as much a product of time as it is of space. Dominated by the fluid, constantly revised spatial-temporal sites, narrative explodes into narratives, primary text into texts: "As the rigid demarcations between formerly discrete texts become fluid liminal zones, and then simply markers within an ever-shifting nodal system of narrative information, the Aristotelian story arc, with its beginning, middle, and end, becomes something else again" (Lunenfeld 15). With its collapse into space-time and imageword, the electronic age, Peter Lunenfeld argues, frees us to "invent nonlineal illogics" (21) and nonlinear time lines, manifesting the enactment of lateral literacy.[12]

The aim of lateral literacy is to increase the fluidity of our meanings and increase our opportunities to transform our imagistic and rhetorical practices. Lateral literacy serves a survival function, enabling us to evolve narrative practices that help us respond flexibly to the challenges posed by a multifaceted reality subject to its own randomness. Bateson has argued that survival goes not to the creature best adapted—physically and rhetorically—to its environment. The Burgess Shale represents as much, filled as it is with the fossilized remains of extinct species all perfectly adapted to their environments. Rather, survival goes to the creature with the greatest flexibility, one that can respond to the random reordering of the ecology within which it is immanent. Lateral literacy endows us with flexibility. It mitigates the human desire for closure, for completion, by keeping us open to transformation. Lateral literacy demands that we continually struggle with the multiplicity, the split nature, of our identities and of our worlds. "The narrative urge," Anne DiPardo writes, "is as ubiquitous as our desire to understand our condition, and just as important as knowledge gleaned through more systematically rational means" (63). But, she continues, in order for our stories and our students' identities as storytellers to affect our curriculum and instruction, "our working definitions of narrative must be enlarged and enriched, as must our sense of its relations to the whole of thought and language" (63). Lateral literacy accomplishes this.

Immersion, Emergence, Transformation

Embodied literacies provide a shape for a poetics of teaching, leading us to new questions for and new techniques of literacy praxis. A major shift in our approach to teaching writing-reading heralded by embodied literacies concerns the dynamic by which we structure our courses, the dynamic by which we decide what to teach when. Embodied literacies implicate a particular rhythm for the class-room, a tempo for learning experiences. That dynamic involves the cadence of immersion, emergence, and transformation. Whether we focus on invention or audience, on writing-reading process or cultural studies, on personal expression or social construction, the pedagogical questions we put to ourselves in regard to our students concern our connectiveness within an imageword ecology, our egress into a critical awareness of the formative rules of that connectiveness, and our re-formation of those rules into different imagistic and rhetorical practices, into different narratives. Shaped by embodied literacies, we are impelled to consider ways in which we can invite our students to immerse themselves in the multilay-ered and tangled loops of an imageword ecology. We are impelled to provoke our students into an awareness of the rules—the ways of seeing and being—that limit their ability to discover, to invent, to mean. We are impelled to elicit transformations, new imagistic and rhetorical practices, that enrich our students and offer opportuni-ties to renarrate the imageword ecologies within which they live. Thus, even as we are subject to our participation in an imageword ecology, that teeming nexus of bodies, cultures, times, and places, we are also able to exercise embodied literacies to act on that image-word ecology, to recraft both the meanings and the systems that give us birth.

Like embodied literacies, the dynamic of a poetics of teach-ing is a cyclical one, existing not as a linear progression from im-mersion to emergence to transformation, but as an interwoven loop of rhythms. In addition, even as each beat of the dynamic privi-leges a specific material literacy—immersion somatic literacy, emer-gence polyscopic literacy, transformation lateral literacy—it is em-bedded within all literacy. Similarly, each embodied literacy offers egress into each pulse of the dynamic (fig. 3.2). For example, im-mersion clearly relies on and enhances the connectiveness of so-matic literacy, but it is also central to polyscopic literacy, to ways of seeing. Similarly, emergence suggests a shift to polyscopic literacy, to different ways of seeing connectiveness, but it is also crucial to

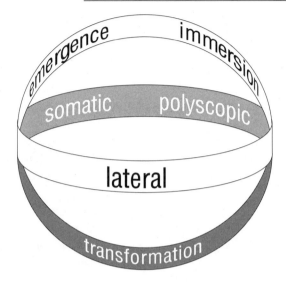

Fig. 3.2. The dynamic of a poetics of teaching

lateral literacies. Finally, transformation is an essential trait of lateral literacies, but it is also necessary for somatic literacy. The question that we need to ask ourselves, then, as we prepare to teach embodied literacies and to teach with embodied literacies, is how to invite immersion, provoke emergence, and elicit transformation, knowing that we can separate these experiences only artificially.

Immersion

Regardless of whether we are committed to teaching tropes, technical writing, or writing with technology, regardless of whether we are in a writing center, literacy center, or traditional classroom, a necessary part of a poetic of teaching is the invitation to immerse, to experience a visceral-emotional connectiveness so that the demarcations between subject and object, individual and situation, word and place dissolve. Privileging the corporeal *is* logic of imagery, immersion is the process of unmarking the boundaries that separate students so neatly and artificially from their embodiment and emplacement within the world. Immersion ties students' literacy experiences to what Gesa E. Kirsch and Joy S. Ritchie, quoting Adrienne Rich, call a "politics of location" (7), which "reconnects our thinking and speaking with the body of this particular living human individual, a woman" (Rich, qtd. in Kirsch and Ritchie 7). A politics of location validates our lived experiences as knowledge, as a way of knowing. Immersion brings students nearer to the realization that bodies, communities, and literacies are mutually infused, mutually porous. Thus, the social-political vigor of a particular community cannot be abstracted from the physiological-psychological vigor of a particular individual. Each is woven within the other.

One way to invite immersion is to focus on the sensuous connections among imagewords, bodies, and places by literally shifting students to a different venue for writing-reading. Randall Roorda explores just such a strategy by having students write in nature as they study nature writing. Writing in nature, Roorda argues, makes students more sensitive to the interweaving of the words they use and the places within which they dwell. "Writing may function not just to record but to embody one's presence in place" (Roorda 397). For instance, Roorda cites the note-taking habits of nature writer Gary Nabhan. While in the field, Nabhan focuses in his field notes on re-creating in language the bird songs he hears. "In the field, there is a chance that some of the sounds I hear in that landscape will carry over into sounds of words I use to describe a place" (Nabhan, qtd. in Roorda 397). These on-site sounds, Roorda writes, weave throughout the language created in place, achieving for this discourse "a virtue borne of its origin in the place itself, a qualitative difference from any language he [Nabhan] can generate elsewhere" (397).

By connecting to place—both an environment and a body—students situate themselves on the shifting boundaries between words and somatic reality, discovering the inescapable connection between our words and our worlds. We do not need to take our students outside to do this. We can invite connectiveness to place by focusing their attention on their immediate "print setting," a term Robert F. Carey and Jerome Haste use to describe the physical environment within which we write-read, opening us to the paradox of place: that connection to place can be one of alienation, can be alienating. The writings exchanged by students in Michael Blitz's and C. Mark Hurlbert's classes poignantly demonstrate the power of a print setting to close down language, to cut off options for actions. As one student so insightfully reveals:

> What's wrong with this picture? An eighteen year old kid comes home to find his mother totally drunk, as usual. His little sister has most of her clothes off with her boyfriend who is older and bigger than the eighteen year old so what can he say? The father? Well he's no place, nobody knows where he is or if he is dead. The eighteen year old finds a pile of dirty dishes and empty bottles and the baby brother is crawling around in garbage. So the eighteen year old picks up the baby and puts him in his chair while he starts to clean up the kitchen and make dinner. [. . .] The eighteen year old will be too tired to study again and he won't have time to write his paper for the only class he thinks he can do good in. What's wrong with this picture? (6)

These sensuous connections among literacies and sites can also be explored in the more traditional and more privileged school literacy. Immersion invites students to explore the blurring of school literacy, with its conformation to assessment and its service to middle-class values, and the material and discursive constraints (and agendas) of academic institutions (Fleckenstein, "Writing Bodies"). This exploration serves as a prelude to the realization that other places give rise to other literacies, literacies ostracized from school places but equally valid, equally capable of creating meaningful realities. Deborah Brandt's approach to writing-reading through "sponsors of literacy"—"agents, local or distant, concrete or abstract, who enable, support, teach, model, as well as recruit, regulate, suppress, or withhold literacy" ("Sponsors" 166)—provides insight into how such invitations to immerse can be supported. Here Brandt examines not only the scenes of literacy, with a perceptive eye toward literacy (and literacy workers) as exploitable resources, but also the performance of literacy, performances that include an appropriation of literacy for the writer-reader's own purposes, separate from those of the sponsor. The acquisition and use of literacy within a work setting, as well as the acquisition and use of literacy to further the user's own agenda, underscore the material performances of literacy practices within specific places by individual people. We are tied to place "undetachably and without reprieve," Edward S. Casey tells us (xiii), and so are our literacies. By providing opportunities for immersion, we help our students learn to halt or limit the inevitable shrinkage that occurs "as signs come to surpass the body [escaping] its sensuous control, dissevering themselves from the material world and dominating that which they are meant to serve" (Eagleton qtd. in McLaren 147).

A second technique for fostering immersion involves empathy.[13] Empathy extends our emotional connections across borders. Martin L. Hoffman defines empathy as a vicarious emotional response to another person's situation. It is a match between the observer's feelings and those of the model ("Interaction" 103). Thus, it requires connections between at least two people who do not share the same immediate situation. However, the power of empathy extends far beyond the dyad of victim and observer, Hoffman argues. Empathy is the basis of our community building and thus the basis of our survival as a species and our identity as human beings. "This human capacity for empathic distress [. . .] may thus be a major cohesive force or glue in society," Hoffman argues ("Empathy and Justice" 151). To feel empathy, people subordinate their own situation to that of the victim. The major process by which an individual experiences empathy, Hoffman says, is that of role-taking: imagining oneself in another's place, an act that intrinsically taps imageword's double logics ("Interaction"). Role-taking can take two major forms: other focus and self focus. The first role-taking strategy—that of focusing on the model—involves imagining how the model is feeling, visualizing the model's behavioral responses so that missing nonverbal cues are provided, and responding to the images as if the situation were physically perceivable. The second strategy, that of focusing on self—or identification—is one in which the individual pictures himself or herself in the model's position instead of just imagining the model's feelings. Perceivers immerse their values, drives, and behavioral patterns in those of the model, merging identities. Both techniques depend on blurring the boundaries between the place the perceiver inhabits and the place the victim inhabits, a process that enables victim and perceiver to experience similar physical reactions.[14]

As Hoffman points out, the richness of empathy extends beyond the victim-observer dyad to embrace the entire imageword ecology. As a result, immersion through empathy reconfigures traditional divisions of writing-reading. Invention, the art of finding the available means of persuasion, becomes inextricable from our connectiveness to the specifics of a physical situation. Invention becomes a material act. Audience is similarly reconfigured, requiring us to "flesh out" the fiction of audience by reminding our students that readers read in real places, in specific bodies. "From my wheelchair," Nancy Mairs wryly notes, "nothing looks the same" (*Voice* 46). The inescapability of body and place feeds directly into response so that reading as a writer means more than an enhanced sensitivity to style. It means resonating to a writer's situatedness, to the scene of action. *How* we invite immersion is not the crucial question for a poetics of teaching. *That* we invite it is.

Emergence

While immersion is a necessary element of a poetics of teaching, it is not sufficient. An entire semester inviting immersion might enable our students to plumb the depths of connectiveness, but it will not help them gain a greater critical awareness of the implications connectiveness holds for their literacy practices. Immersion must work in conjunction with emergence, or immersion can too easily morph into its own end, trapping writer-readers in one place, one body, one literacy, one reality. It can result in a glorification of the personal as an end in and of itself. As Rich warns, the "personal-for-its-own-sake," an "individualistic telling with no place to go," has no power to change the disenfranchisement of women

(*Of Woman* x) or the disenfranchisement of anyone. A necessary corollary to immersion is emergence, an identification of the imagistic and rhetorical strategies that maintain our emplacement within a particular imageword ecology.

We invite immersion, but we provoke emergence. The aim of emergence is to create a classroom praxis that requires our students to become more cognizant of the extent and the implications of their multifaceted immersion. Our participation in a culture results in our second naturing, our development of habits or ways of knowing that are drawn from our involvement with the very tools we create in the places we create them. Emergence aims at inciting an awareness of these habits and the price we pay for them.

One way to provoke that critical insight is by juxtaposing contrary ways of seeing. Ways of knowing are also ways of seeing, what Martin Jay, borrowing from Christian Metz, calls scopic regimes: the visual rules by which we see one way and not another (*Downcast*). These rules, however, become so deeply internalized that it is difficult to recognize their existence or to recognize their cultural embeddedness. However, important to scopic regimes is the existence of multiple ways of seeing. While one regime tends to dominate in a particular time and place, many less privileged ways of seeing are in contention within a single regime. Increased cognizance of a scopic regime, then, can be elicited by requiring our students to shift regimes. Disciplinarity, especially as configured through a communication-across-the-curriculum or writing-in-the-disciplines focus, is one way to do this. For example, literacy practices in the arts and literacy practices in the sciences are predicated on two very different ways of seeing. The ways of seeing in the arts correspond to what Schachtel calls allocentric seeing, a participatory seeing in which a writer-reader merges with the object of study, such as a poem.[15] On the other hand, the sciences are based on a different kind of seeing, that commonly referred to as Cartesian perspectivalism.[16] The scientific observer remains detached from the observed, an invisible witness to the unveiling of a reality to which the witness has unmediated access (Haraway,

Modest 23–45). The disciplines are differentiated not only by their methodologies and languages but also by the way of seeing privileged with that academic community. Literacy practices are linked inextricably with habits of seeing. Thus, juxtaposing different literacy practices—for example, writing a lab report of a poem or a poem of a frog dissection—enables our students to emerge from and recognize the influence of habituated ways of seeing that govern their progress through school, highlighting the degree to which their success in the academy rests, in part, on their ability to segue from one way of seeing to another.[17] On the basis of this realization, students will then be able to turn around on their disciplinary knowledge and on the world situations within which they honed a particular way of seeing so that they can identify the presence of alternative ways of seeing throughout their multifaceted lives.

In addition, when students acquire and validate multiple ways of seeing, they will inevitably find themselves in the position where these ways of seeing present them with oppositional visions of reality. "Struggles over rational accounts of the world are struggles over *how* to see," Haraway reminds us (*Simians* 196, her emphasis). This conflict in ways of seeing opens up gaps in the visual field or, more accurate, highlights the gaps already there. These gaps can then serve as points of resistance to the dominant ways of seeing, points where we can question the truth presented to us by our eyes. As Gilles Deleuze reminds us, "The point of critique is not justification but a different way of feeling, another sensibility" (vii). So, too, a different way of seeing.

Furthermore, confronted with these disparate versions of reality, students are then required to negotiate among these competing visions. This experience provokes the realization that a complete accounting of reality is impossible, that what we can hope for at best is an epistemology of partial perspectives, which is exactly what Haraway advocates: it is in "the politics and epistemology of partial perspectives that the possibility of sustained, rational, objective inquiry rests" (*Simians* 191), that the possibility of knowledge rests.[18] Within the epistemology of partial perspectives we are subject to neither the totalization of a vision from everywhere nor the relativism of a view from nowhere, both of which Haraway calls "god-tricks" and common myths in the rhetorics of science. Instead, caught as we are "in an echo chamber and a house of mirrors, where, in word and image, ricocheting mimesis structures the emergence of subjects and objects," we can turn emergence into an ethical and accountable way to write-read (Haraway, *Modest* 179).

Transformation
Immersion invites sensuous connections, emergence provokes partial perspectives, transformation elicits change in imagistic and rhetorical practices, opening the way to change in an imageword ecology. Transformation radically alters the imagistic and rhetorical rules by which a system functions, by which it maintains the homeostasis of all its elements. Speaking within the context of art and the African American experience, bell hooks calls this the process of "set[ting] our imaginations free," necessary for the "invention of the decolonized self" (4). Because both minds and imaginations are "colonized," what is required is "a revolution in the way we see, the way we look" (4). Feminists have similarly argued for radical shifts in the way we write, a turning around on the rhetorical practices that maintain the supremacy of a patriarchal structure (Joeres and Mittman). Transformation effects such changes, on micro and macro levels of the imageword ecology.

One strategy for eliciting transformations in our classrooms consists of changing the medium within which traditional rhetorical and imagistic habits are practiced. The World Wide Web offers a rich possibility for such a change. The confluence of image and word in cyberspace, the hypermediated as well as the hypertextual structure of cyberspace, requires subtle and obvious shifts in our literacy practices. Craig Stroupe calls such imagistic and rhetorical transformations hybrid literacy, arguing for "visualizing English," an approach based on the "dialogically constitutive relations between words and images [. . .] which can function as a singly intended, if double-voiced, rhetoric" (609). Stroupe argues that

Web-based environments, through a "class of living, social intentions rather than formal arrangements" can result in "illumination" rather than illustration (620). Illumination is the transformed literacy practice in which words and images talk, respond, and resist: they illuminate each other rather than merely illustrate each other (620). "Seams and margins" between words and images become "contact zones," gaps within which new rhetorical and imagistic practices materialize (628).

A second technique that elicits transformation is empathy, particularly the cognitive or critical face of empathy. While empathy provides a valuable strategy for immersion, it also provides a starting point for transformation.[19] Empathy enables not only the sharing of situations and perspectives but also the changing of situations and perspectives. It is an agent of transformation. Hoffman has written repeatedly that empathy is the basis for prosocial activism, which he defines as "sustained action in the service of improving another person's or group's life condition either by working with them or by trying to change society on their behalf" ("Empathy and Prosocial" 65). Empathy initiates action, and it does so through the fusion of emotion and critical cognition. This critical aspect of empathy is clearly evident in the attribution of causes for the distressful situation and in application of principles, values, and ideologies (79). For example, when we encounter someone in distress, we automatically begin to assign reasons for the distress, and those reasons affect how empathy is experienced. If we conclude that victims have no control over their plight or if we conclude that we have contributed in some way to that plight, very different empathic responses occur, each of which lead to different kinds of civic actions. A critical leap is also necessary for the shift between empathy for another's specific situation and for another's life condition. We must recognize that that life condition is not limited to one individual but is endemic to an entire group or class of people (70).

Empathy in its emotional and cognitive aspects elicits radical changes in imagistic and rhetorical practices by reconfiguring narrative. First, it mitigates our reliance on a single story or a single image by breaking the temporal backbone of master narratives. One of the dangers of immersion is that a particular situation can easily become a representation of all situations. For example, one woman's story of her struggle to craft an identity outside patriarchal structures morphs into all women's stories. It is this shifting from *a* situation to *the* situation that women of color point to when they argue that the feminist movement has essentially been a movement of white, middle-class women who have had the luxury of wealth, time, space, and education to ask the "woman's" (their "woman's") question. A multifaceted empathy disrupts "story" by crisscrossing stories, including counterstories that pulse to different rhythms, different times, different places. Thus, feminist researchers deliberately incorporate multiple voices—subjects and researchers—in an effort to highlight the multiplicity of stories within any construction of knowledge.

Second, empathy transforms the tyranny of first person singular, the rhetorical "I." Feminists assert that the construction of the rhetorical "I" in Western autobiography and essayistic writing has been founded on the existence of the unified Cartesian subject: white, middle-class, and male. This is the "I" that Virginia Woolf points to as shadowing, barring the first person Mary Seaton-Beaton in *A Room of One's Own*. By practicing empathy, however, students learn to question the authority, the singularity of the first person pronoun in published writing, in their own developing texts, and in the images "they" create. By disrupting their imagistic and textual stories, students embed multiple identities within that singular instance of "I," transforming a rhetorical stance inherent in Western essayistic practices.

Experiencing our connectiveness to bodies and places, recognizing the scopic regimes that morph out of connectiveness, and transforming in large and small ways our rhetorical and imagistic practices—this is the dynamic of a poetics of teaching. It is a dynamic that relies on, as well as enhances, the development of somatic, polyscopic, and lateral literacies.

Three years ago in first grade, Lindsey announced: "Don't call me Lindsey Mouse. I won't hear you."

"Oh?" I asked, assuming that she no longer wished me to use her nickname of Mouse. "What name will you hear?" "My name is Junie Beatrice Jones Fleckenstein. And I want my hair cut so," she said, assertively placing under my nose the book cover of a popular series about a lively kindergartner. And so for a span she became Junie B. Fleckenstein, signing her diary entries "Junie B." practicing Junie B. mischief, and peppering her conversation and her play with Junie B. witticisms. Then Junie B. morphed into Ash Ketchum. Yesterday afternoon, Ash Ketchum Fleckenstein stepped off the school bus, brandishing her sister's copy of *Harry Potter and the Sorcerer's Stone.*

"Mom, I need a wand and a cape. I'm going to fight He-Who-Cannot-Be-Named." She has discovered Hogwarts, so I expect that soon the Pokémon posters will come down, Ash will be relegated to a garage sale, and Lindsey will transform herself into a wizardling.

Through a continual weave of embodied literacies, through a rhythm of immersion, emergence, and transformation, Lindsey, like our students and ourselves, constructs a place for herself in the world, flexibly recrafting mind and body so that it resonates to the powerful imageword contexts within which she is interwoven, mirroring those multiple contexts in both her life and her writing-reading. By shaping our literacy teaching to embodied literacies and the dynamic of immersion, emergence, and transformation, we hold for our students, our children, and ourselves the hope of connection, of critique, of change.

4 / Slippery Texts: Artifacts for a Poetics of Teaching

> As kinetic, probable, and interactive forms of expression, they [images] attest to the conjectural and fluid nature of life lived in the middle zone. They help us organize and make sense of the floating world, or milieu, stretching considerably below certitude and somewhat above ignorance.
> —Barbara Maria Stafford, *Good Looking*

> "If I didn't draw this [picture], I wouldn't have this [paper]."
> —Janey, portfolio narrative

The muffled thuds of a hammer hitting a wall finally catch my attention. Usually, nothing piques a parent's suspicions more effectively than silence, but I had ignored the pattern of quick moving feet, the spreading quiet, and the muted whispering. Now, alarmed by the sound of forbidden tools, I stand in the open door of Lindsey's room. Lindsey does not sleep in a bedroom. She sleeps in a Pokémon shrine. Bookshelves are filled with Pokémon balls from Burger King, key chain Pikachus, Pokémon action figures, felt markers, and change purses, as well as Pokémon novels, reference books, and ring binders full of carefully categorized cards. Despite parental prohibition, Anna stands on top of Lindsey's bureau mounting her sister's new Pokémon posters. Seated on the floor, surrounded by Pokémon stuffed toys, Lindsey slips between words, images, and objects, whispering while her sister changes her environment. As I linger at the door, barred by my ignorance, they look up at me with eyes clouded by other worlds.

At that moment, Lindsey and Anna inhabit a place constituted out of artifacts that slip and slide across the boundaries of an image-word ecology. These are the artifacts that we also need to use in our classrooms. The shape and the dynamic of a poetics of teaching are drawn from the edges that blur. Embodied literacies and the · rhythms of immersion, emergency, and transformation situate our students and us within this anomalous, indeterminate realm. But a poetics of teaching requires more than embodied literacies pulsing to a provocative dynamic. It also relies on the use of particular kinds of texts, what I call in this chapter slippery texts, the kinds of texts manifested in Lindsey's bedroom.

Loosely defined, slippery texts are artifacts that keep us positioned on the edges that blur, the edges where literacy evolves. Slippery texts inhabit what Barbara Maria Stafford calls the middle zone and the floating world, the realm in which life and knowledge are fluid and conjectural. As imageword continually reminds us, we make and unmake boundaries in our meanings and our realities, shaping an image even as it morphs into a word, shaping a body even as it solidifies into a second nature, and splintering time as it crosses place. This constant movement of marking and unmarking is the movement within which embodied literacies are born. Thus, the texts that we select for a poetics of teaching must be similarly dynamic, similarly slippery, similarly blurred, and the first area of slippage occurs with my use of the term *text*. What constitutes a text is just as unstable, just as fluid as imageword, for it is imageword. Thus, text refers not only to textbooks but also to any artifact that might help us attend to the edges that blur: digital poetics, moos, hypertext, films, art, architecture, city planning, and so forth.

Regardless of the artifact or process chosen, our texts need to blur across three borders: those demarcating topics, genre, and media. The ideal goal is to choose texts that shift across all three, but even texts that slide across one would be a good starting point. Let me describe the possibilities of slippery texts for a poetics of teaching by first exploring in more detail the three areas of slippage. Then I slip across chapter borders to pick up the embodied literacies and the dynamic I described in chapter 3, interweaving them with texts to present three enactments of a slippery praxis for a poetics of teaching.

Slippery Texts

The first area of slippage is subject matter. Simply stated, the topics that we select for our classrooms need to be drawn from the point at which bodies, cultures, places, and times flow into one another. We deliberately choose subjects that challenge the neat categorization and tidy processes of exclusion and inclusion on which our construction of reality rests. We also look for topics that highlight the system of rules that we impose in an effort to reify borders and ban ambiguity. Let me offer a specific illustration of a topic that resides where edges blur: monsters, especially the cyborg monster.

Donna J. Haraway explains in "Cyborg Manifesto" that she chooses cyborg as her metaphor of social and bodily reality because it destabilizes our tidy boundaries between human and animal, human-organism and machine, and physical and nonphysical (*Simians* 151–53). A science fiction buff since I read my first Edgar Rice Burroughs in fifth grade, I have had a lifelong love affair with BEMS (bug-eyed monsters) and cyborgs. When I read Haraway's "Cyborg Manifesto" along with "The Promise of Monsters," long past my fifth grade year, both resonated with my reading history and my desire to challenge my students to think differently about their humanity and their writing-reading. So I gathered together a group of texts that I felt would invite my students to explore the edges of their human identities, jointly and individually.

A recent manifestation of this approach, one that involved an honors first-year composition course, includes three sets of materials—William Gibson's *Neuromancer* coupled with the Wachowski Brothers' *Matrix*, Philip K. Dick's *Do Androids Dream of Electric Sheep?* paired with Ridley Scott's director's-cut version of *Blade Runner,* and Marge Piercy's *He, She and It* partnered with Susan Seidelman's *Making Mr. Right*—and a packet of essays.[1] *Neuromancer,* the 1984 publication that marks the birth of cyberpunk fiction and introduced the term *cyberspace,* offers the story of Case, a data thief who is able to "jack in" to the matrix—cyberspace—via a computer keyboard and electronic hookups, leaving his "meat" behind and hijacking information stored in the matrix. Characters, such as Molly the samurai razor girl, are a combination of human and surgical-mechanical enhancements. In addition, the conflict within the story is initiated by the desire of an artificial intelligence to escape the bonds of its programming, to evolve into something different. With its disorienting narrative style and splintered story line, *Neuromancer* calls into question our beliefs in what we are, where we are, and what we can know. These designations are further destabilized by the film *Matrix*, which explores a life that exists merely as a computer simulation through the stimulation of the cortex. Human bodies lie quiescent, their electrical energies feeding the computer that creates the program—the Matrix—through which they seemingly live.

Dick's *Androids,* a novella about a futuristic police officer assigned to a squad that executes androids on Earth, directly explores the question of what makes us human. Barring a surgical procedure performed after death, the sole criterion by which an android can be differentiated from a human is the Voight-Kampff Empathy Test, and the story opens with a challenge to that test. Throughout the novella, the protagonist Rick Deckard repeatedly doubts his own humanity as he faces the erosion of his empathic abilities and engages in actions that violate his sense of human connection. *Blade Runner* confronts that question even more starkly as viewers are equally repelled and drawn to both Deckard and the replicant-android Roy Batty.

Finally, to offset the male-marked visions of the future promulgated by both novels and films, we end with Piercy's *He, She and It.* A multilayered novel that teeters between the far past and far future, *He, She and It* explores the blurring of gender, time, and human-machine. The novel turns on the creation of a cyborg, Yod, whose physical existence is designed by a man but whose psychological existence is programmed by a female. Crafted to protect the community in cyberspace and real space against incursions by transnational megacorporations, Yod despairs of the tragic paradox of his being—a weapon shaped with a conscience—inviting readers into a similar examination of the ethicality of their being. Seidelman's comedy, *Making Mr. Right,* presents a humorous look at a similar dilemma of humanness. A public relations executive is hired to elicit popular support for the deployment of an android created by a scientist to pilot a deep space mission. The rationale behind the android's existence is that he—because he is a machine—is better able to tolerate the physical and psychological isolation of long-term space travel. To her dismay and confusion, however, the main character discovers that the android is, in fact, more "human" than the scientist who creates him.

The subject matter explicitly and implicitly requires my students to question what it is that makes and keeps us human. It positions and repositions them, not always comfortably, on the unstable boundaries among bodies, cultures, places, and times. In a group presentation, three students illustrated their efforts to tackle this elusive question of humanness. They chose to explore the quality of emotions, a theme central to all three novels, focusing specifically on the assertion that humans are separated from all other creatures neither by their intelligence nor their language but by their empathy. As part of their presentation, the students invited their classmates to engage in an informal study of empathy by completing an on-line empathy questionnaire, one that assessed their empathic abilities. We all enthusiastically participated, completing the questionnaire in class only to discover that many of us (including me) scored fairly low on the empathic scale, low enough that the on-line program (the irony did not go unrecognized) counseled us to seek professional help. John, a student who also did not score well on the questionnaire, took this topic as the subject of his final paper, exploring explicitly Dick's assertion that empathy separates humans from all that is nonhuman. He opens his paper with the following:

> I recently took an empathy test online. I failed. According to Philip K. Dick, this single test is enough evidence to prove that I am not human. However, I know I'm human. Yet this empathy test's results prove that I am not, so I would be "retired" as an android in Philip K. Dick's world. This would be a terrible mistake with irreversible

consequences. So why would Dick choose empathy as the definitive point of humanity? Is empathy what determines humanity outside the pages of a book? Are all humans capable of empathy? I will explore these ideas and attempt to find an answer to an age-old question: "What defines a human?"

Through this combination of texts and through the encouragement of class discussion, John crafted his own slippery text, one that positioned him on the edges that blur, for he is unable to answer this question; he is unable to define his humanness.

The second area of slippage is that of genre, a category of knowledge that resists easy definition and teaching. From our early training in elementary school, we are taught that all writing fits into a particular class or category of texts. Our literature textbooks are divided by both genre and chronology; our rhetoric textbooks at one time (and even now) were arranged by genre, for modes are a facet of genre. However, writing-reading has never been comfortable with genre designations, seemingly more at home on the border between particular genres than within a specific genre. The morphing of genres in cyberspace, not merely the production of new genres, has pretty much exploded our struggles to corral the recalcitrance of text and the recalcitrance of writing-reading roles. Many feminists deliberately court genre slippage, both in cyberspace and print media, because they see in traditional genre designations and traditional essayistic conventions the patriarchal hand (Guyer; Joeres and Mittman; Page).[2] Genre slippage does more than site our students at the point of dissolving textual boundaries. It also sites them at the point of dissolving identity boundaries, introjecting private space and public space, private lives and public lives. Inviting our students to interact—through both writing and reading —with texts that challenge their accepted notions of textual stability bids them to test simultaneously their accepted notions of where they are and who they are, and the recalcitrance of the words they use to articulate both.

One example of such genre slippage is that provided by Gloria

Anzaldúa's *Borderland/LaFrontera*, a work that has evoked wildly
different responses from both undergraduates and graduates.
My first-year students in a second-semester composition class that incorporated literature and research writing (a course deliberately
configured to blur genres) responded enthusiastically to Anzaldúa's
crisscrossing of languages, poetry, research, and polemic.[3] Freed
from what many of them perceived to be the constraints of traditional research writing, they used Anzaldúa as a model of what they
might do as writers, even when writing in the academy. Although
few of them crafted papers that integrated other languages, as does
Anzaldúa, many of them experimented by pushing the edges of the
conventions they were taught in high school, interposing poetry,
stories, and graphic designs in their projects. On the other hand,
a core of my graduate students, differently positioned, differently
focused, actively resisted Anzaldúa, scorning her efforts to perform textually that which she espoused philosophically and politi-
cally. Because Anzaldúa deliberately conflates intellectual, textual,
and geographical "place," my students were likewise called to slip
across the unstable boundaries designating these areas. That act
countered efforts they were simultaneously performing to define
and maintain those exact boundaries. My graduate students, so in-
tent on crafting for themselves a professional identity that kept sliding away from them on a variety of fronts, were unable to experiment with the slippage Anzaldúa performed for fear that all of their
hard-won territory would be lost. I could view with sympathy their
struggles because I, too, as a graduate student enacted (continue
to enact) the same battle to carve out and shore up a professional
identity. As Celeste Schenck wryly notes, "women, never having
achieved the self-possession of post-Cartesian subjects, do not have
the luxury of 'flirting with the escape from identity,' which the de-
constructed subject may enjoy" (qtd. in Snyder 25). What I must do,
in my life and in my classroom, is highlight not the dangers inherent
in slippage but the possibilities for richer definitions, more multifaceted constructions of identity, including professional identity.
Both sets of reactions illustrate important ways that genre slippage

opens up our teaching to the evolution of literacies at the point where boundaries collapse and coalesce. The third area of slippage is that of medium. Questions concerning the content appropriate to a poetics of teaching are not limited to just subject matter or genre. They also encompass medium. Thus, we look for texts that challenge the neat demarcations among media. A startling realization of this cybernetic age is that texts dissolve. Yet we are trained by our traditions and our print history to perceive our textual reality as a material one, reified in the undeniable weight and cost of textbooks. We are trained in the epistemology of presence because of these material tools, so says N. Katherine Hayles. But that is a specious stability. A text remains lodged within a single medium only temporally, and sometimes not even then. All we need to do is look at the Pokémon craze, which began as a video arcade game, morphed to cards and board games, traveled from there to television cartoons, then slid over to films, cyberspace Web sites, and back to video games, this time as Game Boy games. We witness daily the dissolution and evolution of texts across media. It is no wonder that Craig Stroupe insists on our need to learn to navigate multiple symbol systems.[4] This multimedia quality, particularly when media are layered within a single artifact, is an important point of slippage for the texts we choose to teach with.

One way in which we can consistently evoke this slippage is by shifting between media as our students craft texts. An easy and productive strategy is to incorporate drawing and sketching as an integral part of students' literacy instruction, using such drawings to facilitate revision and assessment. In portfolio narratives, students can also reflect on the shifts between drawings and essays, juxtaposing the evolution of their texts with the evolution of the drawings that accompany those texts. To provide a quick illustration, I offered my first-semester composition students the concept of dilemma as the initiating idea for an assignment. Rather than beginning with a journal or other invention technique, I invited them to draw the feelings a dilemma evoked. Janey responded by drawing a heart cracking. From this, she moved to an essay in which she explored how daughters of divorced parents can still have a good relationship with their absent fathers. She paused midway through drafting this essay to craft another drawing, one that helped her envision what she wanted her readers to feel as they read. It consisted of a figure on a pedestal. In the course of revising her essay, which frustrated her efforts to bring it to a close, she returned to her original drawing—that of the breaking heart—and juxtaposed it with her later drawing—the figure on the pedestal. The two images clashed, which she saw as the source of her writing problem. She brought the problem to me, and I suggested that she might draw what she feels, rather than what she wants the reader to feel, and use that as an organizing principle for the revision. She returned with another drawing, this one of the figure on the pedestal being toppled by a giant hand, an image that guided a massive revision of her essay from one praising the possibilities of close father-daughter friendships to one urging daughters to make peace with the reality of a father who is unable to act like a father. In her conference with me to discuss her portfolio, Janey explained that she planned to revise her final essay one more time before the end of the semester because, in her words, she "wimped out" in her conclusion. Failing to hold faith with her image, she offered the unrealistic promise of close friendships in lieu of father-daughter relationships. What was required for a further revision, she explained, is a conclusion that offers a friendly relationship, which, though tepid, palliates bitterness and hatred. By slipping between writing-reading and drawing, Janey inhabited a middle ground emotionally and rhetorically, reseeing both emotions and rhetoric. As she wrote later, "If I didn't draw this, I wouldn't have this."

Slippery texts are a necessary but not sufficient criterion for a poetics of teaching. If imageword has taught us anything, it is that texts are not intrinsically stable or slippery. These are linguistic designations. Even a slippery text can be reified into stable form. Therefore, it is necessary to teach so that texts are experienced as disruptive, so that texts can confuse ways of knowing and ways of seeing. We need to use these slippery texts in such a way that we engage our students in slippery learning.

Slippery Learning

To elicit slippery learning, the kind of learning that enables our students to grapple with immersion, emergence, and transformation, we must combine embodied literacies, imageword's fluid dynamic, and slippery texts. I do not believe that merely providing a step-by-step account of "what I did last Monday" will honor the poetics of meaning that I have espoused through this book. Therefore, I slip across chapter boundaries to catch up the threads of embodied literacies and the provocative dynamic from chapter 3, knitting those threads into my accounts of slippery learning. I provide a specific approach to somatic literacy—body biographies—that helps our students immerse themselves in experiences; I then turn to polyscopic literacy, using spatial geographies to help our students recognize the partiality of their vision, of their literacies. Finally, I address lateral literacy, using splintered narratives to disrupt the linear time frame of their autobiographical identities and their belief in the stability of their rhetorical identity, thereby opening up gaps for change, for transformation. The artifacts that I teach with and teach from throughout each of the three examples parallel the three kinds of slippages that I have described above: across subject, genre, and media.

Somatic Literacy, Immersion, and Body Biographies
Somatic literacy lends itself well to slippery learning, evolving as it does out of the collapse of bodies into words.[5] Through somatic literacy, we can teach students to straddle the shifting boundaries among bodies, places, and languages, to inhabit floating worlds. One technique for enhancing immersion through somatic literacy is body biographies, an activity that I derived from a work of Peter Smagorinsky and Cindy O'Donnell-Allen with high school students. Body biographies are life-sized human outlines crafted out of images

and words that represent students' understanding of a text. Concerned with broadening conceptions of literacy beyond reliance on language-based sign systems, Smagorinsky and O'Donnell-Allen experimented with a multimedia approach to reader response. They had a small groups of high school students collaboratively construct body biographies of Shakespeare's Laertes as they read *Hamlet*. Smagorinsky and O'Donnell-Allen assert that this mode of response, which collapses words and images, serves three functions: it points to the potential of multimedia composing to open up avenues for exploratory discussion, it provides alternative modes by increasing the cultural tools at students' disposal, and it offers mental and artifactual representations that can serve as the basis for reflection, mediation, and subsequent new forms of representation.[6]

Although Smagorinsky and O'Donnell-Allen allude to the neurological basis of multimedia literacy systems, they do not focus on the overtly somatic nature of the technique they study; rather, their concern is to increase the available tools in students' cultural toolboxes. I wanted to use body biographies, which collapse media and subjects, to help my student recognize the multileveled situatedness of their learning. Therefore, I used the fusion of graphic imagery and language in body biographies to highlight the corporeal nature of the imagewords at play in their constructions of meaning. The examples below are taken from an upper division writing intensive class that focused on the role of cultural contexts—in this case, gender and class—on literacy. I used biographies twice with this class, once to plot their own body biographies and once to plot the body biography of Nancy Mairs as evoked in a collection of autobiographical essays, *Waist-High in the World*. By focusing on her life as a writer with multiple sclerosis (MS), someone disabled in a world of the enabled, Mairs invites us to consider the extent to which we define our humanity on the basis of our physical well-being.

Crucial to *Waist-High in the World* is Mairs's contention that one cannot take the mind out of the body, an orientation that is particularly representative of what she calls the FOF, or fornicating old fart (*Voice Lessons* 106; *Remembering* 5). "Who would I be if I didn't have MS?" she asks. "Literally, no body. I am not 'Nancy + MS,' and no simple subtraction can render me whole," she answers. Would I be a writer? she queries anew. "In all likelihood, I would," she replies. "But I could not conceivably have become the writer I am" (*Waist-High* 8–9). To elicit a similar awareness of one's particular body in the process of crafting meaning, I asked my students to create their own body biographies, to construct out of imagewords a sense of their self-identity (fig. 4.1). I supplied them with the oversized paper and instructions, sending them home to complete the assignment out of class. They returned the next class period with their body biographies, which we taped to the wall. We proceeded around the room to look at each biography as though we were in an art gallery, and students interpreted and responded to the various imagewords. The sketches were wildly dissimilar: one a half-body, one an arm, one faceless, one headless. Even the full-body portraits were similar only in outline. One had an oversized heart, another a gigantic derrière, a third had a jagged spear of lightning piercing the head. All integrated language in various ways: a curved line of words forming one side of one body biography; the word *pain* inscribed in the position of the heart, the word *God* in another in the same position; words forming a chain around the neck of another. As the student illustrators guided the class through their biographies, we learned of the commitments and passions that guided them through their academic and personal lives—God, music, family, success, tradition—all symbolized within the porous imagewords of the body biography.

The second body biography was constructed collaboratively to instantiate their shared sense of Mairs's identity and meaning as they interpreted her words through their own inescapable bodies (fig. 4.2). A prelude to body biographies was provided by student leaders. Working in pairs throughout the semester, students assumed responsibility for initiating discussion on various assigned readings. My student leaders in this case had volunteered at the beginning of the semester to guide discussion on the second chapter of Mairs's collection. Rather than offering questions for a verbal

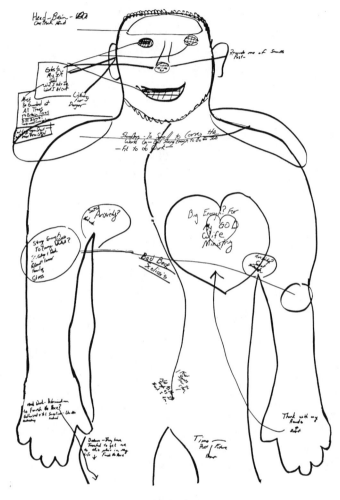

Fig. 4.1. Josh's body biography

discussion, the leaders involved their classmates physically. They first solicited volunteers (a request met with a number of good-humored jeers and abstentions). When the leaders bribed their classmates with the lure of free cans of pop, four students volunteered with alacrity. The leaders then proceeded to blindfold two

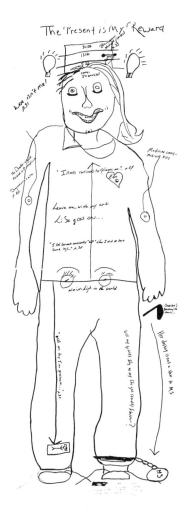

Fig. 4.2. Group body biography

students and tie the hands of two other volunteers. The volunteers were given tasks to perform: opening a can of pop and reading a book. The rest of the class was instructed to record their observations of their classmates' processes. This activity led to a lively discussion of the ways in which we take for granted our grounding in our bodies as we write-read, concluding with students generating similes and metaphors based on their experiences and their reading of Mairs.

Building on this activity, I asked my class to work in self-selected groups to create a body biography based on their understanding of Mairs's first group of essays in *Waist-High in the World*. On body-sized sheets of paper, students worked on the floor to draw the outlines of their bodies with multicolored markers. This process in and of itself made students aware, some uncomfortably so, of their bodies in the classroom. Then they began the process of designing their rendition of Mairs's body biography. I allowed forty-five minutes of the seventy-five-minute period for the composing activity. Then I had students tape their biographies on the walls of the classroom. We all studied the biographies as the students guided us, again, through an interpretation of their imageword.

The body profile that one group crafted highlighted their efforts to traverse the circular pathways tying Mairs's body and her words about her experience of her body to their reading of those words from the orientation of their own bodies (see fig. 4.2). A figure drawn as half-man, half-woman (to reflect, they explained, their differing gender orientations), the body biography consisted of a body outline infused with imagewords. At waist level of the standing figure, the group drew two wide-open eyes to reflect Mairs's view of the world from the confines of her wheelchair. At the time they composed this part of the body biography, one student, standing on a chair, held up the paper so that his partner, on his knees with his eyes at the figure's waist level, could peer out at the world. A small supine figure was tattooed around the ankle of the right leg, adumbrating the eventual time when Mairs's degenerative MS would leave her with a bed-high view of the world. However, a hatchet also appeared in the body biography, as well as a peace sign and the word *Zen* in the heart; the hatchet is there, they explained on the body biography, so that Mairs can chop through the chain of MS, something that she does, they say, with her word pictures. The peace sign is there because Mairs has made her peace with her life as an MA sufferer. Inscribed throughout the body are quotes from the essays, one major quote written in giant letters atop the biography: The Present Is My Reward. The quotes, the group explained to the class, highlight that for Mairs, words cannot be separated from the body: they are in it, around it, on top of it.

I trace two kinds of slippery learning in body biographies. First, students consciously began to tie together their response to Mairs and their responses to their own bodies. They began to look more critically at the ways in which bodies impinged on their writing-reading in and of the world, finding in these connections new worlds to explore in writing. Hannah, a first-generation American whose home language was Vietnamese, was particularly struck by the permeability of words and bodies in her writing-reading. At the end of the semester, for their semester portfolio, each student was required to write an overview of their class derived from weekly summaries (My Life in English 403WI) and a reflection of their learning (What I Learned over the Spring). In both her overview and her reflection, Hannah spoke of the reverberations generated by these imageword activities. Her papers throughout the semester focused on different aspects of embodied experiences (her first on the impact of childhood play, both place and physical activity; her second on the importance of honing a new vocabulary of body language for her upcoming interviews for a position in business management at the corporate level). In her course reflection, she wrote: "Writing about my body was a great way for me to take a look at myself and to see how I felt about my body." In her narrative as well, her "Life in English 403WI," Hannah noted the value of writing about her body: "I enjoyed writing about this subject because it made me look closer at my body and to express how I feel about it. I actually worked on this writing [an informal essay] early which was unusual." She also tied her personal body biography to the one she crafted jointly with Peter, Carolyn, and Josh. She writes in her reading response journal on Mairs:

> For many years she didn't want to be a part of body parts. She thought of them as separate from herself: 'The left hand doesn't work anymore.'" She didn't say "my" left hand

as if it didn't belong to her. Loving herself was struggle. I, too, could understand what she was going through. It's as if your body parts had minds of its own.

Hannah's own body biography consisted of a half-body dominated by a bionic arm, which she explains in her course narrative as follows:

> I brought my oversized paper home and starting thinking about what were some of my experiences. Since I had a hard time thinking about what to put on my hand, knee, or arm, I drew a symbolic body. I drew one like a superhero, a bionic woman of some sort. The next class period, we each went around and explained our body biographies. I had to explain why there were dots on my face connected to each other [map of her identity].

Thus, Hannah wove connections among her own body image, her own way-of-being-in-the-world, and her textual image of Mairs.

The second area of slippery learning to derive from these imageword activities concerned the students' choice of writing topics. Judging from their formal and informal essays, my students across the board were absorbed by the interplay of their bodies and lives with the embodiment of Mairs's essays. From the body biographies, they leaped into their essays, tackling subjects directly related to their sense of presence in the world: the cost of celibacy in an age of sexual license; the problematics of a well-fleshed body, so woefully out of style, but so necessary for the resonance required for operatic singing; the physical loss of identity, as well as the sadness, when a child must become the mother to the parent; the erosion of physical and psychological boundaries as one parents a toddler. Numerous students noted the overlap of bodies-places in their configurations of authority, success, and religious faith.

Of special note is one student's acknowledgement of bodies as a terministic screen for literacy itself. Kelly chose as the topic of her final research essay the resistance of African American male teenagers in her high school to academic success. Inspired by her male peers, who jeered at her academic success, accusing her of selling out, and supported by a variety of sources, Kelly argued that black male teens resisted academic literacy because of their perception that academic success meant a denial of their African American bodies. School literacy, Kelly asserted, was identified as white literacy; therefore, to retain and to honor their sense of themselves as black men, they refused to accede to the training necessary for school literacy. As long as literacy was perceived as a white institution, Kelly concluded, many black teenage males would continue to resist writing-reading because it constitutes a violation of their bodies. In her narrative response to her research essay, Kelly pondered the extent to which the young men she initially condemned in high school may have been right. If successful school literacy is about class and gender, as my class emphasized, is it not also about race? Is it not also about her gendered, racialized body? She was left with no easy resolution to these questions.

Polyscopic Literacy, Emergence, and Geography
Somatic literacy emphasizes the generative and shaping power of physiology and place in our meaning making, highlighting the literacy that evolves from the permeability of bodies, places, and words. But physiology and place can easily become tyrants, determining what is and is not real on the basis of the single vision of a single body lodged in a single place. Polyscopic literacy concerns the development and deployment of the ways of seeing immanent with culture and the constellations of imageword—icons, architecture, urban planning, metaphors, and so forth—that both support and manifest a particular way of seeing. A technique that I have used to invite my students' emergence into polyscopic literacy is that of spatial geographies, a strategy that asks them to trace the connections between their ways of seeing and the places within which they came to language.

Because maps combine visual and textual elements, they can expose the tensions between these semantics, tensions that highlight the constructedness of spatial positioning (Blunt and Rose 10).

I use the tensions implicit within a map to help my students become more aware of the habituated ways of seeing and language using that they bring with them into the classroom. I introduced spatial geographies to my upper division students as we read the opening chapters to Lillian Rubin's sociological narrative of working-class families in the San Francisco Bay area. First published in 1972 and republished in 1992, *Worlds of Pain* defies the traditional genres of sociological research by presenting its results in narrative form, a form that Rubin concedes challenges accepted discourse conventions in sociology; however, she argues, it is the genre that best suits the nature of her data. I wanted my students to reflect on their reactions, many of them resistant, to Rubin's stories of working-class families, by plotting their responses and Rubin's text against the grid of their own home space: one site of their cultural second naturing. The tool for this reflection consisted of the creation of floor plans, two-dimensional graphic diagrams of the dwelling or dwellings and the rooms where the individuals in my class spent most of their time growing up. Students all drew, with varying degrees of elaborations, a grid of their home spaces, marking their grids with names for rooms and a brief list of memories associated with various spaces. We then worked with house plans on three levels: against Rubin's text, against their own experiences, and against two academic essays on class and writing (Lynn Z. Bloom's "Freshman Composition as a Middle-Class Enterprise," in which she argues that first-year composition evolves from and reinforces middle-class values, and Linda Brodkey's "Writing on the Bias," an account of her growth to literacy in a working-class family).

Spatial geographies are predicated on the slippage between cultural-physical environment and a way of seeing that environment. Bateson points out repeatedly that human development for the individual and species is an outgrowth of the organism-in-its-environment, not an organism excerpted from its environment. Similarly, geneticist R. C. Lewontin has argued that the development of an embryo cannot be separated from environment: "A living organism at any moment of its life is the unique consequence of a development history that results from the interactions of and determination by internal and external forces" (63). Consider, for a moment, the slipperiness of optical illusions. All people experience optical illusions, moments when the eye is confused by its own perception. But not all people are confused by the same optical illusions. Citizens of the Western world who grow up in a carpentered environment are misled by illusions that pose no confusion to people who grow up in an environment dominated by horizontal lines (Bolles 115). Where we are imprints how we see and how we write. Spatial geographies help students experience more consciously this slippage involved in their own processes of second naturing.

After my students read Rubin, Bloom, and Brodkey, I assigned them to small groups. Working together, they abstracted a list of working-class characteristics based on these readings, a list that could be compared and contrasted to the list of eleven middle-class "virtues" that Bloom explores in her essay. Reminding them of Rubin's comment on her own working-class background that "no matter how far we travel, we can never leave our roots behind" (13), I then asked them to set these lists aside and to turn to the floor plans they had drawn of the house they remembered most vividly from their childhood. Finally, I asked them to map their lists of characteristics and virtues against their blueprints by offering them the following prompt: "What virtues-characteristics do we identify after growing up in a particular physical space and how do these virtues-characteristics impinge on writing-reading?"

To get them started on this very nontraditional sort of writing-reading activity, I shared my own spatial geography, unlocking the door to my childhood home and walking with them through its rooms (fig. 4.3). Against the image of my house plan displayed on a screen with an overhead projector, I wove the story of my childhood for them, wove a history of the merger between a way of seeing and a way of language using.

I begin with a picture, passing around a photograph of my home taken in 1950 when it was new. I tell my students that until I left for college, I was raised in a five-hundred-square-foot two-bedroom home in a post–World War II subdivision where sixteen

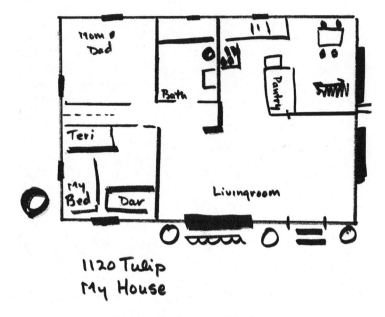

Fig. 4.3. The house on Tulip Street

houses faced each other across an unpaved, dead-end street, just within the city limits of a small Michigan town on the banks of the Grand River. Using overhead markers, I draw on my transparent house plan, explaining that my neighborhood was girded by a Lutheran Church to the west, a Seventh Day Adventist school and campground (off limits) to the east, and farm fields to the north and south (also off limits). The sixteen small tract houses, only superficially different, were situated on plots unmarred by fences of any kind, making the neighborhood an open field that children traversed at will during the summertime, a welcome counterpart to the constrained space of the tiny homes.

As they gather in loose groups around the overhead screen, I introduce my students to my family. Five people filled our four-room house, I tell them: three daughters, a stay-at-home mother who decorated cakes for extra money, and a father who worked two jobs, one on the line at Fisher Body in Lansing and one doing independent body work at night and on the weekends. Outlining with my finger the small, front, left-hand rectangle on my house plan, I tell them about my sisters. We three were crammed into a small eight-by-ten bedroom with two windows, three beds, and one chest with sticky drawers. My mother tried to create additional play space by sawing off the ends of the chest to fit it within a small clothes closet, only to discover that we couldn't open the drawers when we put the closet doors back on. In the small space marked on my overhead, I draw little lines for beds. My two sisters and I, I continue, slept in beds close enough to touch each other at night, sharing everything within this space: fights, underwear (fights over underwear), nightmares, and secrets.

Backlit by the imagewords of my spatial geography, I face my students: What way of seeing the world is habituated by living in this environment? I ask them and myself. How am I, how is my literacy, marked by my liaison with the space I return to with my children as frequently as I can? For my students, I describe the way of seeing and the way of language using that seep out of everything I write.

I learned osmotically, I tell them, that entropy is not just the first law of thermodynamics; it is a way of life. It is impossible to keep a small house filled with active children tidy, especially one with little storage space, governed by the need to retain everything (for the chances of replacement were slim to none). Regardless of my mother's herculean efforts, she could not hold back the flow of disorder, the breakdown of order. Nor was entropy limited to the house itself; everything fell into disorder: shoes lost heels, clothes lost buttons, furniture lost legs, games lost pieces, and dolls lost heads. I admit to my students with a certain degree of chagrin that in grade school I struggled with the concept of neatness; my penmanship, my assignments, and my workspace all reflected my automatic belief in entropy. Now, as a teacher-writer, I expect writing-reading to be messy; I expect order to teeter on the edge of chaos, subject to inevitable erosion and recycling. I might long for closure in my thinking, tidiness in my life, clarity in my vision, but I am always uneasy with the unnaturalness of each, braced for the breaching of all.

Continuing to shape my polyscopic literacy, I tell my students that I grew up learning through my skin that entropy also extended to ego boundaries. Life in my small home tended to truncate first-person identity, creating a hesitant, "osmotic I." I trace for them with my finger the lines marking the walls between the rooms of my house plan. Because of the physical limits set by the walls of my childhood home, my family and I had little to no personal space. My sisters and I might have staked out our individual beds as protected territory, but everything else was common ground. Sharing wasn't a virtue; it was a necessity. To survive as a family, we could only rarely come first individually. Instead, we had to come first as a family, a process that required a subordination of first-person drives. Even now, I confess to my students, I am uncomfortable assuming a first-person identity when I write because it asserts a stark, cleanly defined self that I am never entirely sure exists outside that rhetorical act. As Mairs says of her own autobiographical writing, "The not-mes dwell here in the me. We are one, and more-than-one. Our stories utter one another" (*Remembering* 11). As a result, I tell my students, I can dive with enthusiasm into their first-person accounts, lurking in the background of their ego structure, but I am less eager to offer my own for their enjoyment.

This "osmotic I" also plays into my struggle with the expository process of evolving a point to argue. I view with sympathy their efforts to determine a thesis to argue, I tell my class, because writing as if only one valid perspective exists continues to frustrate me. As the middle child living in such close proximity with other people I loved, I had to adjust to the myriad perspectives crisscrossing any single point. Thus, I am never sure on a visceral level if a single point ever exists. Nor am I ever exactly sure where my audience begins and I end. For me, the border between what I believe and what my reader believes is always fuzzy, causing me to doubt the existence of some sort of autonomous idea, as well as my ownership of that autonomous idea.

Finally, weaving an overhead marker in a sinuous pattern through the small rooms and doors of my house plan, I share one last aspect of my polyscopic literacy, a last osmotic boundary: the publicness of privacy. As they could tell from my house plan, like many of their own, I grew up in a very limited space. And when life is lived with a growing family within the space of four rooms, privacy dies a quick death because life enacts itself always on a public stage, within a public space. Thus, we children could not be separated from the low, tight-toned conversations about bills that my parents conducted at the kitchen table. My sister's rebellious teenage years were blocked out on the kitchen stage for all to witness. We each participated, played a part; no one was exempt. Because privacy was framed on a public stage, I ruefully confess to my class, the disembodied rationality—the Cartesian perspectivalism and Baconian empiricism so privileged by the academy—remains for me a most uncomfortable guise. The requisite emotional distance demanded of academic writing-reading violates my way of seeing, formed where the demarcations between public and private blurred. Even now, that painfully acquired way of seeing fostered by schooling in the West can only take me so far before the habits of a lifetime and a home space erupt on the page in a revelation of my working-class roots.

With these uneasy confessions as their model, my students respond with their own examinations, teasing out the ways of seeing that evolved from their liaisons with a cultural place. For instance, Jennifer was unable to generate a spatial geography in the form of a specific floor plan because she had moved so much in her childhood (six times since her eighth birthday). However, she did draw a single room with a door and closet, filling both with words that narrated her childhood. Wherever her family moved, she wrote, she always had a room of her own because she was the only girl out of four children. With an arrow starting from the words in her room and arcing to a list outside the walls of that room, she recites the value she finds in her peripatetic childhood, underlining aggressively her academic success. Her ability to adjust easily to the differing expectations of teachers and writing-reading situations,

Jennifer explained, derived from the flexibility she developed as a result of melding into myriad new spaces.

Carolyn, through her spatial geography—a series of grids super-imposed on one another—explored the bridges between the difficulties of a poverty-stricken childhood marked by a succession of temporary homes and the difficulties of writing in anything but the invisible (and protected) third person. If she is not seen, she says, then she cannot be harmed. Joanie, a single mother of a three-year-old boy, carried her inability to take control of her writing—to assert her position and say "this is my point"—back to her home space. Circling her written discourse and connecting it with a line to the room marked "kitchen," Joanie explained that her family was controlled by a patriarchal father, a dynamic typical of many working-class families. To a large extent, he dictated what could be said, when, and where. Children were to be seen, not heard. Thus, she explained, even as an adult with a child of her own, she hesitates to speak, waiting for some kind of permission from a teacher-authority.

Many of the working-class students, especially those prepping for their long-awaited shift from working-class home to corporate culture, cited the painful experience of shifting ways of seeing. They described physical discomfort—dizziness, nausea, headaches—as they attempt to fit themselves into new work spaces so disparate from home space. They pointed to the high anxiety they experienced just attempting to produce a written memo in a corporate environment, tracking their rhetorical difficulties to physical roots. The way of seeing habituated in one space violated the way of seeing privileged in another. Fitting into corporate culture was not just a process of code shifting; it was a process of vision shifting. "We feel our way to success," Michael Polanyi tells us, a process inextricable from our way of seeing different realities (63). What became evident to my students was the way in which a tacit dimension, over which they had little conscious control, guided their interpretations of texts, self, and culture. Creating meaning could not be severed from ways of seeing habituated by the liaison between bodies and culturally coded places.

By the time we returned to Rubin's, Brodkey's, and Bloom's
writings, students were already making the leap between the eleven
virtues of successful writing, the academic failure of many working-
class children, and ways of seeing, fostered by the spaciousness of
a middle-class existence, that were privileged in the academy. They
discovered the partiality of their own vision, the partiality of their
rhetorical choices.

Lateral Literacy, Transformation, and
Telling the History That Wasn't

Lateral literacy helps us keep our realities and our options
for action, including rhetorical action, open. By evolving a higher
tolerance for ambiguity—for slippery learning and for dissolving
boundaries—we are less likely to careen toward destruction, taking
the planet with us, and more likely to evolve practices that ensure
the survival of an imageword ecology. To make a difference, Haraway argues, we must discover ways to conceive of reality that do not
replicate the errors of the past. And to discover those ways, we
evolve transformative and transforming imagistic and rhetoric practices. Fostering lateral literacy helps our students and ourselves
experience the power of transformation, for it disrupts the stories, what Haraway calls the figurations, that structure our realities (*Modest* 11). I offer one strategy that I developed to help students experience the openness, the restiveness of their identities.
My goal was to diffract my students' autobiographical time lines,
then carry that diffraction over into a public arena of their lives. To
do this, I crisscrossed two different media: writing and photography, a medium typically overlooked in writing classes. Shifting from
word to photography fostered slippery learning of lateral literacy
because photography destabilizes the unitary self. In *Prosthetic Culture*, Celia Lury argues that photographic images have a central role
in effecting a transformation from what she calls the "possessive
self"—the self-determining, self-knowing singular individual—to a
prosthetic or extensive self. Photographs contribute to this shift
through their ability to "*frame, freeze, and fix*" their objects (3, author's emphasis). Framing changes the context of the object scene,

but even more, Lury argues, it invites outcontextualization: a view of the object from multiple positions at once (3). Freezing or fixing invites indifferentiation: "the disappearance or infilling of the distance between cause and effect, object and subject" (3). Both processes contribute to an evolving sense of restive identities.

In an upper division writing-intensive course that focused on culture and writing, I crafted a multilayered writing assignment called "Playing Games" that attempted to evoke outcontextualization and indifferentiation as a first step to destabilizing unitary identity. The assignment covered about four weeks and comprised a series of overlapping activities. It included photographs, game playing, writing, reading, and a return to photographs. I would like to share one student's work in response to this multifaceted assignment, following her moves from photograph to formal writing (what she called her "first freakin' paper") and back to photograph.

In fall 1996 Ashley was a married student in her mid-twenties in her last semester of college. A pro at multitasking, she was finishing up her course work for an accounting degree, studying for her CPA exam, and courting employment in one of the Big Six accounting firms (now the Big Four), a goal she achieved midway through the semester and celebrated with the entire class. Her background was working class, a subject that cropped up as she prepared for interviews and agonized over wardrobe choices. She supported herself and paid for college by working as a waitress. Her husband worked as a mechanic, and they both found her entry into a highly prestigious accounting firm an occasion for hilarity as well as for celebration.

The unit begins with students bringing in and sharing a photograph from their childhood, exploring the scene, the dynamic at play, and the relationships within that photograph.[7] Ashley brought in a photograph of her brothers and her in front of a Christmas tree taken on a Christmas morning when she was five years old. One brother was on a tricycle, another stretched out on the floor under the tree, propped up on a football. Ashley, the only one standing, was rigged out in cowboy boots, fluffy nightgown, cowboy hat, and a six-gun strapped around her middle. During her turn to tell the story of her photograph, Ashley spoke with affection of her desire to be just like her brothers when she was young, scorning the games and toys typically assigned to little girls. After we shared stories and images, I broke the class into small groups and everyone played a self-selected game reminiscent of those they played as children. One group played Monopoly; another Sorry; a third Yahtzee; a fourth jumped rope. Ashley and a fellow student played with Barbie dolls. Finally, the groups spent time compiling journal entries listing the "rules" they learned from playing particular games as children. In her journal entry, Ashley listed what she learned as a child from playing with dolls: life was open-ended, noncompetitive, integrative, and imaginative. Before the end of the period, I returned the class to their photographs, asking them to develop a similar set of rules that seemed to permeate the scene. Their final journal assignment was to consider the multiple "rules" they juggled during their childhoods, the multiple identities that they felt free to explore as children.

In conjunction with this activity, students were also reading Evelyn Fox Keller's *Reflections on Science and Gender,* a careful exploration of the ways in which gender figures in the construction of scientific knowledge and scientific knowing. Keller's work effectively destabilizes the sacredness of knowledge, especially scientific knowledge, and highlights the role that one's childhood has in approaches to knowledge making. When students returned to class, we examined more closely the lessons that the rules of their childhood inculcated in them, testing Keller's hypotheses against the fabric of their games and photographs.

With this wealth of contradictory material to pull from, we began to shape our formal papers. On the basis of our discussions, readings, and informal writings, I asked students to evolve a subject that they would like to address that would be important for a public audience to read. The only stipulation I made was that they had to describe to their classmates and me how their particular choice of audience and topic evolved out of our shared activities. They were to offer this narrative when they presented their final papers to the class as a whole.

Ashley's topic for her "first freakin' paper" concerned the troubling realization that she, a budding career woman on the verge of a lucrative professional position, personifies "some of the traditional female roles." Addressed to married women on the verge of shifting to a demanding career, Ashley's paper explores how she and they had arrived at this impasse, a question resonating with the desire of the little girl who wanted to be a cowboy and the little girl who found enjoyment in Barbie dolls. Disappearing and reappearing through the paper are the children Ashley rescues: the child who wants to sacrifice the game rules in order to keep the relationships going and the child who wants to finesse the rules so that she can win the game. Derived from the same lifeline, these children splintered Ashley's narrative of her life, her sense of identity. She explores the cost and the necessity of juggling these multiple identities for herself and other adult women who struggle with similar children within. Central to her exploration is her enactment of outcontextualization and indifferentiation.

Outcontextualization is the process of examining a specific scene from all views at once, as if one inhabited a spatial continuum. Ashley does exactly this by returning to her photograph and her experiences playing with dolls. A rule of her life is the maintenance of relationships, which, she says, quoting Carol Gilligan, is not unexpected, given the ways in which child care is handled predominantly by female caregivers. Her behavior within her marriage is guided by the rules she learned playing with dolls: interactive, imaginative, open-ended, the focus on keeping the process going rather than honoring the rules. Ashley explores the caregiver dynamic at play in her marriage, a dynamic that she says "shocks me with its accuracy. The house could be cleaned by me from top to bottom, and my husband will empty the dishwasher and want a cookie for his effort."

But this is Ashley from only one angle. Contending with this identity, this need to enact the caregiver game, is the need to enact the doer role, the one who knows the rules, plays by them, and wins by them. As her childhood photograph reveals, from a different point on the spatial continuum, Ashley is the child who wants to call the shots, who wants to lead the way, regardless of the reactions of her brothers, and this is the Ashley who aggressively pursues a challenging career in a field long dominated by men, specifically zeroing in on a firm long controlled by men. Relationships, caregiving, she ruefully points out, will be less important to her advancement in her career than it seems to be in the advancement of her marriage. Thus, she accepts the shuttling between roles, the not always comfortable fit between the Ashley who cares and the Ashley who wants to win in a career that she construes, with pleasure, as a battlefield.

The process of indifferentiation, the infilling of the spaces between cause and effect, object and subject, complicates an already complex picture. To move with joy among the various facets of her restive identity, Ashley recognizes that her husband must also nurture a restive identity, one that complements the facets of hers. She explains that if her roles are multiple, then her husband's roles must also be multiple, or the marriage risks failure, a failure that would strip her of one of her most valued identities. As she moves to embrace a demanding career, she recognizes that she must find some way to invite her husband to craft a new role as caregiver. "I want to convince my husband that he would [sic] perform all the duties of the house if I was not around. This would hopefully show him that we should share all the duties, and not just perform those set by tradition." Without such a move, her ability to foster her restive identities is truncated by a single identity imposed upon her by a loved one.

Through an exploration of the children who weave her adult life, Ashley finds something crucial to say to many women in our culture who struggle with their multiple identities as professionals and as caregivers. More important, however, I believe that she glimpses the identities and the stories bubbling beneath the surface of what she once saw as a linear time line. During her presentation of her paper to the class, Ashley returns to her childhood photograph, looking behind and through the image. There is more than one person smiling back at the camera, she tells us, more than one way to play out this scene. But pleasure and joy in that discovery are dimmed by her realization that the actualization of those multiple Ashleys is not entirely within her control. Manifesting those identities, telling those stories, is an act dependent not only on her ability to tell a lateral narrative but also on the ability of others around her to tell their own lateral narratives. Stories are not story "lines"; they are story networks, woven in highly interactive patterns.

Texts that we choose to teach with, like the embodied literacies we teach, and the rhythms we aspire to, should untuck all of our neatly tucked edges, reminding us that we cannot learn a particular literacy by keeping precise lecture notes, recording note cards, or filling in cloze tests. Just as literacies evolve out of and into kaleidoscopic patterns, so must the texts that we choose to teach with and from. In addition, contributing to the fluid dynamic of literacies and texts is the fluid dynamic of process. Literacy in whatever guise it takes is a performance, an act. Texts do not exist outside that performance, as Louise Rosenblatt has reminded us for more than sixty years. And how we teach, how we organize our instruction, is as integral to teaching embodied literacies as is what we teach—goals and subject—and what we teach with—texts. I address next this question of how we organize our instruction so that we poise our classrooms on the threshold of being, resonating to a poetics of meaning.

5 / Double Mapping: The Organization of a Poetics of Teaching

> The manner of the search is plain to me and might be called
> the *method of double or multiple comparison.*
> —Gregory Bateson, *Mind and Nature*

> Mapping is a distinctive form of spatial representation because
> it can be interpreted as visual and/or textual. [. . .] [T]he
> spatial imagery of mapping can expose tensions between the
> dynamics of the visual and the written.
> —Alison Blunt and Gillian Rose, *Writing Women and Space*

> Staring blankly at the huge white paper taunting her she was
> speechless.
> —Patti, portfolio narrative

A group of my first-semester composition students clustered around the table that I had staked out as mine four weeks into the fall term. Vying for my attention, they waved their illustrations, pointing fingers, and talking in a wild cacophony of overlapping voices. All except Patti. Bright, vibrant, and articulate, with a dry sense of humor that cracked me up regularly, Patti hung back, her illustration wound into a tight tube. The flock around my desk dispersed until only Patti and I remained in the now quiet room. On the verge of tears, her frustrations and fears came boiling out.

"I can't do this. I don't know what you want. I can't figure out where you're going with this." In full tilt, Patti's staccato sentences offered me no opening for response. "This class is driving me nuts. I wasn't taught this way. I can't write this way." "Here," she shook her tube in my face, "you asked us to draw something. I did draw something. But I don't know why I did it. How is this teaching me to be a better writer?"

If I am not troubled on a Sunday night by questions of what I should teach on Monday morning, I am troubled by questions about how I should teach on Monday morning. Regardless of whether we are in a traditional classroom, a writing center, or a computer lab, teaching consists of more then deciding the shape, dynamic, and texts of a classroom. It also consists of deciding how to coordinate those course materials and how to craft an environment conducive to learning. As I argued in chapter 2, literacy evolves from the site where imageword shape-shifts across the permeable planes of bodies, cultures, places, and times. I bridged a poetics of meaning and a poetics of teaching by means of this fluid dynamic, sculpting out of embodied literacies a poetics of teaching. In chapters 3 and 4, the questions of what to teach and what to teach with were addressed through this same liquid movement. Now we are confronted with the tricky question of how we organize the embodied literacies that evolve from the flux of imageword so that we retain the mercurial movement of immersion-emergence-transformation so integral to a poetics of meaning and of teaching. In this chapter, I argue that we organize embodied literacies according to the double logics of imageword. To teach through the alternative imaginary of imageword requires that we position our teaching at the same unstable sites from which we draw our literacies. By so doing, we can better stave off the reification of embodied literacies into a set of core texts or a set of protocols assessable through standardized testing.

The organizational strategy I describe in this chapter is that of double mapping, a process by which we deliberately juxtapose the corporeal logic of image and the discursive logic of word so that at some level they are always contending with each other. As Alison Blunt and Gillian Rose remind us, "[T]he spatial imagery of mapping can expose tensions between the dynamics of the visual and the written" (10). By uncovering these tensions, even as we rely on them to say that which could not otherwise have been said, we continually subject our course content and our teaching to self-disruption. Double mapping our teaching, both our instructional materials and our environments, enables us to teach embodied literacies without arresting the dynamism of their evolution and thereby altering their identities. I begin with a brief explanation of double mapping, following that with three examples of double mapping embodied literacies in the classroom. I focus first on somatic literacy, providing an assignment sequence that loops language with physical activities and physical displays, attempting through this activity to highlight the physiological aspects of our literate identities. Next, I turn to polyscopic literacy and a four-tiered writing sequence that shuttles between words and word images. This unit aims at helping students recognize the ways of seeing within which they are immersed. Finally, I conclude with lateral literacy, yoking words with graphic and spatial images to transform our students' belief in the stability of a text, the stability of an identity. Although I lay these assignments out in a linear fashion and treat them as separate units, they, like the embodied literacies they manifest and serve, function to double map each other.

Double Mapping

Double mapping is a process of deliberately layering different ways of making sense of reality on one another.[1] It explicitly relies on the value of double vision or double description. "May God us keep/ From Single vision and Newton's sleep!" William Blake writes in a letter to Thomas Butts, expressing in those two lines from a larger poem his deep concern for the ways in which humans impoverish their senses (420). "For man has closed himself up," he despairs in *The Marriage of Heaven and Hell*, "till he sees things thro' narrow chinks of his cavern" (129). To explode those chinks, Blake the engraver develops what he calls his "infernal method," using corrosives on copper plates to unite images and words within a single plate, "cleansing the doors of perception" and thereby "melting apparent surfaces away, and displaying the infinite which was hid" (129).

The dynamic at play in Blake's work (and life) is that of double mapping, the process of juxtaposing one semantic against another, for, as Blake says, "[w]ithout contraries is not progression" (123). Double mapping cleanses "the doors of perception" by fusing the mutually constitutive but dissimilar logics of image and of word, affording us what Gregory Bateson calls double vision. To know about the world around us and about our part in that world requires double description or double vision, Bateson argues (*Mind*, ch. 3). Double description provides us with something other than just an addition of one species of information (discourse) to another species of information (image). Double description results in the creation of an extra dimension. "[T]he combining of information of different sorts or from different sources results in something more than addition," he argues; it results in "[a] momentary gleam of enlightenment (86). Such is the goal of double mapping. By structuring our course content so that meaning is sifted through different semantics, our students and we gain fluid literacies where mimetic representation is tugged out of shape, destabilized by the differing logics in imageword.

The need to double map literacy is implicitly acknowledged in a range of pedagogical and theoretical orientations to literacy. Stuart Greene and John M. Ackerman, in "Expanding the Constructivist Metaphor," advocate an approach to literacy focusing on "the means and circumstances through which readers and writers represent and negotiate texts, tasks, and social contexts" (384). This requires attending to the role of media in literacy activities, they argue. The textual space readers and writers inhabit is actually intersubjective and intertextual, crisscrossing "graphic, aural, imagistic, and physical systems of meaning" (384). In the penultimate section of their article, Greene and Ackerman review approaches to literacy research, especially those based on Bakhtin's heteroglossia, materialism, and social validity, as well as those based on Peirce's triadic model of meaning, to illustrate the ways in which acts of meaning "carry an imprint of the social and cultural ecology," and the ways in which "linguistic and informational 'coherence' in texts echoes the proximal and spatial relationships from built environments and their inhabitation" (409). Understanding literacy, then, requires double mapping. On a similar theoretical level, Peter

Smagorinsky, in an article aimed at deconstructing the idea of pure data dominant in the hard sciences by means of Vygotsky's zone of proximal development, simultaneously underlines the double mapping of physical place and literacy, highlighting these reciprocal loops in the development of mental abilities, telos, and a researcher's interpretation of those abilities ("Social"). More explicitly, Stephen Witte builds on C. S. Peirce's semiosis and includes the object as part of the triadic flow of meaning. As Witte argues, Peirce's three-pronged theory of meaning enables us to factor in the influence of place and object on the writer, both of which become enmeshed in the semiotic process themselves.

To account for the myriad aspects of literacy—textual and imagistic—we are required to double map our understanding. Therefore, we can do no less than double map our organization of literacy activities in the classroom. To do otherwise is to promulgate implicitly a theory of literacy that fails to recognize its own double nature. At this point, however, it is also necessary to keep in mind both the pleasures and the pains of double mapping. On the one hand, double description affords our students and us the possibility of insight, inspiration, and transformation. Historian of science Arthur I. Miller traces the doubling of imageword in scientific creativity, plotting through case studies the importance of Poincaré's reliance on "sensual imagery," Einstein's reliance on visual imagery, and Heisenberg's transformation of imagery into an amalgamation of image and mathematics. Throughout, Miller argues for the central role that imagery in various modes and language in various modes play in the radical reconfiguration of our notions of space, time, and causality.

On the other hand, double description disrupts meaning, undoing our conviction in our own truths, our confidence in the stability of our reality. Double vision refers not only to the marvels of a binocular vision that becomes stereoscopic vision. It refers also to the pathology of diplopia, a visual disorder characterized by blurred vision and not infrequently accompanied by uncoordinated movement, even nausea. Cursed rather than blessed by double vision, we are forced to "feel" our way in a world bereft of clear-cut edges and durable boundaries. Within this realm of double borders and double centers, we have to construct an alternative order, an alternative knowledge that always teeters on the edge of no order, no knowledge. And that is not a pleasant process. Blake's struggles with, as well as commitment to, the rigors of double mapping meaning attest to that. The struggles of many of my students attest to this as well. But those struggles may be a necessary prelude to transformation.

Patti experienced acute anxiety in the midst of exploring ideas for her first formal writing assignment. We had journaled in response to an assignment that asked students to resurrect significant moments in their lives, including their writing lives. We had plotted these "moments" on the board, analyzing the array for patterns, for motivations, for potential readers. We had watched as student volunteers "pushed" their moments in different ways: networking, brainstorming, cubing. At this point, I invited my students to take a break from the traditional approaches to invention that we had been experimenting with and to play a bit: by sketching. What happens to your ideas, I asked them, when you try to draw not the idea itself but the feel of it, both for you and for your reader? I wished to shake my students out of their previous training with an efficient, linear model of writing: get an idea that fits the assignment, figure out some good examples for illustration, set it up, and write it out. I did so by inviting them to double their vision, to see those nascent ideas through what Susanne K. Langer calls a different semantic, hoping in the process that they would discover unexpected depths and nuances to those ideas, adding richness to the entire process of creating meaning. So I brought in eleven-by-fourteen sheets of copy paper, along with crayons, colored pencils, and markers. When we finished, student volunteers mounted their sketches above the blackboards, and their classmates milled around the room, using the blackboard beneath each sketch to write their responses to and interpretations of the drawings. The artists by turn took us through their sketches and the emotions they hoped to evoke.

Many of the students engaged in the activity enthusiastically, delighted by the opportunity to think in different ways; others followed through on my suggestions because they perceived it as a welcome break from the usual class cycle of talk-write and more talk-write. Patti, however, goal-driven, fixed in her writing regimen, found the process of drawing so disorienting that it was emotionally disturbing. Doubling her vision of her topic did not increase her perception; it blurred it. And that lack of clarity, that lack of stability in her meaning, almost paralyzed her. Not only did she come to me after class but, she later told me, she also called her family, convinced that she was going to fail. Patti and I exchanged e-mails over the next few days, with me directing her attention to both her initial journal and her sketch, using each to elicit more thinking about her topic, which was food. Finally, she sent an e-mail indicating a breakthrough had occurred. Filled with her usual energy, she wrote:

> Ummm . . . ok wow. Dr. Fleckenstein you're like my best friend, Christina!! We always think the same thoughts and it's real weird. I talked to my Mom tonight and told her how I was stressing about the paper, I told her some of your ideas and mine and she gave me pretty much your exact idea! She was reminding me about when I was little and came home from having dinner at a friend's house and was always surprised that no other families ate together every night like we did. I came up with a very rough draft for this paper, but one question: we can use "I" can't we? Like "I eat dinner with . . . " I sure hope so!! I guess I'll ask you in class if I don't hear back before class tomorrow.

Struggling and discarding a number of "almost" ideas, Patti finally found the link she wanted to explore: family dinners as an expression and anchor of love for children. In her portfolio narrative, titled "A Traumatic Birth," Patti reviewed the difficult process of bringing this paper into the world. Written in third person, the portfolio history chronicled Patti's struggles and triumphs.

> After the huge struggle with a topic came an even bigger problem to grapple with, crayons! Patti never was, nor probably ever will be, an artist by any definition of the

word. Staring blankly at the huge white paper taunting her she was speechless. She was apparently wrong in thinking that with high school graduation she could leave her crayons behind. But then, something happened. Someone asked, "how did you feel when Molly [Patti's sister] had cancer?" Patti thought in her head, "my world crumbled around me." When she again looked down at the pristine white paper it was covered in scribbles! She had subconsciously completed the assignment and was looking at a sequence of events on her paper that described just what she felt, her world crumbling around her in .02 second. Patti had won the battle with art and was ready to turn her paper in.

Nonetheless, in spite of this success, she also admitted that she did not wish to draw anymore. The price was not worth the reward, a sentiment shared by many of her classmates. Before I assign any more drawing, another student recently warned me, I needed to read the portfolio narratives to see how some students really felt about double vision.

Crucial to my argument is my belief that Patti could not have arrived at her final paper except by going through the process of double mapping. She would have come up with another paper, perhaps one that resonated to the school literacy within which she had been trained so well—what she described in her portfolio narrative as "manipulating assignments in high school"—but it would not have had the intensity, the emotional dimension, the resonance of a paper encouraging families to love each other regularly around the dinner table. The anxiety evoked by the destabilization of meaning in double vision is perhaps a necessary prelude to transformation, to a different kind of literacy.

Regardless of the resistance our students and we may initially feel to double vision, I advocate double mapping as the means by which we can keep our teaching poised on the site of dissolving boundaries. In the next three sections, I provide examples of ways to double map embodied literacies using three different "maps." The first involves juxtaposing a specific physical activity, in this case, playing with dolls, with writing-reading; the second involves jostling word and the word images in metaphors; the third involves tangling words and graphic-spatial imagery.

Double Mapping Somatic Literacy

Central to Blake's drive to double map reality as a means of perceiving reality was his fear that print threatened to disembody voice, and an art separated from the body of the speaking subject was an art of dead matter (Hecimovich). We could easily extend his argument: any meaning separated from the body of the thinking subject may well be dead meaning. Therefore, I begin with a double mapping of somatic literacy because we learn and live in the world through the connectiveness of our bodies and places. By teaching somatic literacy, we teach our students that a necessary fusion exists between situation and literacy, between bodies and texts, between imagewords creating their bodies and environments and the imagewords they create as writers-readers. One way to foster this realization and enhance the evolution of somatic literacy is by double mapping bodies and words. Let me begin with one student's essay.

Marie opens her first essay in an upper division writing-intensive course with her grandmother's birthday party at a local restaurant. Isolated behind a plate of birthday cake—white with white frosting and golden roses—she sits among family members and family friends. The double weight of her mother's gaze and of her grandmother's gaze rests on her. Sleek, stylish women dressed in sleek, stylish clothes, they watch, waiting to see Marie eat her slice of birthday cake, waiting, in Marie's words, to pounce. For Marie is neither sleek nor stylish, she writes, and two generations silently reject her: You aren't my daughter; you aren't my granddaughter. My daughter, my granddaughter is thin, is graceful, is not you.

From this poignant starting point, Marie draws us into a paper designed for women struggling with the pressure from family, from culture, from boyfriends to be slender, lithe, and pliable. She counts the cost in her life of her failure to achieve this ideal, an ideal physically manifested in the bodies of her mother and grandmother and in their pressure on her to reshape her body to fit that ideal. Beyond the physical price exacted by fad diets and intense but episodic exercise, Marie insightfully points in her essay to the psychological costs. She grew silent, she writes, in and out of school. If she spoke, she would draw attention to herself, to what she perceived to be an ungainly voice in an ungainly body. So she denied herself a voice, she confesses to her readers, as she tried to deny herself a body. She also denied herself risks, especially the risk of original thought. She sought to uncover exactly what a teacher wanted her to say, wanted her to be, and attempted to replicate that desire as closely as possible. How many words should I write? she admits asking her teacher. Tell me the point you want me to argue, she would beg. If her body failed to meet the standards set by her mother and maternal grandmother, perhaps she could reshape her mind to better fit their ideal.

This paper was not easy for her to write, Marie states baldly in her portfolio narrative. Not only was it painful to resurrect these memories of a part of her life she continues to agonize over, but the act itself of speaking forcefully to other women, to anyone, was also foreign to her experience. It was both exciting and frightening, Marie notes, and while she likes the end product very much, she is not sure if she wants to go through something like this again.

How did Marie reach this point of crafting an essay that both mattered passionately to her and spoke persuasively and cogently to readers outside her immediate circle? How did she manage to enact somatic literacy, writing as an embodied voice, rendering an embodied meaning? Part of the answer to that question rests with the array of activities that Marie engaged in during four weeks prior to completion of her paper, activities that asked her to turn around on her experiences and resee them from multiple angles but especially from the angle of her writing-reading body. I offer the following classroom experience to illustrate the possibilities of double mapping texts and bodies to enhance the evolution of somatic literacy. For this particular assignment, which the students named the Barbie Caper,[2] my goal was to immerse my students in an array of physical activities that reminded them in various ways of their identities as writing-reading bodies, identities that wove in subtle ways through the imagewords they created as writer-readers. I wanted my students to be more aware of the web of images that they mirror in their bodies, in their spatial orientations, and in the subject positions they embrace in their literacies. I helped them achieve this goal by organizing a series of textual activities and physical activities that double mapped the world of play against a world privileging particular literate behaviors. My materials consisted of a willing group of fourteen students, four weeks of a sixteen-week upper division writing-intensive course, a modest packet of poems, essays, Web sites, and illustrations about Barbie dolls, an embarrassingly rich collection of Barbie dolls, and my five-year-old daughter's desire for a prince.

"Dear Santa," Anna writes in her first unsolicited letter to Santa. "I want a real live prince to fall in love with me, and I want him to be five years old." Spontaneously composed in the first semester of her kindergarten year, Anna's letter illustrates the pervasive influence of an array of material images that structured her childhood years—rumba panties, Disney films, fairy tales, and Barbie dolls—culminating in a letter soliciting the gift of the imageword dominating that array: a five-year-old prince who loves her. I begin with Anna's letter for two reasons. It reminds my students, separated so decisively from their childhood by time and circumstances, of the truth of Wordsworth's words: the child is father to the man (mother to the woman). The toys we play with directly implicate the fantasies that we create, the goals we set ourselves, the identities we hone. So, with Anna's letter as a starting point, we begin talking about the immediate situation that brings her to this point, where the most important Christmas present in her five-year-old life is a "real live prince who loves her." I point them to Anna's imaginative play with her sister's Lego castle, a castle replete with king, knights, horses, griffin, and princess (who, with a flick of her hat, becomes a witch). "Where is the princess," I asked Anna during one of the many times she sat in front of the castle whispering her way through her imaginary world. "Why, Mama," she answered, surprised at my ignorance. "She's up in the tower waiting to be rescued." As I tell this story to my students, I lay out on my desk for display the clothes that Anna wore as a toddler—a red velvet Christmas dress, white tights with lace ruffles on the panty portion, and black patent leather shoes—and a sampling of the clothes she chose at five—lace socks, Beauty and the Beast underwear, and dresses (no skirts, no jeans, no shorts). We shuttle between clothes and rules, highlighting the paradoxes little girls experience. Keep your skirts down, mothers tell their children, simultaneously dressing them in rumba panties with pretty lace trim that no one can see unless the skirts go up. Is it no wonder, I ask my students, that during a Christmas program before a church full of amused parishioners, a three-year-old Anna kept flicking up her skirts so everyone could see her pretty panties, decorated with layers of lace and tiny embroidered candy canes? As a class, we begin constructing from these materials the imagewords drawing Anna to her prince.

Then we turn to subject positions, to the rhetorical identities that we craft for ourselves in both our lives and our literacies. Look at the dynamic that undergirds Anna's letter, I instruct them. Where is Anna in this dynamic? How does she position herself in terms of the rhetorical action? She is a petitioner, they point out, a petitioner who, like the princess in the tower, waits for the prince to deliver himself to her. She does not cast herself as actively pursuing the prince, finding him for herself. Rather, she constructs for herself a passive role, one in which her most aggressive action is the demand in her letter: I want you to give me a prince because I'm supposed to have one.

We spend a significant portion of the period discussing Anna's letter, exploring the connections between childhood and adult literacy as a necessary prelude to their own explorations of the dynamic at play in their lives. They follow the discussion of Anna with their own journal entry. It is here that Marie reveals that she has collected Barbie dolls since her childhood, a collection she continues to maintain. Encouraged by her mother and grandmother, Marie has an impressive assortment of Barbies in sundry garb from sundry eras, all hermetically sealed in tidy boxes intended for display, not play. It is at this point that one student, a sociology major who, as a single woman, was unable to obtain a loan that, she was told, would be made available to her if she were married, writes of the fights in her family over Barbie dolls. The only girl in a family of boys, the children would argue over who gets to do what to the dolls: chop off the heads, bury them under sand, run over them with GI Joe action figures. Another student, an African American career soldier in his late forties with a Japanese wife and three adult children, taps memories of war games, cops and robbers, and neighborhood football games. The remaining students explore their memories of toys, games, and pastimes—marathon Monopoly games, baseball cards, and statues—that they unearth from their childhoods.

Against the text of Anna's letter and their resurrected memories, we move to a physical activity: thirty to forty-five minutes spent playing with an array of Barbie dolls and paraphernalia that I supplied.[3] They all sat on blankets on the classroom floors—no desks—surrounded by dolls, clothes, shoes, purses, dishes, food, furniture, and cars, literally playing with the toys. Notebooks at their sides, they kept field notes of their experiences so that they would have a written record of those experiences and their observations of classmates. For instance, drawing from my own field notes, I noted the kinds of activities students enacted: role-playing in which pairs of students evolved elaborate scenarios for Barbie action; parallel play in which, for example, one older male student struggling with Barbie's hair reminisced to another student about his trouble trying to braid his daughter's hair when she was a child; and resistant play where students created new Barbies (Boozer Barbie, Super Barbie) and new accessories (a chapel for the Catholic Barbie, a church for the Fundamentalist Barbie). Students then turned around on their field notes, interpreting what they experienced and observed, seeking patterns in behaviors at play and behaviors in the world. We shared and discussed both field notes and interpretations, responding to each other's and exploring the ways in which we all saw different structures, different rules organizing the class play. To illustrate, one student wrote a spirited rebuttal of my interpretation of the play, an interpretation that focused on the reinforcement of Barbie as the eternal virgin who enslaves Ken by always saying "no." As he argued in response, what I missed was the element of parody, of mockery, that wove through their play, especially in his case. By exaggerating those aspects of Barbie that are already exaggerations, he insisted, he and Marie, his self-selected partner during playtime, challenged the belief system whereby women accrue power in relationship to their sexual desirability. Sometimes, he concluded, men and women have to change a system by undermining its foundations first.

On this heavily textual activity, we layered a second physical activity: field trips into the community to identify the marketing of Barbie dolls. Some students went to the local Toys 'R Us, to the local Wal-Mart, and to a boat show where Barbie and Ken were featured. Other students brought back sketches of window displays; descriptions of a popular car commercial featuring a pseudo-Barbie who ditches a preppie Ken and a colonial mansion for a GI Joe in a muscle car; and samples of print ads for Barbie dolls, including collector's editions. Students again wrote in response to their observations, analyzing the import of double imagewords. What is being marketed? How does that marketing implicate us? How does it require that we develop a certain kind of literate stance in relationship to toys and to ownership? What about the spatial implications of Barbie, especially in stores where rows and rows of Barbie materials press on parent and child? How do we align ourselves physically and rhetorically in response to this bombardment?

With these experiences as a touchstone, we turn to a modest packet of print materials including illustrations, cartoons, essays, poems, and Web sites on Barbie dolls. What have other people said about Barbie dolls and how have they said it? What is her status as a cultural icon and how did she acquire it? To what degree does her mythos permeate our immediate lives? Is Cindy Jackson, a British woman who has systematically engaged in extensive plastic surgery to recreate herself in the image of Barbie, an anomaly or an exemplar of the motivation that drives men and women across cultures to undergo cosmetic surgery? What kind of resistance does the Barbie mythos elicit and how is that resistance manifested? What are the media of that resistance? Integrated into this packet of readings that I provide are the "readings" that students themselves provide: feature-length cartoons of Barbie, lyrics of songs on Barbie, children's books featuring Barbie, CD-ROMs of Barbie computer games and fashion games. We play these imagewords against each other, looking for patterns that we construct as they construct us.

The fourteen students in my upper division writing-intensive class began at the same point—with Anna's Christmas letter, on the floor in a college classroom playing with Barbie dolls, Ken dolls, and an embarrassing richness of clothes, cars, houses, and furniture—and all ended up at wildly disparate destinations four weeks later. But the one common factor that united their very different papers was a renewed sensitivity to the bodies that we inhabit, the bodies that we write-read with, the bodies through which we communicate. Let me offer a sampling of the papers that evolved from this assignment. Michael's paper dealt with the martial arts, a discipline he had begun practicing in childhood. Central to the paper was Michael's concern with the necessity in merging the inner and outer, the soul and the body, in martial arts programs. Parents need to be wary of martial arts training that did not fuse the discipline of the body with the discipline of the spirit, he warns, for attending to one without attending to the other offers not freedom but enslavement. In a totally different vein, a single female student wrote an essay that begins with an incident in a bar where a complete stranger smacks her on the bottom, then gets miffed when she protests. From here, she argues that too much of American culture is aimed at yoking women to men. We are pressured to link ourselves to a man for our protection, so that we have access to spaces and places denied us as single women. We are pressured into "couplehood" for money, using as an illustration her own failure to acquire a loan because she was young, female, and single as opposed to young, female, and married. Finally, we are pressured by an entertainment culture that offers for our pleasure activities involving male-female couples. At every turn, the writer protests, women are told to harness themselves to a man. Lena, a student from an east coast Italian family who had married a Missouri state trooper, wrote a paper in which she advocated a regimen of systematic self-help. During the Barbie Caper, Lena brought in, at our request, videos of her elaborate wedding, along with photo albums and keepsakes. She brought as well her self-help books, books that she had put together throughout her life filled with articles, illustrations, pictures, and her own writing, all on topics designed to help her grow and change. It is these self-help books that she incorporated into her paper, weaving the story of her own desire to improve herself into the advice she offers to other young women. A musician who earned extra money by playing the organ at wedding ceremonies explored the symbols associated with wedding ceremonies, explaining to young brides the messages they were sending as their fathers "gave them away," as they walked down the aisle veiled, and as they exchanged with their groom bites of cake. Tracing the history of these symbols, this student writer highlighted the physical promises behind the rituals that most brides actively solicit without understanding what their performances promise. Finally, an African American student, committed to success through assimilation for his children and other children, wrote an open letter to Mattel pleading for them to create ethnic dolls that reflected positive images for African American children. These positive images included not only the incorporation of physical markers other than skin color by which African Americans identified themselves but also appropriate apparel and careers that invited African American children into the American middle class and a better way of life.

We carry the weight of our physical lives into our literate lives, turning around in a reciprocal fashion to knit our literacies back into our bodies and our places. We cannot shed that weight or edit it out of our discourse. By looping and relooping physical experiences within a specific situation with literacy experiences across an array of media, these fourteen students were able to gain and to confirm a sense of the sensuous connection between the imagewords they use and the imagewords they live. We found in our unique positions things important to say to other people and to ourselves, carving out of those situations connections to the larger world within which we live. These double-mapped activities serve to reacquaint students with the materiality that infuses their lives and their literacies, spinning them into physical and rhetorical orientations difficult to separate.

Double Mapping Polyscopic Literacy

A pulse point for a poetics of teaching is immersion, and somatic literacy enables us to plunge into our own positionality. It highlights the degree to which meaning is a product of our physical emplacement within a specific site and scene. By teaching somatic literacy, we encourage our students to attend to the sensuous connections between words and living, focusing their attention on the degree to which what they see as meaningful is a product of where they are. However, a second pulse point of a poetics of teaching is emergence —our awareness of the multiplicity of our visions and the partiality of those visions. Fostering polyscopic literacy fosters emergence. Through polyscopic literacy, students expand not only their repertoire of imagewords but also their ways of constituting valid imagewords. We cannot live in the world until we have an image of the world. But we also cannot allow our world to be dominated by a single web of reinforcing images. By teaching polyscopic literacy, we can increase the presence and frequency of imageword webs in our classrooms as well as increase our ways of seeing in the world. Toni Morrison illustrates the absolute necessity of such polyscopic literacy.

In *The Bluest Eye*, a novel that focuses on the creation and disintegration of black identities in the 1940s, Pecola, the novel's tragic focus, escapes neither the web of images nor the pain of her life situation. Rather, after her rape by her father and her fruitless efforts to secure her mother's love, Pecola escapes into a fantasy in which she mirrors the culture's dominant web of reinforcing imagewords. She believes that she possesses the bluest of Shirley Temple eyes and the world's adoration: "Are they really nice?" Pecola asks a phantom self. "*Yes, very nice,*" the phantom self whispers back. "Just 'very nice'? Really, truly, very nice? *Really, truly, very nice.* Really, truly, bluely nice?" (194). On the other hand, Claudia, Morrison's ten-year-old narrator, identifies and resists the same reinforcing web of imagewords manifested in the Shirley Temple doll, the celluloid figure who dances with Bo Jangles, and an array of Shirley Temple paraphernalia. Unlike Pecola, Claudia destroys every Shirley Temple doll she is given; she actively resents Bo Jangles for dancing with the celluloid Shirley Temple when he should have been dancing and joking with little girls like Claudia; she discards her Shirley Temple cup. Claudia notes the disjunctures within the particular web of images she is called to replicate, finding cracks that enable her to resist the lure of reflection. In spite of the prevalence of the Shirley Temple mythos, Claudia, unlike Pecola, can say, "I could not love it. But I could examine it to see what it was that all the world said was lovable" (20), proceeding to smash and dismember every Shirley Temple doll she is given.

How do we double map our teaching so that our students more easily recognize the webs of imagewords dominant in a culture and more easily disrupt those webs? How do we teach them to recognize and dismember *their* Shirley Temple dolls? In this section, I explore a double-mapping approach to polyscopic literacy. The double map that I describe below involves a four-stage writing assignment juxtaposing word and image—marking and unmarking— in metaphors.

Metaphors have always been problematic sites, structures that both control and emancipate. For instance, Patricia Yaeger's study of women writing is predicated on both faces of metaphor. Concerned with the dominance of metaphors of silence that circulate throughout feminist criticism, Yaeger undertakes to uncover a countertradition in women's writing, "a tradition that involves the reinvention and reclamation of a body of speech women have found exclusive and alienating" (2). She identifies an alternative metaphor, an alternative mythology of feminine speech, that of the writer as a honey-mad woman, as "someone mad for the honey of speech" (3–4). By recovering this metaphor, she establishes "a matrix of images that will emphasize women writers' empowerment," a web of images that offer different reflections, different ways of seeing and speaking for women.

I sought to evoke this formative and transformative power of metaphor in a four-part assignment sequence fashioned for a group

of upper division students enrolled in a class on writing and composition theory. I illustrate the possibilities of this assignment by
using the work of one student—Aletha—a five-feet-eleven, sophisticated, highly literate, and brilliant third-year medical student who
had and continued to model professionally (see also chapter 1).

The double-mapped assignment sequence cycles students through
an in-depth examination of a metaphor that they generate to describe themselves. Drawing heavily on George Lakoff and Mark
Johnson's *Metaphors We Live By*, I began the unit with a discussion
of metaphors, exploring their formal aspects and their presence
within the meanings we create. After playing with metaphors in
class, I asked my students to answer the following question—Who
am I?—using a metaphor of the form "I am?" They were to set up
two columns, one for the tenor and one for the vehicle (see below).
They were to brainstorm the vehicle first, tapping all the associa-
tions they had with it. Then they were to turn to the tenor, writing
down everything they knew about it. Next they were to shuttle
across the state-of-being verb *am*, exploring the ways in which their
understanding of both vehicle and tenor shifted under the weight of
the other. Aletha produced the three-column list shown here.

I am like a	black	doll
not the norm/majority	beautiful powerful	wanted pretty
shelved unwanted	blacker the berry, the	delicate held
not the cultural	sweeter the juice	played with
standard of beauty	afrocentric	dresses little girls
left out forgotten	rich heritage	white blond
not accepted	symbol of bad or evil	Barbie standard
looked over	in society	perfect loved
ashamed of	racism bigotry	porcelain fad
different awkward	civil rights 1960s	blue eyes
not there	shut out depth	models
	derogatory negative	representatives
	southern food	babies expensive
	unique	Cabbage Patch

After their exploration, students were to produce in whatever
genre they wished an informal journal entry that captured the various

senses of their metaphor. Aletha chose to speak through the voice
of a doll abandoned on a store shelf: "I am a black doll left behind." At the core of the journal were her struggle and her perceived failure, in spite of her modeling, to participate in the American iconography—its dominant web of imagewords—encompassing
beauty. She could not achieve any sort of satisfactory (and persuasive) match between her physical form and that web of imagewords.
As an American of African descent (her preferred means of identification), she was barred from reflecting the iconography of American beauty, which was predicated on blond hair and blue eyes: the
white Barbie. She describes how she, like other black dolls, had
been left on a shelf, "waiting for hands to want me," eventually
questioning whether she was as attractive and intelligent as the
blond, blue-eyed, perfect dolls who never collected dust. Then she
traveled to Europe, where doubts about her attractiveness and intelligence disappeared. "In Europe," she writes, "I actually became the
revered, sought after, precious doll. I was the center of attention because I was different. It was then that I realized what it was like to
be the wanted doll." As a result of her participation in a different
iconography of beauty, she realizes that she remains on the shelf
in America because she is not "the cultural standard, the wanted,
white Barbie" that she is told through the "media, through literature, through everyday experiences" that she should be.

The second assignment within this sequence loops back on
the first part. Taking as my starting point Warren McCullough's
question—What is a number and what is a man that he knows a
number?—I asked my students to return to their original metaphor
and reexamine the vehicle by asking themselves who are they that
they would describe themselves thusly. Aletha asks herself the following: What is a black doll, and who am I that I know myself as a
black doll?

Struck by the contradictions between iconographies of beauty,
Aletha extends her thinking about dolls in this informal paper,
turning dolls into mirrors, which can be broken. Change is possible; children do "revolt against perfection." The standard dolls
in eighteenth-century America, she begins, were porcelain, pink-

cheeked, delicate, and beautifully dressed. However, "little girls were found pulling off their [dolls'] heads and burying them in the backyard. The reason: they were too pretty, too clean, too perfect and did not look or reflect the newfound American [frontier] persona."

From this promising opening, Aletha turns to the contradictions that mar the unity among women, regardless of color. She first veers back to the pressure to mirror the dolls that mirror American society. Dolls are a selective looking glass for American society, reflecting back what the majority wants to see and requiring all female children to model themselves after that image. Because Aletha is a black American woman, she is invisible in this mirror. But she is not invisible as a black American; instead, she is given an image to reflect that is untenable: one of laziness and dishonesty. As a result of these internal contradictions, Aletha concedes that she has limited empathy for white women who claim a gender disadvantage:

> From my point of view, the white female has a great advantage because she does not need to worry about her color. She will always come before a black girl in our society. For example in the business world the white female is more likely to move up in position before a black female. In an expensive store, the more likely shoplifter may be a white girl, yet the black girl is closely eyed and followed.

Finally, in the third turn on the metaphor, I asked my students to look at their metaphor from one more angle: what constraints are operating both on the evocation of the metaphor and on the identity constructed by means of this metaphor? What are the limits on identity implicit within the medium we use to represent it? For Aletha, the answer is the limits of double consciousness. The doubleness of vision is the topic of her last informal paper. Following a head quote from W. E. B. Du Bois on double consciousness, Aletha's paper opens starkly: "I use two mirrors," one a real mirror and one the mirror in the eyes of others. For her, the reliance on other's eyes is a defense mechanism: to figure out how she is being perceived so that she can assess the situation and decide whether she needs to arm herself and prevent an unwanted outcome. How am I being seen by others? she asks herself. A threat? A victim? She must read this mirror in order to protect herself in a culture where her being is disrupted by their seeing.

The assignment culminates in a request that they fashion a work intended for an audience other than self. Aletha integrates her three previous assignments into a formal paper, deliberately titled "Untitled," that explores the ramifications of her female black identity in America, where a particular configuration of beauty and female identity dominates. Here she pulls together the contradictions and tensions she has exposed and in the process crafts for herself a different way of seeing and a different image. She begins with a headnote taken from Morrison's *The Bluest Eye* in which Claudia expresses her hatred for the Shirley Temple doll (20). From here Aletha reprises points explored in her informal papers until she comes to her crucial turn: her brother's popularity in high school. Here her argument morphs from her status as a *black* female to her status as a black *female,* for, she argues, the rejection that she suffered as a teenager was not replicated in her brother's experiences as a young black male. He was chosen, she was not. Iconography is not about women's beauty; it is about men's ideas of women's beauty. "Men have always been the choosers, not the choosees." The bottom line, Aletha says, is not that she is black but that she is black and female. It is not merely an issue only of race. It is also an issue of gender. The doll she, like Claudia, wishes to dismember is that which privileges a particular race as well as a particular gender. "Perhaps for the dolls that are chosen," she concludes, "none of this is visible. But for those of us left sitting on the shelf, the view is very clear."

As Aletha's essay illustrates, double mapping webs of imagewords offers us an opening within which we can create a different way of seeing; it fosters our students' acquisition of polyscopic literacy. This is not an escape from one web of imagewords to no web of imagewords, which is impossible. Rather, it is an opening within which we can create an alternative vision. Aletha's story ends not with her final paper, a discursive act, but with her performance at our last meeting of the semester, a material act. After struggling with imagewords of beauty during the last weeks of our class, a struggle she shared with peers through collaborative workshopping, Aletha walked through the door on the last day of class wearing form-fitting jeans, red boots with two-inch heels, and a grin. Turning to her classmates, who rippled in responsive humor, Aletha displayed her newest acquisition: vividly tinted blue contact lenses. Laughing at the reactions her parody elicited from her classmates and me, pleased with her revision of an American beauty mark, Aletha enacted a different web of images, one that offered her egress into a different iconography of physical agency. Such a process is worth fostering in our classrooms, in our lives, and with our children.

Double Mapping Lateral Literacy

Regardless of our efforts to encourage openness, exploratory thinking, and intellectual risk taking in our classrooms, we have all fielded the same question asked in different words: how long do you want this paper? How many words, pages, paragraphs? One of the most difficult lessons we must teach in a public school culture that uses standardized tests as a means to assess education progress is to court transformation by resisting closure, by keeping a search open, by leaving a question only partially answered. In this last section, I explore the potential of double mapping for teaching lateral literacy, a literacy that encourages students to court transformation and resist closure by disrupting the linearity of texts and lives. The assignment sequence focuses specifically on eroding our students' belief that a text holds a single meaning that they must ferret out. If we begin to teach lateral literacy by destabilizing our students' faith in the singularity of a text, we also take the first step in destabilizing their faith in the singularity of their lives. On subtle levels, we link texts and lives. We refer to a body of work, to an author's corpus. We call the introduction to an essay the head and the middle the body (where ideas are developed in some sort of digestive process).

An argument in the West possesses a forward momentum, a forward progression, like a life. On multiple and frequently inaccessible levels, the identity of a discourse and the identity of a life are fused. Critique of our writing, thus, is frequently experienced as critique of our lives, our identities. Double mapping lateral literacy to disrupt the unity of text opens the door to a similar disruption of individual identity.

One of the first bars to lateral literacy is our students' belief in the inviolability of the text. Therefore, one of my first concerns in my classes, both first year and upper division, is to violate the primacy of print text. Our students are trained from kindergarten to regard print texts as sacred. Preschoolers are taught not to color in their storybooks, grade school students are taught not to write in their reading books, and high school students are taught not to deface their library materials. Furthermore, our assessment procedures inculcate the belief that there is a "real" retrievable meaning in a text, and the closer students get to that meaning, the higher their grades will be. So trained, our students might engage enthusiastically in evolving diverse interpretations to a thorny text, but they will inevitably turn to us as authorities and ask for the "real" answer ("What does this really mean?"), seeking the one answer we expect on a test, an essay, a paper. It is this attitude, reinforced in so many ways by the academic environment, that must be disrupted before students can experience the validity of lateral literacies. To enhance my students' enactment of lateral literacy, I want them to experience what Barbara Page, commenting on hypertextual fiction, calls the "restive text," the text that splinters ownership, time lines, and meaning. And I do this by importing hypermedia techniques into traditional pen-and-paper classrooms, that is, classrooms that are not technology enriched.[4] Twice within the sixteen weeks of a first-year composition course, once in response to a literary text and once in response to an academic essay, I ask my students to craft hypermedia responses. Rather than soliciting written or sketched journal entries, I form my class into groups and assign each group the task of constructing a paper Web site of a primary text, a Web site that must consist of a range of hotlinks. Let me offer an illustration of one such activity focusing on William Stafford's "Traveling Through the Dark."

Depending on the size of the class, I allow three to four class periods for this activity. I begin with familiarizing students with the complexities of Web site design, using overhead transparencies to chart the fluid movement of a multimedia Web site. Their assignment, I explain, is to construct a Web site of Stafford's poem, incorporating a variety of texts, images, and audio cuts that they have selected according to a logic that they evolve. This process, I point out, requires that they do more than read and respond to the poem. They must also research the poem, research their response to the poem, and research others' responses to the poem. Then they must sift through those materials to construct a Web site that serves a purpose they determine. We discuss the logistics of a paper Web site. They must have a home page, a point at which they start, although it may not be a point at which their readers start. They must also have links to other pages, and for each lexia, they must have a paper, drawing, video clip, or audio clip to display to the class, a hardcopy of the experience they want available for their readers-users. Finally, they must have a flow chart diagramming the layout of the Web site. Each Web site will be presented visually and aurally to the class, I remind them, so consider the factors involved in setup. I then divide students into groups, making sure that students with Web site expertise are distributed evenly through the class. Groups spend the remaining class time organizing their own responsibilities on the basis of discussions of the poem, as well as on their individual strengths and interests.

We meet the next class period in the library, where I set up an area at which we all congregate. Students drift to and from this area, soliciting input from their classmates and me, jump-starting stalled group work. We deal with the knotty issues of audiovisual support, ensuring that I have the necessary hardware on hand to support their "paper" Web sites.

Depending on the progress and the needs of the students, we present final projects on the third or fourth day of the unit. First, all groups post their paper Web sites, either taping or tacking the Web sites around the room. One particularly enterprising group scotch-taped home page and links to a student volunteer with paper arrows running down legs and arms to various links. One group, blessed with an elementary ed major, arrived with elaborate poster boards arrayed with hand-cut block letters and illuminated renditions of the poem linked to photographs. The Web site's links were connected with threads to specific elements of the illuminated poem. Throughout the class, links elaborating elements of the poem ranged from biographical information and critical commentary on Stafford to Stafford's own comments. One group linked to other Stafford poems, while another focused on wildlife information, recommendations about night driving, and geographical information about the Pacific Northwest, where Stafford once lived, and Kansas, where Stafford was born and raised. Students incorporated audios of Stafford reading poetry and of night sounds. One group included a video clip from the Disney film *Bambi*, while another included an inked sketch of a member's responses to the poem. Finally, a last group wrote up and decorated their individual responses to the poem that they then linked in a kind of imageword collage. Presentations consisted of classmates gathering around the Web sites while the group members guided us through the site, explaining the logic underlying their choice of materials.

The presentations and the Web sites serve as the starting point for additional discussions. With the Web sites still on display, I ask students to track the number of ways that classmates can get into and out of the primary text. Weaving back and forth between the physical poem and the Web sites, we trace the array of hotlinks, discussing the differences and similarities in the words and phrases students considered important enough to link to other pages; we discuss the changes that traversing the links in various ways effected in our reading of the poem. We cross correlate not only specific graphics and audio clips students imported but also the degree to which people integrated diverse media and the impact of that media on our sense of the primary text. We also begin the process of linking the individual Web sites to each other so that we can craft a network of Web sites. Finally, we return to the poem itself, addressing the question that bedeviled us at the beginning: what does it mean? When the paper Web site activity is successful, students point out that this question cannot be answered with any definiteness. What a poem means depends on how and when and why we enter it and what we link to (what is available to link to) or what we choose not to link to.

The paper Web site activity is designed to underscore the restiveness and the intertextual-intermedia nature of a published piece of literature, and it has served me well with first-year students in a composition class devoted to writing in response to texts. At least for the sixteen weeks they spend with me, students are more relaxed about challenging a static reading of a short story or an essay. It is the anchor we return to when our discussions of readings get too heated (or not heated enough). How do we get to a certain reading, we ask each other? What are the invisible links that fragment our illusion of a single, stable text? On the other hand, when we get trapped in a static meaning, we ask what factors should be fragmenting that complacency.

The paper Web site also implicitly undermines the inviolability of identity, the belief that self-identity is evident and immutable. Grown within the hothouse of western Enlightenment, students take as a given the one-to-one correspondence between one body, one identity, and one individuality. Anything else is tantamount to insanity (multiple personality disorder) or criminality (aliases for nefarious purposes). However, destabilizing textual unity opens the door to further assignments that similarly double map restive identities, underscoring the hypermediated and splintered nature of our physical, psychological, and spiritual lives.

"Now I a fourfold vision see, / And a fourfold vision is given to me," Blake both exults and despairs in a letter to Thomas Butts (420). He issues to our students and to us a similar invitation to teeter on the edge of despair, on the edge of a fourfold vision, for here the doors of perception are cleansed. By requiring my students to double map and double map again, I have issued the same invitation, summoning them to both the exultation and the despair. Patti, Marie, and Aletha can attest to the experience of double mapping, for good and for ill; they have eaten the fruit of Blake's fourfold vision and created something different, something more. As their teacher, I have called them to double map, solicited the disruption of their hard-won truths, with the hope that they will connect more closely to their bodies in their words, that they will split vision into a rich array of imagewords, and that they will challenge the linearity of their texts and their lives. How do I organize a poetics of teaching? By double mapping, hoping to help my students evolve embodied literacies that open them to something beyond Barbie dolls, something beyond silence, something beyond the myth of the one text, the one life, the one story, the one meaning. And so I close with a hopeful story, a retelling of a daughter who wished for a prince.

Anna stands at the plate, her batting helmet slipping over her forehead, her uniformed body flexible, her concentration focused on the ball. "We don't play with Barbie dolls," her teammates chant from the dugout. "We just play with bats and balls. We don't wear no miniskirts, we just wear our dirty shirts. We don't drink no lemonade; we just drink our Gatorade." This eleven-year-old child with chipped blue fingernail polish and a picture of her "boyfriend" in a silver heart-shaped frame in her bedroom cracks the pitch over the diminutive second baseman. Infused with her own complicated and conflicting array of embodied literacies, she lofts that twelve-inch softball past the infield into the green and sprints for first base, determined to beat the ball home. Hit, run, score.

Conclusion

Teaching in and as an Imageword Ecology

In this way we might become answerable for what we learn
how to see.
                              —Donna J. Haraway, *Simians, Cyborgs, Women*

I do not like drawing pictures.
                              —Cathi, portfolio assessment

"You make me so mad. You never listen to me," my younger daughter raged and, in a completely atypical response to fury, burst into
tears. My fighter, my competitor, my rebel, who would rather eat
brussels sprouts than cry, sobbed as she stomped her way up the
stairs to slam into her room. Engaged in one of our innumerable
wranglings about Pokémon and good choices, I had pushed too
far, asked one too many "but, Lindsey" questions about the troubling ethics infusing the Pokémon world. In my self-assigned role
as parent provocateur, I had provoked more angst than order, more
resentment than repositioning. And, through my actions, I had
unintentionally replicated the very Pokémon dynamic I wished
to undercut: dominance-victimhood, master-slave, captor-captive,
user-used. I have misjudged similarly in the classroom, crafting a
teaching stance that called forth rebellion—"I refuse to write the
way you want me to"—and resentment—"I do not like drawing pictures." Neither response was my aim, and both were, in part, a result of how I constituted myself as teacher.

Positioned where the edges blur, our literacy classrooms are
sites of and opportunities for provocation. As teachers we initiate
the dynamic of immersion, emergence, and transformation. Students may contribute to the focus of a dynamic, but we offer (and

163

withdraw) the invitation to participate in the construction of a certain kind of meaning. With that role of provocateur, however, comes a necessary commitment to our own answerability. Imageword calls us to an ethicality of double positions, one that must be replicated in our teaching stance, our teaching identity. We are stretched throughout a specific loop of imageword—body, culture, place, and time—forging and fusing with connections on a particular level of that ecological web while we are simultaneously dispersed and diffused throughout the entire web of imageword's evanescent relationships. Because of our immersion within and our dependence on an imageword's porous ecology, we are bound to its double-sited system, bound to a classroom identity that is similarly positioned and dispersed. This final chapter explores the double-sited ethics of imageword and the teaching stance it evokes. I begin with a description of imageword's corporeal-discursive logics, extending my earlier discussion of ecological meaning in chapter 1. I then enact that doubleness by reweaving my actions in and responses to a troubling moment in a graduate seminar. By returning to this moment, by rewriting this story, I hope to transform my teaching stance, positioning and dispersing myself in the classroom in ways more congruent with the double-sited ethics of imageword and the dynamic of a poetics of teaching.

Framing a Double-Sited Ethics

Imageword is not just a conceptual category, although it is that, without a doubt. It is also the world we live in and the means by which we live in it. In this section I ferret out the ethics implicated in that theory of imageword. A theory of meaning always involves our actions in the world, even if only implicitly. An epistemology inevitably frames a way of acting as well as a way of knowing. Thus, an objectivist orientation suggests that moral values-actions exist outside specific situations and are discovered via a system of rational, procedural testing. At the other extreme, a subjectivist orientation leads us to moral values-actions that exist solely within an individual's feelings. It is this connection between epistemology and ethics that troubles poststructuralism, especially deconstruction with its deliberate erasure of originary, material reality by the action of the word, a process that undermines the possibility of both a system of ethics and ethical action in the world (Norris). David Lehman argues that Paul de Man's deconstructive philosophy enabled him to construct a morality that justified both his World War II anti-Semitic writings for a Paris newspaper and his later silence about that Nazi collaboration. Similarly, Geraldine Finn argues that Louis Althusser killed his wife, rather than a student or a colleague or a stranger, because of the patriarchal implications of his ideological-philosophical orientation. Meaning and action are inextricable. Therefore, I must tease out the ethics weaving throughout a theory of imageword. In this section, I begin with an imageword's double logics, proceed to its creation of and immanence within an ecology of meaning, and return to doubleness and the resonance it produces.

Above all else, imageword is characterized by its doubleness. On the most obvious level, imageword is an image and a word, a collage of material and linguistic relationships fusing. In this dynamic transaction, corporeal and discursive logics mark and unmark themselves in a constant, fluid movement. We might talk about image and word as separate categories, but we find them joined in mutually constitutive loops of circular causality, where one is both the cause and the effect of the other. Imageword is a phenomenon of interfaces, of fusions. At another level, imageword is doubled because it exists as a border rider, shifting constantly among the porous planes of bodies, cultures, places, and times. As I described in chapter 2, imageword multiplies itself within and across these planes in important ways. Its doubleness is complicit in the physiological creations of bodies—both as chemical matrix and as coding in the cellular process of embryogenesis. Its doubleness is also evident in the cultural construction of bodies, the second naturing wherein humans are remade by the tools they make. Bodies and cultures collapse and coalesce in a new configuration, in a double helix of imagewords. In addition, even as imageword is doubled by bodies and cultures so is it doubled again by places and times, both of which seep into bodies and cultures via imagewords to reconfigure that which has already mutated into different identities. We have layers within layers, doubles crisscrossing doubles until we can no more trace back points of origin than we can predict points of culmination.

The enactment of this inextricable doubleness results in an ecology of meaning. I introduced the concept of meaning as an ecology in chapter 1. Let me briefly summarize the points that I made then before turning to a teaching stance. As an ecology, meaning consists of a complex system of imagewords exchanging information and creating themselves as they communicate throughout a web of interlocking relationships. Meaning is evoked from that movement; it is a statement about that movement. As an ecology, meaning is triadic, involving at least two organisms within an environment, all of which are mutually constitutive, mutually dependent.[1] Neither organisms nor environment evolves separately. Instead, the context, or meaning, evolves. Bateson illustrates this dynamic neatly with his description of the evolution of horses and grassy plains. Unlike the narrative of evolution chronicled by Darwin, Bateson argues that neither the horse nor the grassy plain could have evolved without the other. Instead, the protohorse and the protoplain were locked within a complex relationship whereby minute changes in one elicited minute changes in the others, resulting not in the evolution of horse or grass, but in the evolution of the context: the entire array of relationships comprising horse and grass. Thus, Bateson concludes, it is always difficult to determine with any precision where the horse starts and the grass stops because to understand one we must also understand the other. To render this picture even more complex, in order to maintain the arbitrary designations of horse and grass, the context is engaged in a constant process of marking and unmarking as pathways shift in response to random elements (*Steps* 155). Neither passive nor inert, context, instead, is fluid and living.

For a teaching stance, we need to keep in mind two essential elements of an imageword ecology. First, meaning is always about an identity that has no existence outside that system: horse, grass, environment. Identity for any single aspect of meaning is embedded within the dynamic of the jointly crafted context. We cannot excise one element and attempt to define it outside its immersion within a system of relationships. Nor can we point to a single site within the system and say that identity starts or stops here. It is dispersed throughout the entire system. Meaning is a statement about the relationships comprising the entire system. Second, to maintain the health of the ecology of meaning, we must consider the health of the ecology as a whole, as well as the health of the individual strands within its web. We can no longer cavalierly mark off one level of an ecology—image or word, body, culture, place, or time—and say that this sole element is alone critical to the survival of the ecology. We can no longer so easily bracket mind and text, private and public, image and word, teacher and student in meaning. Such designations are continually marked and unmarked within an ecology so that we cannot determine with any consistency where one starts and the other stops. Let me offer an illustration of such an ecology, one drawn from a recent incident in my teaching.

I brought a draft of my introduction to chapter 4 into my first-semester composition class for my students' critical review, something I do regularly with all my writing classes and much of my writing. This was my first effort to share my work with this group of students, and the reaction was typical: moaning and groaning that they had nothing to offer me, that the text was too hard, that they were not my audience, so why should they have to respond. In the face of my insistence, my students reluctantly acceded to my request for critical input. As I paced around, Janey changed the entire dynamic of the class and the course. One of my class leaders, Janey was the first student to volunteer her draft for class examination, the first to wear her leopard-spotted fuzzy slippers to class, the first to object vocally to sketching. She began reading my three-page introduction immediately, while the rest of the class was still caught up in their protest rituals. She stopped reading in the midst of her classmates' grousing, looked at me jiggling nervously in front of the room, and with a mischievous grin, silenced her classmates with a single sly demand: "We need a picture." In a parody of my own words, she added, "Draw us a picture that centers us, that evokes a feeling." The resentful muttering halted, and twenty-four expectant faces turned to me with glee. I went to the dry erase board, paused, then drew my stick figures. The class burst into laughter, relaxed in the face of my artistic incompetence, and for the first time that semester, welcomed me into their ranks, at ease with their struggles in the face of my own.

At that moment, a moment in which I was the student grappling with the requirements of the course, I became a teacher. What evolved was an ecology of meaning, a context from which emerged a complex system of teaching and learning where participants shifted positions fluidly from student to teacher and, in so doing, became both student and teacher. Within an ecology of image-word, teachers become teachers only in the moments when students learn. Students become students in the moments when teachers teach. To trope Paulo Freire, learning occurs in the instances when people jointly configure themselves as teacher-students. We have no identity as teachers outside the network of pathways by which people simultaneously become students. Because of these linkages, the designation of teacher and student blur.

Bateson once challenged his graduate students with the following epistemological question: is a blind man's cane part of him? If information flows into the man as he walks via the cane, and if we wish to understand the man walking, then is not the cane a part of the man? We designate the system, the "man," by drawing our lines around all the pathways by which information is communicated through the system (the very pathways that determine the existence of the system in the first place). Therefore, if it is the walking man that we seek to comprehend, we must conceptualize the identity of the man as extending beyond the boundaries of skin to encompass the cane (*Steps* 318). So, too, with classrooms. If it is literacy learning that we wish to understand, then it is the entire complex of interlocking pathways through which information flows that we must embrace.

An imageword ecology, then, exists on multiple, transacting levels joined in intricate feedback and feed forward loops. Such an ecology encompasses the unity of corporeal, social, environmental, and temporal organizations of physical and mental systems. We cannot demarcate the borders of our worlds by using the boundaries of our skins, our neighborhoods, our species, our rhetorics, or our images. We are all linked in a permeable network, a complex system of meaning. If we disrupt the health of one part of the system, we endanger the health of the entire system of meaning, risking meaninglessness (chaos-pathology) not only on one level but also throughout all levels. Thus, Bateson can talk of the pollution of Lake Erie as a process of driving a lake insane, for it is an insanity that will surely turn around and infect us because we are inescapably linked.

From this holistic and deeply imagistic perspective, we can no longer comfortably talk about inner and outer, emotional and rational, private and public. Instead, we must consider the character of the entire system; we must be double positioned, both as part and as whole, as inside and as outside, as margin and as center, as image and as word. And it is in this doubleness that we find our ethics, our principles of right action by which we construct our teaching stance.

I now make my circular way back to my starting point, back to the doubleness of imageword and a poetics of teaching. Our teaching stance is poised within this doubleness, evolving from the resonance between corporeality and discursivity, image and word, student and teacher. The doubleness of a theory of imageword means that we serve both the survival of the local loop—community, classroom, students—and the survival of the larger public sphere within which the local is immanent. Furthermore, we serve those dual interests, those two sites not by privileging one over the other, but by privileging the health of the relationships that vibrate between.

Bateson refers to this resonance as aesthetic determinism. He argues that any theory of action, including moral and ethical action, "within large complex systems, where the active agent is himself [sic] a part of and a product of the system," must be understood as an aesthetics (*Sacred* 254). Aesthetic determinism suggests that moral and ethical actions are guided by a holistic response to the resonance across the transacting levels of a complex system. Does a pitcher throw a fastball by engaging in differential calculus? Bateson asks. Does a ballerina leap so gracefully because of an effective plotting of angles and velocity? When we are immersed in an activity so intently that we lose awareness of our external environment and our participation seems to unfold without our conscious contribution, we are in the grip of aesthetic determinism, responding to the resonance of the whole. Thus, Bateson argues, we must approach questions of moral and ethical action as a question of aesthetics, a question of the music of the spheres, the harmony resulting when the planets, and the angels inhabiting them, are aligned in such a way that the songs of the angels reverberate harmoniously throughout the universe.

Elaine Scarry argues similarly, contending that beauty intensifies our "capacity to attend to problems of injustice"; it exerts a pressure to "repair existing injuries" (57). Central to Scarry's argument about beauty leading to justice are two points: aliveness and distribution. The experience of beauty reciprocally links the object and the observer in a feedback–feed forward loop wherein the observer, who endows the object with aliveness by creating and recreating it as the object, is mutually endowed with a parallel aliveness. Distribution spreads this aliveness from the object and observer throughout a system. Scarry likens the movement to that which Plato advocates: from *eros,* the care and passion for one object-person, to *caritas,* the care and passion for the many (79). "[B]eautiful things give rise to the notion of distribution, to a lifesaving reciprocity, to fairness not just in the sense of loveliness of aspect but in the sense of 'a symmetry of everyone's relation to one another'" (95). At the heart of beauty and justice, then, is resonance, and doubleness is necessary for that to occur. Without imageword's paradox in which we are simultaneously in and out, image and word, body and culture, place and time, we would be unable to evoke and experience the resonance of our existence as an ecology.

To enact this double-sited ethics, we have to situate ourselves in the liminal space between imageword, immersed as it is within and through the porous planes of bodies, cultures, places, and times.

We need to tune ourselves to an ecological resonance, as aesthetic determinism. A teaching stance drawn from and answering to imageword imposes on us the need to respond to the pattern of the whole, the context. Simultaneously, it imposes on us the need to respond to the single thread. We must attend to both thread and web because even the smallest loop in an ecology contributes in nonlinear ways to the configuration of the whole. As producers and products of an ecology of meaning, we must be double sighted, double sited: bound to specific sites and spread through the whole. I turn now to an incident that occurred recently in a graduate seminar I taught on modern rhetorical theory, reenacting and thus resituating my teaching through the double-sited ethics of imageword.

Enacting a Double-Sited Ethics

On Tuesday, my graduate seminar in modern rhetorical theory exploded. A compliant group, the students had tolerated my nonlinear teaching style as they struggled to take notes and participate simultaneously. They were obedient discussants, cognizant of their responsibilities as students in a seminar, but never what I would have called enthusiastic—until we read Gloria Anzaldúa. Then four of my seven students co-opted the discussion and left class telling me that it had been the most productive session we had ever had. All because of Anzaldúa. The discussion, however, was not an exploration of the insights evoked by a critically empathic reading of Anzaldúa's *Borderlands/La Frontera;* in fact, just the opposite. The dominant speakers in Tuesday's discussion were, in fact, wildly antagonistic to Anzaldúa.

One student, just returned from the Conference on College Composition and Communication and counting the financial cost of his professional participation, bemoaned his discovery that he could never apply to the scholars for the dream program because as a white male he did not qualify. Struggling financially, working hard at moving forward in this profession, he felt as if preferential treatment were allowing other students a step up on him. A fellow student, a woman working on a literature Ph.D. with a secondary area in critical theory, supported her classmate, speaking from the perspective of a mother of two elementary-age boys. "Look at the pressure put on little boys," she pointed out with justification. "It's not as if they have a free ride." A third voice, then a fourth, chimed in, challenging Anzaldúa's claim to disenfranchisement, accusing her of a narrow, racist vision.

I responded to the barrage with a variety of approaches. I drew them back into their childhood to their toys, their games, their pastimes, pointing out how early a sense of their possible futures was inculcated in them. I led them through the discourses of their upbringing, pointing out the ways in which speech rituals at home prepared them for the speech rituals of preschool and elementary school. We looked at the houses and towns within which they were raised, contrasting these places with those within which Anzaldúa rooted herself. From these coordinates, we plotted the arc of identity and agency. Eventually, I elicited a grudging agreement from my vociferous four that perhaps Anzaldúa had something significant to say, but it was a Pyrrhic victory, an agreement pried from them with an intellectual crowbar, because I could argue better, could spit out more authoritative names. I doubt that I gained from them any substantial change of heart.

Throughout this free-for-all, three students were remarkably silent regardless of my efforts to draw them into the conversation. One student, who had been raised in a missionary community in Papua New Guinea, later said in her journal that Anzaldúa was the only rhetorician with whom she had connected, tracing in Anzaldúa the same unstable boundaries and uprootedness that she experienced both in America and in Papua New Guinea. The second student silent within the storm of hostile words was an international student from China whose first formal paper had been a thoughtful exploration of Edward Said's postcolonialism as a new rhetoric. Finally, the third student who withdrew from the discussion was another international student from Saudi Arabia whose first paper was a painstaking examination of the similarities and differences between the rhetorical theories of I. A. Richards and

Abd Alqahir Aljurjani, an eleventh-century (fifth-century Islamic) Arabic scholar. The three students who inhabited on a daily basis Anzaldúa's borderlands were the three students marginalized by the discussion. With the clarity of hindsight, I imagine a different future, a different discussion with a different outcome in a different class. By altering my conduct in, my conduct of, my graduate seminar, I might have invited my students to engage embodied literacies that were more ecologically healthful, and I might have shaped a public space within which all my students felt comfortable acting out those embodied literacies.

Perhaps the first resonance to heed is that created by somatic literacy, the resonance of bodies, places, and words vibrating. A value of imageword in dissolving the boundary that separates flesh and text is that it turns our attention to the physical nature of our literacies. Thus, our students who come into our classrooms with bodies sculpted by marginalized literacies resist the school literacy that requires them to change their bodies as they change their writing-reading. The dynamic is no different when students sculpted by school literacy are asked to change bodies and thinking as they write-read with marginalized literacies. Therefore, I must act out of this resonance of somatic literacy in imageword. One way I might do this is to remember that intellectual dissonance and confusion are inextricable from corporeal dissonance and confusion. Dissonance, Todd DeStigter reminds us, changes mental and physical habits but, unless handled with sensitivity, with attentive listening and vigilance, can also drive us back into entrenched ways of thinking and acting (37). Given this insight, I might have more productively guided the students' discussion of Anzaldúa into an explicit examination of the need for empathy in the successful forging of community, the need for building a common ground of affection by opening ourselves to the needs of others (Hoffman, "Empathy and Justice"). The limits of our experiences are also the limits of our understanding of another's experiences. This realization may have opened up a space for students within my class to offer the differing insights derived from their differing somatic literacies.

Such an approach would have built on strengths already present in my class. First, the class itself existed as a cohesive, supportive group. It had already cemented ties of affection in and out of the classroom before they had gathered together as a seminar. Quite simply, they liked each other, and this affection could have served to reduce the anxiety initiated by dissonance, by the failure of known corporeal and mental habits. Second, on the basis of this affection, the introduction of their unique experiences might have been perceived as an extension of that affection rather than a violation of it. Bolstered by the support of communal ties, Dana, my student from Papua New Guinea, could have shared her insider-outsider status with the class and not just in her journal with me as sympathetic reader. This would have allowed Dana an opportunity to initiate and participate in a dialogue that might have laid the groundwork for changing habits of body that, in turn, might have eased our return to Anzaldúa.

Imageword relies on more than the physiological-emotional component of somatic literacy. It also relies on the doubling of perspectives, of views from more than one place. Thus, imageword relies on the resonance of polyscopic literacy with its partial and mutable ways of seeing. The interweaving of imageword and polyscopic literacy leads me to my second lesson for enacting an imageword teaching stance. The discursive logic of imageword marks boundaries, locking us into static positions. Min-Zhan Lu refers to this as the recalcitrance of language. Lu notes that the problem of language in outing privilege is that words essentialize; they hide the ways in which position (e.g., my position as white, heterosexual, middle-class woman employed in a white-collar job) is also a disposition (e.g., my position as the daughter of a quarter Cherokee, blue-collar, Southern father who spent his youth picking cotton as a seasonal worker). Language persuades us to forget the ways in which we are inside and outside privilege simultaneously, the ways in which we are sited in more than one place, see from more than one perspective. Our physical experiences in the world, our boundedness in the containers of our skins, create the bedrock belief that identity is stable and bounded.[2] The complexities of image-word highlight its reliance on a multilevel ecology of meaning that weaves layers of bodies, cultures, places, and times, but those complexities also highlight the paradoxes of that ecology, inhabiting as we do more than one place at once, more than one identity at once. Imageword's reliance on and evocation of polyscopic literacy offers avenues of change for my class and me. One of the distressing aspects of the high-jacked discussion was the switch in focus from *Borderlands* to the students' own narratives of exclusion, of denial of privilege. Thus, in my class discussion, students responded to *Borderlands* with embittered accounts of their exclusions resulting from "invasions of the Other" (Lu 189). Anzaldúa was made a scapegoat, a representative of an Other who had "not sufficiently scrutinized her own complicity with various systems" (Lu 189), becoming, in turn, the victimizer with my students as victims. The lessons I can abstract from the resonance of polyscopic literacy in imageword are twofold. First, it teaches me that I cannot dismiss these students' reactions entirely. I, too, must engage in care-full listening and vigilance, for I, too, am subject to language, am part of this ecology. This care-full listening and seeing ask that I invite my students to explore the parameters of their own sense of exclusion, exploring their "yearning for agency" and the material circumstances that limit that agency (Lu). I cannot ask them to validate another's sense of exclusion if I dismiss their own. Second, the resonance of polyscopic literacy teaches me that I must also engage them in a similar exploration of the limits on Anzaldúa's yearning for agency. For this, I might elicit a deliberate layering of word against image, suggesting a literal mapping of the places they inhabit. Then, I could have invited them to map the places Anzaldúa inhabits in *Borderlands*. Here we could have visually diagrammed both the scope and limits of communal and public places for each of them and for Anzaldúa. This process might have enabled us to witness the overlap of the places of our privilege and the places of our exclusion, tracing the boundaries inscribed around both.

Finally, an imageword teaching stance relies on lateral literacies, the splintering of timelines and lifelines and the resonances created by those multiple vibrating lines. I might have acted more fully out of those resonances, hoping to evoke the same sense of lateral literacy in my students. The permeability of time and place disrupts the stories we tell, fracturing the linear time lines of history and autobiography, of unified identity. We could have performed such a splintering in my class by turning to my students' invocation of Anzaldúa's words to illustrate their belief that she advocated a racist philosophy. Here, we could have taken key passages that they cited, both in class discussion and in their journals, and returned those passages to the context, to the page, the chapter, the book, the ecology from which they were excerpted. As Lu advises, we could have then explored what came before the excerpted text and what came after, seeking a fuller understanding of the use to which we put the words of others, the interpretations we weave. Such a move sets the scene for language-mediated empathy through role-playing, a process that requires visualizing the scene-situation of another person (Hoffman, "Interaction"). By sifting through Anzaldúa's words for a fuller context, we also sift through her verbal images. Returning to these verbal images, we could begin to reconstruct the scene of her experiences, the first step to entering into that scene with her and forming ties of affection. As Deborah Tannen notes,

> The power of images to communicate meaning and emotion resides in their ability to evoke scenes. Images, like dialogue, evoke scenes, and understanding is derived from scenes because they are composed of people in relation to each other, doing things that are culturally and personally recognizable and meaningful. (*Talking Voices* 135)

Thus, interacting with Anzaldúa's language positions us to interact with Anzaldúa's verbal images, inviting us to envision and participate in the scenes those images evoke, creating out of that participation different imagistic and rhetorical practices.

I am the final player in this performance of hindsight. The resonance of embodied literacies in imageword requires that I vigilantly examine my own reactions, decisions, and teaching stance. I cannot set myself outside the loop of the classroom or my embodied literacies without committing what Lu calls "teacher illiteracy." And so I return to that day and see in my reactions a desire to co-opt. By reacting so viscerally to my students' unexpected rejection of Anzaldúa, I appointed myself her spokesperson and, in the process, abrogated my students' responsibility to speak for her and through her for themselves. Caught up in my own somatic understanding, I ignored theirs. Then I cut off polyscopic literacy and all its rich resonance by privileging one voice: mine. My student from China later told me that he appreciated my advocacy of Anzaldúa, a writer who affected him deeply. Why, then, I asked in turn, didn't he add his voice to mine? Honestly puzzled, he responded that he didn't need to. I was saying everything he wanted to say. Lu reminds me that I need to listen care-fully and act attentively, which means that I have to listen for the ways that I inadvertently silence others. I must watch myself for the moments when I fail to see others disappearing from the community. Without such vigilance, I am merely contributing to the erosion of a poetics of teaching in my own classroom. Finally, in my passion to tell Anzaldúa's story—in the singular—I unified, reduced to a single note, that which Anzaldúa deliberately splintered, erasing the enactment of her lateral literacies. Compounding that error, I did not recognize the lateral literacies weaving throughout my class, compressing the complexities of each of my vocal students into a single group, with a single voice, a single motivation. I contributed to the dissipation of resonance, to the erosion of imageword and the ethical action that might evolve out of it.

The resonances ensuing from imageword may not ensure that I handle with any more grace the next class discussion that gets high-jacked, but it offers me hope that I might. And I believe that I must act on that hope, grappling with my own illiteracy as I grapple with my teaching stance. A theory of imageword redefines what constitutes ethical teaching. Something different evolves when we stop talking about teaching as bounded by the skin, the class, the home, the neighborhood and begin talking about teaching as the confluence of places and people mutually constituted. Literacy would then be predicated on the health of the entire complement of elements. Such a stance commits us to situations, to partiality, to networks, to reciprocal actions. Such is the gift and the burden of a poetics of teaching.

We have no border that separates image and word, student and teacher, center and margin, flesh and mind. We have only our shifting movements through osmotic boundaries. In the *Troubadour of Knowledge,* Michel Serres asks the Harlequin-Hermaphrodite where and how he might

> locate the site of suture or of blending, the groove where the bond is knotted and tightens, the scar where the lips, the right and the left, the high and the low, [. . .] the emperor and the clown are joined? . . . What shadow must be cast aside, now, in order to reveal the point of juncture? (xvi)

The answer is that we cannot locate the suture or cast aside the shadow because we are always lodged at the intersection or the interference of the many if not the all (Serres xvii). As literacy teachers, as parents, as lovers, as friends, as colleagues, this is the ethical stance we need to inhabit as we are inhabited by it.

"Lindsey," I coax gently at the closed door. "Come out."

Tears are gone, but anger remains.

"No. I'm staying in here with Pikachu. You just won't listen."

Out of the mouths of babes.

"Okay," I concede. "How about if I come in there? And I'll try to listen—to both of us."

"We shall not cease from exploration," T. S. Eliot writes in "Little Gidding." "And the end of all our exploring / Will be to arrive where we started / And know the place for the first time" (145).

Notes

Works Cited

Index

Notes

Introduction: When Words Take Form

1. All students' names have been changed unless otherwise requested.

2. My decision to hyphenate the terms *writing* and *reading* grows out of my desire to highlight the fusion between both language acts. First, it is impossible to separate writing from reading, either practically or theoretically (see Nelson and Calfee). Writing overlaps reading; reading, perhaps less obviously, overlaps writing, unless we narrowly construe writing as only the act of scripting words on a page. Therefore, I graphically represent through the hyphen how activities bleed into each other. Second, writing and reading morph across disciplinary borders in at least three areas: rhetoric and composition; literature, especially critical theory; and reading theory, which, although lodged within education departments since the early part of this century, draws heavily on linguistics, cognitive psychology, sociology, and anthropology. Attending to writing and reading as writing-reading invites of us and of our students a similar morphing across borders. Third, I have chosen *writing* as the first element of the term in order to work against the historical privileging of reading (Nelson and Calfee). I wish to counter both the institutional valorization of reading and the same valorization in home environments (Brandt, "Remembering").

3. Other historical eras were marked by a similar dominance of imagery. For instance, Stafford argues that the imagery-rich milieu created by Catholicism was disparaged by intellectuals of the Enlightenment in large part because of its promulgation of denigrated imagery. The Enlightenment agenda, regardless of its fascination with optics, is characterized by its reaction against what was perceived as the tyranny of the deceiving image. However, the degree to which imagery penetrates our lives today, literally penetrating the body by means of various medical imaging technologies, is historically unprecedented. For an examination of the impact of visualization technologies and bodies, see, especially, Anne Balsamo's *Technologies of the Gendered Body*. For the intersection between advertising and women's perceptions of their bodies, see Susan Bordo's *Unbearable Weight*. For the influence of television advertising on children's evolving literacy, see Roy F. Fox's *Harvesting Minds*.

4. Interest in imagery has been manifested in a variety of ways: its fusion

with word in all meaning (Fleckenstein, "Image"), the coupling of image and word in technology (Stroupe), rhetoric's reliance on various facets of visuality (Faigley; Fox, *Images;* Groenendyk; Tebeaux), and the use of imagery in the classroom (Fleckenstein, Calendrillo, and Worley; Swearingen; Sadoski and Paivio, *Imagery*). A variety of scholars have linked image and word in mental representation (Paivio, *Mental*), as well as in reading (Sadoski and Paivio, "Dual Coding"; Sadoski, Paivio, and Goetz) and in writing (Berthoff, *Sense;* Witte).

5. Derived from Multi-User Domain, Object Oriented, a moo is a text-based, virtual reality environment that enables synchronous communication and the coconstruction of virtual spaces.

6. As described by Howard Rheingold in *Virtual Reality,* teledildonics refers to sexual experiences shared via a virtual reality interface, a potential rather than a current possibility of technology, and one that also highlights the fusion of image and word.

7. See Ellen Esrock for the denigration of visual imagery in twentieth-century literary studies.

1. Imageword: An Alternative Imaginary for a Poetics of Meaning

1. See Calendrillo; Hobbs; and Yates.

2. In 1971 Canadian psychologist Allan Paivio introduced in *Imagery and Verbal Processes* his dual coding theory (DCT) of cognition, which he refined and expanded more than a decade later in *Mental Representations.* Based on empirical rather than rationalistic studies, the DCT hypothesizes two functionally and structurally distinct systems for representing reality: a visual system (which includes other sensory modalities) for nonverbal objects and events; and a verbal system for language. According to DCT, concrete knowledge is represented by means of imagens, representational units of the image system that are organized synchronously in a type of "nested set" ("Empirical" 309). Within an imagen, smaller units are fused into highly integrated, thickly webbed, recursive levels of meaning. Embedded in larger parts, the entire memory configuration is available for use more or less all at once, like the elements of a fabric ("Mind's Eye" 8). Imagistic constructs easily serve as conceptual pegs, or ideational nodes, around which relationships constituting other information tend to cluster, like metal-mental filings around a magnet. On the other hand, more abstract information is represented via logogens in which information is arranged sequentially, in a linear pattern, with linking, rather than webbing, the major source of connection. Information coded within logogens is not available simultaneously; rather, those data unroll in time. Although separate systems, imagens and logogens communicate constantly through referential ties; in fact, much information is coded via both logogens and imagens. DCT contributes in impor-

tant ways to our theories of meaning, Mark Sadoski, Paivio, and Ernest Goetz argue. First, emotion is integrated into the model, particularly through the construct of imagens. Second, memory is affected in that the extended recall of concrete information is seen as a product of dual coding, that is, coding via both imagens and logogens. Third, flexibility is added to the process of knowledge construction, something that the scaffolding of schema theory lacks.

3. See also David Michael Levin, *The Opening of Vision,* for a critique of the philosophical and cultural cost of ocularcentrism as well as an alternative way of seeing.

4. Although Jay has included Foucault with French philosophers who disdain visual imagery, John Rajchman and Gilles Deleuze in separate works have argued otherwise, claiming that Foucault privileged vision.

5. See Judovitz on Descartes's repudiation of perceptual vision for schematized vision. A similar connection between the denigration of vision and the totalizing influence of perspective is seen in the Renaissance art technique *chiaroscuro,* used to present the illusion of three dimensions. Donna J. Haraway identifies the rise of perspective in art as a decisive moment in Western intellectual history that splits artist from subject. The artist arrays the subject's body (or the scene) on an imaginary grid, guided by the implicit belief that reality can be likewise accurately arrayed on such a grid, adumbrating the desire in science to stretch nature on the X-Y axes of the Cartesian plane. Reality (nature) becomes separated from the artist (scientist) as something that the artist can see and systematically represent as seeable, irrespective of the artist's influence as the seer (*Modest* 180–82; see also Mitchell, *Iconology*). It erases the embodied—constructed and positioned—nature of all imagery. This way of seeing leads American and French scholars to eschew tyrannizing metaphors of sight. Similarly, many teachers recoil from considering imagery as anything but a tool of domination and a manifestation of foundationalism.

6. If there is one type of imagery that has been a consistent focus of interest, it is verbal imagery, especially as it connects with literature and response to literature. However, Ellen Esrock argues persuasively that the verbal imagery of interest in the twentieth century is sound and touch, not vision.

7. Although I focus on the traditional five senses, a dominant way of conceptualizing modes of perception since Aristotle, Robert Rivlin and Karen Gravelle have argued persuasively for at least seventeen different senses: "Five [senses] was obviously just not enough to account for the huge range of sensory possibilities of which the human species is capable; seventeen is a more accurate count" (17), including among that array the trigeminal system (touch and temperature in the face), vomeronasal system (for detecting pheromones), and the pineal gland (essential for responses to light and synchronizing internal body rhythms to the rhythms of the sun) (16).

8. In setting forth this argument, I am aware of the chicken-egg factor.

Visualization might be privileged in our culture because of the prevalence of graphic imagery. Or graphic imagery may be prevalent because of the privileging of the visual. A circular causality is at work, one that also includes the physiological visual system as the major sensory system by which we know our world (to "see" is to "know"). There is no linear cause-effect pattern; rather, there are overlapping, even circular, forces that resist linear representation.

9. See also Fleckenstein, "Writing Bodies."

10. Mental imagery is not the only form of imagery characterized by fluidity. See Marcos Novak for the concept of liquid architecture, a position that undermines the fixity of architectural forms, including the graphic imagery of blueprints that yield a structure.

11. See also Abram.

12. Susan Aylwin's work with imagery in *Structure in Thought and Feeling* confirms this complementary dance between creating relationships and being relationships in imagery. Aylwin, in fact, claims that approaches to imagery split along this very point of relationships. Some theories, she explains, such as those proposed in Paivio's early work, posit an image as a mental entity that exists as a totality, not as a fluid set of relationships. However, she also explains that most of those theories have gradually incorporated the position of image as relationships. Aylwin, like Bateson, argues that images (and words) come to be when our attention actively shifts from one facet of reality to another. The image cannot be traced to that reality; instead, the image is a map of relationships created from that shifting attention. Drawing on the work of Jerome Bruner, Aylwin states that there are three modes of representation: enactive, visual, and verbal (4). These representations correspond to imagined actions, mental pictures (static, as opposed to active), and language (5). These modes of representation constitute conscious and unconscious thinking, and each possesses a unique semantic structure, one that Aylwin says corresponds to Charles Fillmore's case grammars (10). These semantic structures are not amodal propositions (13), nor do they lie behind a mode of representation. Instead, a semantic pattern is evident only in the representation: "Structures are in phenomena, not lurking behind them" (44). The movement of our focus evokes a series of connections between random bits of reality, and it is those relationships that we experience, not the reality. Aylwin's visual image, which serves as the matrix from which enactive imagery and language evolve, manifests itself as a "scene" in which a subject is positioned within a location or environment and possibly engaged in an intransitive action. An enactive image manifests itself as a narrative within which the individual participates in some transitive action that requires multiple related scenes. Aylwin maps the relationships that constitute each. For instance, if our attention flits from an attribute to the subject of attribution (The parrot is colorful) or from part to whole (The parrot has wings) or from subject to spatial location (The parrot is in the forest), then we craft a set of

relationships that yield a visual image. If our attention scoots so that we create relationships that feature an agent (a tiger) with motives (wants lunch) and transitive actions (attacks gazelle) and consequences (eats gazelle), then an enactive image results (32–32).

13. Although Bateson never connects his theory directly to the triadic meaning of C. S. Peirce (he did cite the importance of Peirce's concept of abduction, indicating his familiarity with Peirce's work), other scholars have noted the contiguity of Bateson's work in cybernetics and Peirce's work in philosophy (see especially Brier; Hoffmeyer). The two are also tied by means of semiotics, Peirce obviously as the father of semiotics and Bateson, who, with coauthor Jurgen Ruesch, wrote *Communication: The Social Matrix of Psychiatry*, a text that Thomas Sebeok calls one of the most significant works on the semiotics of communication in this century.

14. Significantly, Louise Rosenblatt refers to Bateson's work, particularly his reciprocal concept of ecology, as an example of the transaction she is attempting to describe ("Reading").

2. From a Poetics of Meaning to a Poetics of Teaching

1. Susanne K. Langer notes in *Problems in Art* that "the first created image is the dynamic image [. . .] the first true art is Dance" (12), an observation that suggests teaching second graders to square dance, as I was taught in the 1950s and my daughters were taught in the 1990s, accomplishes more than honing their social and physical skills. It fosters their evolving literacies.

2. Although I describe these planes as separate and separable, they infuse each other, especially the plane of place, which seeps into bodies, for bodies are a place; into cultures, for cultures are always emplaced; and into time, for time and space are inextricable. This inextricability is foregrounded in chapter 3, but I focus in this chapter on these four "separate" permeable planes.

3. Attesting to the power of words to hurt and heal, Jean admits that it is only since Molly began kindergarten that she has been able to use her hospital experiences in her writing. She explains that the act of writing about Molly's early danger seemed to evoke that danger, placing Molly in some jeopardy from which Jean would be helpless to protect her.

4. See also David Abram's *The Spell of the Sensuous* for connections between language and one's experiences in and of the world.

5. Central to this healing movement across the cusp between body and words is what James S. Baumlin and Tita French Baumlin, borrowing from Thomas Szasz, call iatrology, the utterance of healing words. Working out of a classical tradition, Baumlin and Baumlin suggest that to the Aristotelian *pisteis* of *logos, ethos,* and *pathos* we need to add *mythos.*

6. See Christine Battersby *(Gender)* and Patrocinio P. Schweickart on the

degree to which creativity and canonical literature require a reconfiguration of female bodies into male bodies.

7. Peter L. Berger and Thomas Luckmann pose a similar argument except that they claim humans are born biologically incomplete and therefore incompletely "natured." To complete themselves, humans craft a culture whose created structures reverberate on the creators, finishing their natures, completing their incompleteness. That which we make makes us.

8. Foucault defines spectacle in a more positive light, one drawn from antiquity, than does Debord.

9. A student in Jabari Mahiri's upper division undergraduate class that focused on teaching English in secondary schools, Viviana was the subject of a study jointly conducted by Mahiri and Amanda J. Godley. Using a "life-story" approach that blurs the boundaries between personal and political, between individual and social, Mahiri and Godley trace throughout Viviana's experiences the ways in which personal identity is shaped in part by the social constructs of literacy (416). The authors describe Viviana as bright, articulate, and outgoing. The oldest child of immigrant Mexican parents, one of whom had finished a two-year business degree at a Mexican university and one of whom had stopped going to school in first grade to care for siblings, Viviana was encouraged to succeed in school from an early age. Despite severe financial deprivation, Viviana's parents managed to keep Viviana and her two younger siblings in private schools for much of their education. Her commitment to education was reflected in her impressive academic achievement, including matriculation into and imminent graduation from the University of California Berkeley. Viviana was the first from her extended family of thirty-two cousins to attend college; she also hoped to be the first to receive a graduate degree. Upon graduating from UC Berkeley, Viviana planned to attend the Monterey Institute of Foreign Languages to become a court translator.

10. I track the shifts in Aletha's thinking and literacy practices more extensively in chapter 5.

11. See Le Dœuff's critique of Bachelard's concept of home, which calls into question Bachelard's assumption that all intimate geographies of home recapture the comfort and safety of the womb. Contrast Bachelard with the conflict that Steven Feld and Keith H. Basso report in their introduction to *Senses of Place*. Early work in anthropology focused on the social well-being attached to the rootedness of "home," similar to the emotional connections Bachelard explores, rather than to the contestations and power currents in the "unrooted and the uprooted." As working-class experiences of home reveal, rootedness is always fragile, always infused with unrooted- and uprootedness. Thus, acute issues of "exile, displace, diasporas, and inflamed borders" (4) are central to our inner geographies of place. See Anzaldúa for such a fragmented internal geography.

12. Bachelard's insight concerning the reciprocity of internal and external realities, as reflected in the house of memory, resonates historically with the "house of memory," a common memory strategy of classical rhetoric (Yates), and futuristically with Gibson's configuration of cyberspace as a "consensual hallucination" that comprises elements of internal and external geographies.

13. A reciprocal relationship—an ecological relationship—exists between place and language, not a linear one. Place and discourse are mutually constitutive.

14. The proliferation of cybercafes as well as their transformation into chat rooms, confirms our need for literacy spaces and demonstrates the ways in which real world geography is in part overcome by cyber-geographies. The phenomenon illustrates as well the ways in which the regime of spectacle as a dominant way of seeing is upset by the participatory nature of cyberspace reality.

15. See also Tannen, *Talking Voices*.

16. Perhaps more than any other cognitive model of discourse processes, de Beaugrande's parallel stage interaction model, which attempts to represent all speech acts (speaking, listening, reading, and writing), offers the greatest insight into time. For de Beaugrande, time functions on two axes: the length and the depth of writing-reading, that is, across the entirety of the literacy act and within-between the levels of processes. Time is a factor across the literacy act in terms of its effect on such factors as short-term memory, attention, and so forth. Here, time is the parameter within which literacy must conform. On the other hand, time within processing depth is more fluid. While each of the seven levels are embedded within each other (occurring in parallel interaction), each level also has what de Beaugrande calls processing dominance, where attention is focused on the performance of that specific act, for instance, forming goals (the deepest level) or forming letters-sounds (the shallowest level). The shift between levels is cued by thresholds of initiation and termination, and time can expand or contract up and down the vertical axis of de Beaugrande's model depending on the thresholds set by the literacy task, situation, or writer-reader. Performative time, then, is both sequential and fluid, offering important insights into the myriad faces of time in writing-reading.

17. See also Berman, *Reenchantment*.

18. See also O'Reilley.

3. The Shape and the Dynamic of a Poetics of Teaching

1. I thank Robert Brooke for helping me articulate this.

2. The growing attention within our culture and our classrooms to multiple literacies reflects all of this. For example, Brian Street argues that literacy is too frequently defined as autonomous literacy: a narrow set of discrete skills yielding a culturally valid performance that would by itself (autonomously) lead

to significant social and cognitive changes (13, 76). This is the literacy promulgated by public education, which results in the dismissal of all other literacies as invalid, as illiteracies. In opposition to this, Street advocates a move from autonomous, or school, literacy to multiple literacies. Multiple literacies emphasize the ways in which literacies and their consequences vary across cultural contexts and social practices, fusing oral and print performances. Unlike autonomous literacy, multiple literacies focus on a concrete understanding of literacy practices as specific enactments, a focus that disrupts the narrow construal of literacy as school literacy and as written literacy. Through the lens of multiple literacies, Street asserts, we can integrate into our theory and our instruction the places and practices that give literacy activities meaning.

Street's multiple literacies resonate to the *multiliteracies* advocated by the New London Group. Composed of ten literacy scholars who met for a weeklong discussion in September 1994 in New London, New Hampshire, to discuss the state of literacy pedagogy, the New London Group encapsulates their discussions in a single word—*multiliteracies*—a word, they argue, that describes for them their two important points: "the multiplicity of communications channels and media, and the increasing saliency of cultural and linguistic diversity" (63). What the New London Group adds to Street is the importance of medium. Multiliteracies integrate different media, the visual, audio, spatial, behavioral, and so forth, and honor local diversity amidst global connectedness (64). The New London Group argues that "literacy educators and students must see themselves as active participants in social change, as learners and students who can be active designers—makers—of social futures" (64), shifting from a textual definition of writer-readers to an imagistic one.

Multiliteracies validate and value writing-reading developed outside the venue of the classroom, developed even in resistance to students' sense of marginalization within the classroom. Multiliteracies demand that we work not only within students' "zone of proximal development," as social constructivist applications of Vygotskian perspectives urge us, but also within the students' enactments of writing-reading in specific physical locales and social sites.

Embodied literacies do not discount the value of multiple literacies. If anything, they reaffirm that value. What embodied literacies do is reorganize multiple literacies by highlighting the core literacies—somatic, polyscopic, and lateral—that configure individual literacy. Thus, the fostering of digital or visual literacy relies on a particular deployment of somatic, polyscopic, and lateral literacies.

3. See also Frederic Bartlett, who bases his concept of schemata on body memory.

4. Both Morris Berman and Owen Barfield claim that this way of knowing dominated the medieval mind-set. For example, Barfield describes the medieval way of being in the world as embryonic:

The background picture then was of man as a microcosm within the macrocosm. It is clear that he did not feel himself isolated by his skin from the world outside him to quite the same extent as we do. He was integrated or mortised into it, each different part of him being united to a different part of it by some invisible thread. In his relation to his environment, the man of the middle ages was rather less like an island, rather more like an embryo, than we are. (78)

5. Barfield locates the flowering of what he calls "original participation" in the Middle Ages (see also Bordo's analysis of medieval art in *Flight to Objectivity*). Berman, however, sees the Middle Ages, especially the hermetic wisdom of alchemy, as the final clarion call of participation as a legitimate mode of knowing (see also Keller, *Reflections*), the end to an erosion process begun with Plato's devalorizing of mimesis.

6. Aristotle's rationale for excluding slaves and women from participation in the Athenian political structure rested on a somatic rationale. For instance, both women and slaves lacked sufficient body heat—a corporeal attribute—which resulted in their inability to engage in the deliberative function. An absence of a particular quality of embodiment corresponded to an absence of a particular intellectual quality. Literacy, then, was inextricable from somatic knowing.

7. This imageword dynamic extends into Lindsey's academic work as well. Lindsey prepares for science and social studies tests by writing a keyword on one side of a note card and drawing her answer on the opposite side. When given an option to illustrate or to describe verbally an answer to a science essay question, she will draw and label rather than rely on predominantly textual explanations.

8. See also Bateson, *Mind* 153–54.

9. Scholars situate themselves variously in regard to the reciprocity of imagery and narrative. Susanne K. Langer argues that "the first thing we do with images is to envisage a story" (*Philosophy* 128). Exploring Jerome Bruner's concept of narrative epistemology, Kristie S. Fleckenstein argues that image and narrative are mutually constitutive ("Image"). On the other hand, Gunther Kress has argued that imagery disrupts verbal narrative.

10. While the confluence of space and time can disrupt each other, they also complement each other. Foucault points to this relationship when he analyzes the use of both space and time in schools and in the military to ensure control: "The disciplines, which analyse space, break up and rearrange activities, must also be understood as machinery for adding up and capitalizing time" (*Discipline* 157).

11. As Silvio Gaggi notes, hypertext will "alter our whole notion of what a text is—and what reading is, as well" (102). See also Lanham; Bolter.

12. I do not want to suggest that cyberspace is a utopian environment. The degree to which it is dominated by commercial interests and Western modes of thought (sixty-eight percent of all Web sites on the World Wide Web are in English ["Web Pages"]) suggests colonizing as well as liberating tendencies (see Sardar). In addition, the promise of multiple identities does not erase racist and sexist behaviors (Kang). Finally, it would behoove us to remember that cyberspace is the product of programming; we are bound by the constraints of software and of webmasters.

13. Empathy is a no stranger to literacy studies. See Fleckenstein, "Osmotic"; McLeod; Richmond; Teich.

14. Martin L. Hoffman's concepts of self and other focus are heavily visual and kinesthetic, relying on our ability to visualize another place and emplace ourselves imaginatively within its boundaries. Others working with empathy, however, have emphasized the importance of aurality, of listening. For instance, Susan H. McLeod's account of empathy in the classroom, which draws on the work of Carl Rogers, highlights the value of teachers' careful listening. Richmond similarly underscores the need for "care-full" listening, outlining an ethical framework for such empathic listening. Dale Jacobs, concerned with establishing affective ties in the classroom, advocates "deep listening," which he relates to Krista Ratcliffe's rhetorical listening. Care-full listening, like care-full seeing and feeling, reinforce one another in the same experience.

15. See also Barbara Maria Stafford for the participatory quality of imagistic thinking and perception thinking. See Evelyn Fox Keller, *Feeling*, for an account of participatory seeing in the sciences, specifically in the practices of Nobel laureate Barbara McClintock.

16. Martin Jay describes the way of seeing that undergirds science as Baconian empiricism rather than Cartesian perspectivalism ("Scopic Regimes" 12)

17. See also Laurel Richardson, who recommends writing the results of sociological fieldwork in alternative forms, such as lyric poetry.

18. See also *Modest* 37.

19. Empathy can also be used fruitfully to provoke emergence if students are requested to focus on the different ways of seeing required for an enactment of empathy. The protean quality of empathy and its power to invite immersion, evoke emergence, and elicit transformation suggest that empathy's development individually and communally may be linked in crucial ways to the development and deployment of somatic, polyscopic, and lateral literacies.

4. Slippery Texts: Artifacts for a Poetics of Teaching

1. A work that offers intriguing possibilities that I hope to pursue more fully in future classes is Dennis Todd's *Imagining Monsters*, an exploration of the fraud perpetual by Mary Toft, an eighteenth-century woman who had persuaded

the medical establishment that she had repeatedly given birth to rabbits. At the heart of Todd's study is the belief prevalent at the time that the imagination, especially that of a gravid woman, can transgress the boundaries of the mind and body. Noteworthy in Todd's study is the extent to which language—in official documents, in poetry, in the press of the day—participated in the fraud.

2. We can even take this slippage with genre, especially as manifested through the interactivity of cyberspace narratives, and extend it to a slippage in writer-reader roles. The ease with which a reader in cyberspace can so easily become a writer leads cybercritic Marie-Laure Ryan to insist on the term *wreader*, highlighting the fluidity of not only genre but also rhetorical identities.

3. First-year students struggling to nail the conventions of academic writing were less taken with Anzaldúa's confusion of genres. Reading her text elicited bewilderment rather than enjoyment, suggesting that slippage is itself relative to the position of the student and warning us that we must consider carefully the point at which slippage itself slips into chaos.

4. See also the New London Group.

5. Spatial geographies represent only one possible way to foster the slipperiness of somatic literacy. See Christopher Worthman for an exploration of the connections between kinesthetic imagery training and students' writing. See also Ellen W. Goellner and Jacqueline Shea Murphy's *Bodies of Text: Dance as Theory, Literature as Dance* for an exploration of the connections between dance and the literary experience. For an exploration of dance literacy, see the *Arts in Society's* issue *Growth of Dance in America*.

6. The researchers approach composition guided by the concept of *design* developed by the New London Group, which construes as semiotic any activity that offers "a creative application and combination of conventions [. . .] that, in the process of Design, transforms at the same time it reproduces these conventions," (qtd. in Smagorinsky and O'Donnell-Allen 200–201). Pointing to the diverse sign and tool systems involved in literacy, Smagorinsky and O'Donnell-Allen cite the need to address three aspects of literacy frequently ignored: the influence of individual neurology on the choice of medium, the role of membership in communities that privilege different modes of literacy, and the impact of different developmental levels on a writer-reader's reliance on different ways of expressing and representing meaning.

7. Two international students, one from Taiwan and one from Japan, were unable to contribute childhood photographs, so they substituted more recent photographs.

5. Double Mapping: The Organization of a Poetics of Teaching

1. See Kristie S. Fleckenstein, "Bodysigns," an argument for the necessity of double vision, double speaking, and double living.

2. I have used this assignment with a wide range of classes and students, including workshops with high school teachers. Responses to it vary considerably. For example, in one class, a group of men highly resistant to the entire sequence of activities high-jacked the Barbie and Ken dolls to stage pornographic tableaux, repeatedly soliciting the women in the class, including me, as their audience (for both the tableaux and their antics). I insisted that they maintain careful field notes of the entire procedure and that they provide an equally careful interpretation. I ended up with thoughtful commentary on pornography and gender but also with thoughtful essays on relationships (father-son, individual-God, lover-lover). In the same class, a group of women, all of whom were business or accounting majors with well-articulated career goals, spent the time ignoring Barbie and playing exclusively with the variety of Kelly dolls (Barbie's little sister) my children had collected.

3. Men suggested that in the future I bring in GI Joe dolls and military equipment. It is not that boys don't play with dolls, they explained. It is just that they play with dolls called action figures.

4. The majority of the classes I teach are scheduled in traditional classrooms, those lacking access to digital technologies and the Internet. However, I wanted my students to experience the hypertextual thinking evoked when they develop Web sites. What resulted is the paper Web site activity, one that can be performed in the traditional classroom as well as in technology-rich environments.

Conclusion: Teaching in and as an Imageword Ecology

1. I hesitated over the word *organism* because it implies that two elements of the triad must be living creatures. This question of living is a tricky one, since, for Bateson, an ecology can consist of two cells within an environment, or one T cell and a pathogen, such as a wooden splinter. Also, I might be able to speak of meaning as consisting of the interplay of image and word within a specific environment, but that meaningfulness is predicated on the existence of an organism—anything from a cell to a person to a community—seeking to make that interplay meaningful.

2. See especially George Lakoff and Mark Johnson; see also Christine Battersby (*Phenomenal*) for a critique of this containment metaphor as being based on the male body as the norm.

Works Cited

Abram, David. *The Spell of the Sensuous: Perception and Language in a More-Than-Human World.* New York: Pantheon, 1996.

Adams, Marilyn Jager, and Allan Collins. "A Schema-Theoretical View of Reading." *Theoretical Models and Processes of Reading.* Ed. Harry Singer and Robert B. Ruddell. 3rd ed. Newark, DE: IRA, 1985. 404–25.

Allende, Isabel. "Isabel Allende." *Writers Dreaming.* Ed. Naomi Epel. New York: Carol Southern, 1993.

Anderson, Charles M., and Marian M. MacCurdy. "Introduction." *Writing & Healing: Toward an Informed Practice.* Ed. Charles M. Anderson and Marian M. MacCurdy. Urbana, IL: NCTE, 2000. 1–22.

Angelou, Maya. *I Know Why the Caged Bird Sings.* New York: Bantam, 1970.

Altman, Meryl. "How Not to Do Things with Metaphors We Live By." *College English* 52 (1990): 495–506.

Anzaldúa, Gloria. *Borderlands/La Frontera.* San Francisco: Aunt Lute, 1987.

Aristotle. *De Anima.* Trans. D. W. Hamlyn. Oxford: Clarendon, 1993.

———. *De Motu Animalium.* Trans. Martha Craven Nussbaum. Princeton, NJ: Princeton UP, 1978.

Aylwin, Susan. *Structure in Thought and Feeling.* London: Methuen, 1985.

Bachelard, Gaston. *The Poetics of Space.* Trans. Maria Jolas. Boston: Beacon, 1958.

Balsamo, Anne. *Technologies of the Gendered Body: Reading Cyborg Women.* Durham, NC: Duke UP, 1997.

Barfield, Owen. *Saving the Appearances: A Study of Idolatry.* 2nd ed. Hanover, NH: Wesleyan UP, 1988.

Barthes, Roland. *Image—Music—Text.* Trans. Stephen Heath. New York: Hill, 1977.

Bartlett, Frederic C. *Remembering: A Study in Experimental and Social Psychology.* London: Cambridge UP, 1932.

Bates, Elizabeth. *The Emergence of Symbols: Cognition and Communication in Infancy.* New York: Academic, 1979.

Bateson, Gregory. *Mind and Nature: A Necessary Unity.* 1979. Toronto: Bantam, 1988.

———. *Sacred Unity: Further Steps Toward an Ecology of Mind.* Ed. Rodney E. Donaldson. New York: Harper, 1991.

———. *Steps to an Ecology of Mind: Collected Essays in Anthropology, Psychiatry, Evolution, and Epistemology.* 1972. Northvale, NJ: Aronson, 1987.

Bateson, Gregory, and Mary Catherine Bateson. *Angels Fear: Toward an Epistemology of the Sacred.* New York: Macmillan, 1987.

Battersby, Christine. *Gender and Genius: Towards a Feminist Aesthetics.* Bloomington: Indiana UP, 1989.

———. *The Phenomenal Woman: Feminist Metaphysics and the Patterns of Identity.* New York: Routledge, 1998.

Baumlin, James S., and Tita French Baumlin. "On the Psychology of the *Pisteis:* Mapping the Terrains of Mind and Rhetoric." *Ethos: New Essays in Rhetorical and Critical Theory.* Ed. James S. Baumlin and Tita French Baumlin. Dallas: Southern Methodist UP, 1994. 91–112.

Bennett, Christine. "Genres of Research in Multicultural Education." *Review of Educational Research* 71 (2001): 171–218.

Berger, John. *Ways of Seeing.* London: British Broadcasting, 1972.

Berger, Peter L., and Thomas Luckmann. *The Social Construction of Reality: A Treatise in the Sociology of Knowledge.* Garden City, NY: Doubleday, 1966.

Berman, Morris. *Coming to Our Senses: Body and Spirit in the Hidden History of the West.* New York: Simon, 1989.

———. *The Reenchantment of the World.* Ithaca, NY: Cornell UP, 1981.

Berthoff, Ann E. *Forming/Thinking/Writing.* Upper Montclair, NJ: Boynton, 1982.

———. *The Sense of Learning.* Portsmouth, NH: Heinemann, 1990.

Blade Runner: Director's Cut. Dir. Ridley Scott. Warner Bros., 1991.

Blake, William. *Selected Poetry and Prose of William Blake.* Ed. Northrop Frye. New York: Modern Library, 1953.

Blitz, Michael, and C. Mark Hurlbert. *Letters for the Living: Teaching Writing in a Violent Age.* Urbana, IL: NCTE, 1998.

Bloom, Lynn Z. "Freshman Composition as a Middle-Class Enterprise." *College English* 58 (1996): 654–75.

Blunt, Alison, and Gillian Rose, eds. *Writing Women and Space: Colonial and Postcolonial Geographies.* New York: Guilford, 1994.

Bolles, Edmund Blair. *A Second Way of Knowing: The Riddle of Human Perception.* New York: Prentice, 1991.

Bolter, Jay David. *Writing Space: The Computers, Hypertext, and the Remediation of Print.* 2nd ed. Mahwah, NJ: Erlbaum, 2001.

Bordo, Susan. *The Flight to Objectivity: Essays on Cartesianism and Culture.* Albany, NY: State U of New York P, 1987.

———. *Unbearable Weight: Feminism, Western Culture, and the Body.* Berkeley: U of California P, 1993.

Brandt, Deborah. "Remembering Writing, Remembering Reading." *College Composition and Communication* 45 (1994): 459–79.

————. "Sponsors of Literacy." *College Composition and Communication* 49 (1998): 165–85.

Bridwell-Bowles, Lillian. "Freedom, Form, Function: Varieties of Academic Discourse." *College Composition and Communication* 46 (1995): 46–61.

Brier, Soren. "From Second-Order Cybernetics to Cybersemiotics: A Semiotic Re-Entry into the Second-Order Cybernetics of Heinz von Foerster." *Systems Research* 13 (1996): 229–44.

Britton, James N. *Literature in Its Place*. Portsmouth, NH: Boynton, 1993.

Brodkey, Linda. "Writing on the Bias." *College English* 56 (1994): 527–47.

————. "Writing Permitted in Designated Areas Only." *Writing Permitted in Designated Areas Only*. Minneapolis: U of Minnesota P, 1996. 130–49.

Bruner, Jerome. *Acts of Meaning*. Cambridge, MA: Harvard UP, 1990.

Bryson, Norman. *Vision and Painting: The Logic of the Gaze*. New Haven, CT: Yale UP, 1983.

Bukatman, Scott. *Terminal Identity: The Virtual Subject in Modern Science Fiction*. Durham, NC: Duke University P, 1993.

Burke, Kenneth. *Attitudes Toward History*. Boston: Beacon, 1937.

————. *A Grammar of Motives*. Berkeley: U of California P, 1945.

————. *Language as Social Action: Essays on Life, Literature, and Method*. Berkeley: U of California P, 1966.

————. *Permanence and Change: An Anatomy of Purpose*. Indianapolis: Bobbs, 1965.

Calendrillo, Linda Theresa. "The Art of Memory and Rhetoric." Diss. Purdue University, 1988.

Casey, Edward S. *Getting Back into Place: Toward a Renewed Understanding of the Place-World*. Bloomington: Indiana UP, 1993.

Csikszentmihalyi, Mihaly. *Beyond Boredom and Anxiety: The Experience of Play in Work and Games*. San Francisco: Jossey, 1975.

Damasio, Antonio. *The Feeling of What Happens: Body and Emotion in the Making of Consciousness*. New York: Harcourt, 1999.

Davies, Paul. *About Time: Einstein's Unfinished Evolution*. New York: Simon, 1995.

de Beaugrande, Robert. *Text Production: Toward a Science of Composition*. Norwood, NJ: Ablex, 1984.

Debord, Guy. *Comments on the Society of the Spectacle*. Trans. Malcolm Imrie. London: Verso, 1990.

————. *The Society of the Spectacle*. Trans. Donald Nicholson-Smith. New York: Zone, 1994.

Deleuze, Gilles. *Foucault*. Trans. and ed. Seán Hand. Minneapolis: U of Minnesota P, 1986.

DeStigter, Todd. "The Tesoros Literacy Project: An Experiment in Democratic Communities." *Research in the Teaching of English* 32 (1998): 10–42.

Dick, Philip K. *Do Androids Dream of Electric Sheep?* New York: Del Rey, 1968.

Dickinson, Emily. "1129: Tell all the Truth but tell it slant—." *The Complete Poems of Emily Dickinson.* Ed. Thomas H. Johnson. Boston: Little, 1960. 506–7.

DiPardo, Anne. "Narrative Knowers, Expository Knowledge: Discourse as Dialectic." *Written Communication* 7 (1990): 59–95.

Duffy, W. Keith. "Imperfection: The Will-to-Control and the Struggle of Letting Go." *JAEPL: Journal of the Assembly for Expanded Perspectives on Learning* 7 (2001–2002): 1–10.

Dyson, Anne Haas. "Coach Bombay's Kids Learn to Write: Children's Appropriation of Media Material for School Literacy." *Research in the Teaching of English* 33 (1999): 367–402.

Eliot, T. S. "Little Gidding." *Four Quartets. The Complete Poems and Plays. 1909–1950.* New York: Harcourt, 1971. 138–45.

Esrock, Ellen. *The Reader's Eye: Visual Imaging as Reader Response.* Baltimore: Johns Hopkins UP, 1994.

Faigley, Lester. "Material Literacy and Visual Design." Selzer and Crowley. 171–201.

Farrell, Thomas B. *Norms of Rhetorical Culture.* New Haven, CT: Yale UP, 1993.

Feld, Steven, and Keith H. Basso. "Introduction." *Senses of Place.* Santa Fe, NM: School of American Research P, 1996. 3–12.

Finn, Geraldine. *Why Althusser Killed His Wife: Essays on Discourse and Violence.* Atlantic Highlands, NJ: Humanities, 1996.

Fisher, Walter R. *Human Communication as Narration: Toward a Philosophy of Reason, Value, and Action.* Columbia: U of South Carolina P, 1987.

Flax, Jane. "Responsibility Without Grounds." *Rethinking Knowledge: Reflections Across the Disciplines.* Ed. Robert F. Goodman and Walter R. Fisher. Albany: State U of New York P, 1995. 147–68.

Fleckenstein, Kristie S. "Bodysigns: A Biorhetoric for Changes." *JAC* 21 (2002): 761–90.

———. "Image, Word, and Narrative Epistemology." *College English* 58 (1996): 914–33.

———. "The Osmotic Self and Language Arts Pedagogy." *JAEPL: Journal of the Assembly for Expanded Perspectives on Learning* 3 (1997–98): 40–49.

———. "Resistance, Women, and Dismissing the 'I.'" *Rhetoric Review* 17 (1998): 107–25.

———. "Writing Bodies: Somatic Mind in Composition Studies." *College English* 61 (1999): 281–306.

Fleckenstein, Kristie S., Linda T. Calendrillo, and Demetrice A. Worley, eds. *Language and Image in the Reading-Writing Classroom: Teaching Vision.* Mahwah, NJ: Erlbaum, 2002.

Foucault, Michel. *Discipline and Punish: The Birth of the Prison.* Trans. Alan Sheridan. New York: Vintage, 1979.

———. *The Order of Things: An Archaeology of the Human Sciences.* New York: Vintage, 1973.

———. "Of Other Spaces." Trans. Jay Miskowiec. *Diacritics* 16 (1986): 22–27.

———. *The Use of Pleasure.* Trans. Robert Hurley. New York: Pantheon, 1985.

Fox, Roy F. *Harvesting Minds: How TV Commercials Control Kids.* Westport, CT: Praeger, 1996.

———. Introduction. *Images in Language, Media, and Mind.* Ed. Roy F. Fox. Urbana, IL: NCTE, 1994. ix–xiii.

Francoz, Marion Joan. "Habit as Memory Incarnate." *College English* 62.1 (1999): 11–29.

Freud, Sigmund. "The Ego and the Id." *Standard Edition of the Complete Psychological Works of Sigmund Freud.* 1923. Vol. 14. Trans. J. Riviere. London: Hogarth, 1949. 13–21.

Gaggi, Silvio. *From Text to Hypertext: Decentering the Subject in Fiction, Film, the Visual Arts, and Electronic Media.* Philadelphia: U of Pennsylvania P, 1997.

Gendlin, Eugene T. *Experiencing and the Creation of Meaning: A Philosophical and Psychological Approach to the Subjective.* New York: Free P of Glencoe, 1962.

Gibson, William. *Neuromancer.* New York: Ace, 1984.

Goellner, Ellen W., and Jacqueline Shea Murphy, eds. *Bodies of the Text: Dance as Theory, Literature as Dance.* New Brunswick, NJ: Rutgers UP, 1994.

Goldhill, Simon. "Refracting Classical Vision: Changing Cultures of Viewing." *Vision in Context: Historical and Contemporary Perspectives on Sight.* Ed. Teresa Brennan and Martin Jay. New York: Routledge, 1996. 17–28.

Greene, Stuart, and John M Ackerman. "Expanding the Constructivist Metaphor: A Rhetorical Perspective on Literacy Research and Practice." *Review of Educational Research* 65 (1995): 383–420.

Greenfield, Susan A. *Journey to the Centers of the Mind: Toward a Science of Consciousness.* New York: Freeman, 1995.

Groenendyk, Kathi L. "The Importance of Vision: Persuasion and the Picturesque." *Rhetoric Society Quarterly* 30 (2000): 9–28.

Growth of Dance in America. Arts in Society 13 (1976): 200–358.

Guyer, Carolyn. "Fretwork: ReForming Me." 24 Dec 02 <http://mothermillennia.org/Carolyn/Fretwork1.html>.

———. "Fretwork: ReForming Me, Con't." 24 Dec 02 <http://mothermillennia.org/Carolyn/Fretwork2.html>.

Haas, Christina. "Materializing Public and Private: The Spatialization of Conceptual Categories in Discourses of Abortion." Selzer and Crowley 218–74.

Haraway, Donna J. *How Like a Leaf: An Interview with Thyrza Nichols Goodeve.* New York: Routledge, 2000.

———. *Modest_Witness@Second_Millenium.FemaleMan©_Meets_OncoMouse™: Feminism and Technoscience.* New York: Routledge, 1997.

————. "The Promise of Monsters: A Regenerative Politics for Inappropriate/d Others." *Cultural Studies*. Ed. L. Grossberg, Cary Nelson, and Paula Treichler. New York: Routledge, 1992. 295–337.

————. *Simians, Cyborgs, and Women: The Reinvention of Nature*. New York: Routledge, 1991.

Harding, Sandra. *Is Science Multicultural?: Postcolonialisms, Feminisms, and Epistemologies*. Bloomington: Indiana UP, 1998.

Hariman, Robert, and John Louis Lucaites. "Visual Rhetoric, Photojournalism, and Democratic Public Culture." *Rhetoric Review* 20 (2001): 37–42.

Hayles, N. Katherine. *How We Became Post-Human: Virtual Bodies in Cybernetics, Literature, and Informatics*. Chicago: U of Chicago P, 1999.

Heath, Shirley Brice. "The Children of Trackton's Children: Spoken and Written Language in Social Change." *Theoretical Models and Processes of Reading*. 4th ed. Ed. Robert B. Ruddell, Martha Rapp Ruddell, and Harry Singer. Newark, DE: IRA, 1994. 208–30.

Hecimovich, Gregg. "Technologizing the Word: William Blake and the Composition of Hypertext." Fleckenstein, Calendrillo, and Worley 135–50.

Hobbs, Catherine. "Learning from the Past: Verbal and Visual Literacy in Early Modern Rhetoric and Writing Pedagogy." Fleckenstein, Calendrillo, and Worley 27–44.

Hoffman, Martin L. "Empathy and Justice Motivation." *Motivation and Emotion* 14 (1990): 151–72.

————. "Empathy and Prosocial Activism." *Social and Moral Values: Individual and Societal Perspectives*. Ed. Nancy Eisenberg, Janusz Reykowski, and Ervin Staub. Hillsdale, NJ: Erlbaum, 1989. 65–85.

————. "Interaction of Affect and Cognition in Empathy." *Emotions, Cognition, and Behavior*. Ed. Carroll E. Izard, Jerome Kagan, Robert B. Zajonc. Cambridge, Eng.: Cambridge UP, 1984. 103–31.

Hoffmeyer, Jesper. *Signs of Meaning in the Universe*. Trans. Barbara J. Haveland. Bloomington: Indiana UP, 1996.

Hollis, Karyn. "Material Desire: Bodily Rhetoric in Working Women's Poetry at the Bryn Mawr Summer School, 1921–1938." Selzer and Crowley 98–119.

hooks, bell. *Art on My Mind: Visual Politics*. New York: New, 1995.

Jackson, Cindy. "Cindy Jackson: Official Website." 30 Oct. 2001 <http://www.cindyjackson.com>.

Jacobs, Dale. "Being There: Revising the Discourse of Emotion and Teaching." *JAEPL: Journal of the Assembly for Expanded Perspectives on Learning* 7 (2001–2002): 42–52.

Jay, Martin. *Downcast Eyes: The Denigration of Vision in Twentieth-Century French Thought*. Berkeley: U of California P, 1993.

————. "Scopic Regimes of Modernity." *Vision and Visuality*. Ed. Hal Foster. Seattle: Bay, 1988. 3–23.

Joeres, Ruth-Ellen Boetcher, and Elizabeth Mittman. "An Introductory Essay." *The Politics of the Essay: Feminist Perspectives.* Ed. Ruth-Ellen Boetcher Joeres and Elizabeth Mittman. Bloomington: Indiana UP, 1993. 12–20.

Judovitz, Dalia. "Vision, Representation, and Technology in Descartes." *Modernity and the Hegemony of Vision.* Ed. David Michael Levin. Berkeley: U of California P, 1993. 63–86.

Kang, Jerry. "Cyber-Race." *Harvard Law Review* 113 (2000): 1130–1207.

Katz, Steven B. *The Epistemic Music of Rhetoric: Toward the Temporal Dimension of Affect in Reader Response and Writing.* Carbondale: Southern Illinois UP, 1996.

Keller, Evelyn Fox. *A Feeling for the Organism: The Life and Work of Barbara McClintock.* San Francisco: Freeman, 1983.

———. *Reflections on Gender and Science.* New Haven, CT: Yale UP, 1985.

Kirsch, Gesa E., and Joy S. Ritchie. "Beyond the Personal: Theorizing a Politics of Location in Composition Research." *College Composition and Communication* 46 (1995): 7–29.

Kosslyn, Stephen Michael. *Ghosts in the Mind's Machine.* New York: Norton, 1983.

Kress, Gunther. "'English' at the Crossroads: Rethinking the Curricula of Communication in the Context of the Turn to the Visual." *Passions, Pedagogies, and 21st Century Technologies.* Ed. Gail E. Hawisher and Cynthia Selfe. Logan, UT: Utah State UP and NCTE, 1999. 66–88.

Lakoff, George, and Mark Johnson. *Metaphors We Live By.* Chicago: U of Chicago P, 1980.

Landow, George P. *Hypertext 2.0: The Convergence of Contemporary Critical Theory and Technology.* Baltimore: Johns Hopkins UP, 1992.

Langer, Susanne K. *Mind: An Essay on Human Feeling.* Vol. 1. Baltimore: Johns Hopkins UP, 1967.

———. *Philosophical Sketches.* Baltimore: Johns Hopkins UP, 1962.

———. *Philosophy in a New Key.* Cambridge, MA: Harvard UP, 1942.

———. *Problems in Art: The Philosophical Lectures.* New York: Scribner, 1957.

Lanham, Richard A. *The Electronic Word: Democracy, Technology, and the Arts.* Chicago: U of Chicago P, 1993.

Le Dœuff, Michèle. *Philosophical Imaginary.* Trans. Colin Gordon. Stanford, CA: Stanford UP, 1989.

Lehman, David. *Signs of the Times: Deconstruction and the Fall of Paul de Man.* New York: Poseidon, 1991.

Levin, David Michael. *The Opening of Vision: Nihilism and the Postmodern Situation.* New York: Routledge, 1988.

Lewontin, R. C. *Biology as Ideology: The Doctrine of DNA.* New York: Harper, 1991.

Lindberg, David C. *Theories of Vision: From Al-Kindi to Kepler.* Chicago: U of Chicago P, 1976.

Lofty, John S. *Time to Write: The Influence of Time and Culture on Learning to Write.* Albany: State U of New York P, 1992.

Lu, Min-Zhan. "Redefining the Literate Self: The Politics of Critical Affirmation." *College Composition and Communication* 51.2 (1999): 172–94.

Lunenfeld, Peter. "Introduction: Screen Grabs: The Digital Dialectic and the New Media Theory." *The Digital Dialectic: New Essays on New Media.* Ed. Peter Lunenfeld. Cambridge, MA: MIT P, 2000. xiv–xxi.

Lury, Celia. *Prosthetic Culture: Photography, Memory, and Identity.* London: Routledge, 1998.

Mahiri, Jabari, and Amanda J. Godley. "Rewriting Identity: Social Meanings of Literacy and 'Re-visions' of Self." *Reading Research Quarterly* 33 (1998): 416–31.

Mairs, Nancy. *Remembering the Bonehouse: An Erotics of Place and Space.* 1985. Boston: Beacon, 1995.

———. *Voice Lessons: On Becoming a (Woman) Writer.* Boston: Beacon, 1994.

———. *Waist-High in the World: A Life among the Nondisabled.* Boston: Beacon, 1996.

Making Mr. Right. Dir. Susan Seidelman. Orion Pictures, 1987.

Marschark, Mark, and Allan Paivio. "Integrative Processing of Concrete and Abstract Sentences." *Journal of Verbal Learning and Behavior* 16 (1977): 217–31.

Matrix. Dir. Joel Silver. Warner Bros., 1999.

McCulloch, Warren S. "What Is a Number, That a Man May Know It, and a Man, That He May Know a Number?" *Embodiments of Mind.* Cambridge, MA: MIT P, 1989. 1–18.

McLaren, Peter L. "Schooling the Postmodern Body: Critical Pedagogy and the Politics of Enfleshment." *Postmodernism, Feminism, and Cultural Politics: Redrawing Educational Boundaries.* Ed. Henry A. Giroux. Albany: State U of New York P, 1991. 144–73.

McLeod, Susan H. *Notes on the Heart: Affective Issues in the Writing Classroom.* Carbondale: Southern Illinois UP, 1997.

McRae, Shannon. "Coming Apart at the Seams: Sex, Text and the Virtual Body." *Wired Women: Gender and New Realities in Cyberspace.* Ed. Lynn Cherny and Elizabeth Reba Weise. Seattle: Seal, 1996. 242–63.

Miller, Arthur I. *Imagery in Scientific Thought.* Cambridge, MA: MIT P, 1986.

Mirzoeff, Nicholas. *An Introduction to Visual Culture.* London: Routledge, 1999.

Mitchell, W. J. T. *Iconology: Image, Text, Ideology.* Chicago: U of Chicago P, 1986.

———. *Picture Theory: Essays on Verbal and Visual Representation.* Chicago: U of Chicago P, 1995.

Mitchell, William J. *City of Bits: Space, Place, and the Infobahn.* Cambridge, MA: MIT P, 1996.

Morrison, Toni. *The Bluest Eye.* New York: Plume, 1970.

Mulvey, Laura. "Visual Pleasure and Narrative Cinema." *Screen* 16 (1975): 6–18. 10 July 2002 <http://www.bbk.ac.uk/hafvm/staff_research/visual1.html>.

Nelson, Nancy, and Robert C. Calfee. "The Reading-Writing Connection Viewed Historically." *The Reading-Writing Connection*. Ed. Nancy Nelson and Robert C. Calfee. Chicago: U of Chicago P, 1998. 1–52.

New London Group. "A Pedagogy of Multiliteracies: Designing Social Futures." *Harvard Educational Review* 66 (1996): 60–92.

Norris, Christopher. *What's Wrong with Postmodernism: Critical Theory and the Ends of Philosophy*. Baltimore: Johns Hopkins UP, 1990.

Novak, Marcos. "Liquid Architectures in Cyberspace." *Cyberspace: First Steps*. Ed. Michael Benedikt. Cambridge, MA: MIT P, 1992. 225–54.

Nussbaum, Martha Craven. "Rational Animals and the Explanation of Action." *The Fragility of Goodness: Luck and Ethics in Greek Tragedy and Philosophy*. Cambridge, Eng.: Cambridge UP, 1986. 264–89.

Ong, Walter J. *Orality and Literacy: The Technologizing of the Word*. London: Routledge, 1982.

O'Reilley, Mary Rose. *Radical Presence: Teaching as Contemplative Practice*. Portsmouth, NH: Boynton, 1998.

Page, Barbara. "Women Writers and the Restive Text: Feminism, Experimental Writing, and Hypertext." *Cyberspace Textuality: Computer Technology and Literary Theory*. Ed. Marie-Laure Ryan. Bloomington: Indiana UP, 1999. 111–36.

Paivio, Allan. "The Empirical Case for Dual Coding." *Imagery, Memory, and Cognition*. Ed. John C. Yuille. Hillsdale: Erlbaum, 1983. 307–32.

———. *Imagery and Verbal Processes*. New York: Holt, 1971.

———. *Mental Representations: A Dual Coding Approach*. Oxford Psychology Series 9. Oxford: Oxford UP, 1986.

———. "The Mind's Eye in Arts and Science." *Poetics* 12 (1983): 1–18.

Pearson, David P., and Diane Stephens. "Learning about Literacy: A 30-Year Journey." *Theoretical Models and Processes of Reading*. 4th ed. Ed. Robert B. Ruddell, Martha Rapp Ruddell, and Harry Singer. Newark, DE: IRA, 1994. 22–43.

Peirce, Charles Sanders. *Peirce on Signs: Writings on Semiotic by Charles Sanders Peirce*. Ed. James Hoppes. Chapel Hill: U of North Carolina P, 1991.

Pennebaker, James W. *Opening Up: The Healing Power of Confiding in Others*. New York: Morrow, 1990.

Piercy, Marge. *He, She and It*. New York: Knopf, 1991.

Polanyi, Michael. *Personal Knowledge: Towards a Post-Critical Philosophy*. Chicago: U of Chicago P, 1958.

Pylyshyn, Z. W. "What the Mind's Eye Tells the Mind's Brain: A Critique of Mental Imagery." *Psychological Review* 87 (1981): 16–45.

Rajchman, John. "Foucault's Art of Seeing." *October* 44 (1988): 89–119.

Ratcliffe, Krista. "Rhetorical Listening: A Trope for Interpretive Invention and a 'Code of Cross-Cultural Conduct.'" *College Composition and Communication* 51 (1999): 195–224.

Reeve, C. D. C. "Philosophy, Politics, and Rhetoric in Aristotle." *Essays on Aristotle's Rhetoric.* Ed. Amélie Oksenberg Rorty. Berkeley: U of California P, 1996. 191–205.

Reynolds, Nedra. "Composition's Imagined Geographies." *College Composition and Communication* 50 (1998): 12–35.

Rheingold, Howard. *Virtual Reality.* New York: Simon, 1991.

Rich, Adrienne. "Contradictions: Tracking Poems—29." *Your Native Land, Your Life.* New York: Norton, 1986.

———. *Of Woman Born: Motherhood as Experience and Institution.* New York: Norton, 1986.

Richardson, Laurel. *Fields of Play: Constructing an Academic Life.* New Brunswick, NJ: Rutgers UP, 1997.

Richmond, Kia Jane. "The Ethics of Empathy: Making Connections in the Writing Classroom." *JAEPL: Journal of the Assembly for Expanded Perspectives on Learning* 5 (1999–2000): 37–46.

Rinaldi, Jacqueline. "Rhetoric and Healing: Revising Narratives about Disability." *College English* 58 (1996): 820–34.

Rivlin, Robert, and Karen Gravelle. *Deciphering the Senses: The Expanding World of Human Perception.* New York: Simon, 1984.

Roorda, Randall. "Sites and Senses of Writing in Nature." *College English* 59 (1997): 385–407.

Rose, Gillian. *Feminism and Geography: The Limits of Geographical Knowledge.* Minneapolis: U of Minneapolis P, 1993.

Rose, Mike. *Lives on the Boundary.* New York: Penguin, 1989.

Rosenblatt, Louise. *The Reader, the Text, the Poem.* Carbondale: Southern Illinois UP, 1978.

———. "Reading Transaction: What For?" *Developing Literacy: Young Children's Use of Language.* Ed. Robert P. Parker and Frances A. Davis. Newark, DE: IRA, 1983. 118–35.

Rubin, Lillian B. *Worlds of Pain: Life in the Working-Class Family.* 1972. New York: Basic, 1992.

Ruesch, Jurgen, and Gregory Bateson. *Communication: The Social Matrix of Psychiatry.* 1951. New York: Norton, 1987.

Rushing, Janice Hocker, and Thomas S. Frentz. *Projecting the Shadow: The Cyborg Hero in American Film.* Chicago: U of Chicago P, 1995.

Ryan, Marie-Laure. Introduction. *Cyberspace Textuality: Computer Technology and Literary Theory.* Ed. Marie-Laure Ryan. Bloomington: Indiana UP, 1999. 1–28.

Sadoski, Mark, and Allan Paivio. "A Dual Coding View of Imagery and Verbal Processes in Reading Comprehension." *Theoretical Models and Processes of Reading.* 4th ed. Ed. Robert B. Ruddell, Martha Rapp Ruddell, and Harry Singer. Newark, DE: IRA, 1994. 582–601.

———. *Imagery and Text: A Dual Coding Theory of Reading and Writing.* Mahwah, NJ: Erlbaum, 2001.

Sadoski, Mark, Allan Paivio, and Ernest Goetz. "Commentary: A Critique of Schema Theory in Reading and a Dual Coding Alternative." *Reading Research Quarterly* 26 (1991): 463–84.

Sardar, Ziauddin. "alt.civilizations.faq: Cyberspace as the Darker Side of the West." *Futures* 27 (1995): 777–94.

Scarry, Elaine. *On Beauty and Being Just.* Princeton, NJ: Princeton UP, 1999.

Schachtel, Ernest G. *Metamorphosis: On the Development of Affect, Perception, Attention, and Memory.* New York: Basic, 1959.

Schilder, Paul. *The Image and Appearance of the Human Body: Studies in the Constructive Energies of the Psyche.* New York: Wiley, 1950.

Schweickart, Patrocinio P. "Reading Ourselves: Toward a Feminist Theory of Reading." *Gender and Reading: Essays on Readers, Texts, and Contexts.* Ed. Elizabeth A. Flynn and Patrocinio P. Schweickart. Baltimore: Johns Hopkins UP, 1986. 31–62.

Sebeok, Thomas. *Semiotics in the United States.* Bloomington: Indiana UP, 1991.

Selzer, Jack, and Sharon Crowley, eds. *Rhetorical Bodies.* Madison: U of Wisconsin P, 1999.

Sennett, Richard. *Flesh and Stone: The Body and the City in Western Civilization.* New York: Norton, 1994.

Serres, Michel. *The Troubador of Knowledge.* Trans. Sheila Faria Glaser with William Paulson. Ann Arbor: U of Michigan P, 1997.

Smagorinsky, Peter. "Snippets: What Will Be the Influences on Literacy in the Next Millennium?" *Reading Research Quarterly* 35 (2000): 277–78.

———. "The Social Construction of Data: Methodological Problems of Investigating Learning in the Zone of Proximal Development." *Review of Educational Research* 65 (1995): 191–212.

Smagorinsky, Peter, and Cindy O'Donnell-Allen. "Reading as Mediated and Mediating Action: Composing Meaning for Literature Through Multimedia Interpretive Texts." *Reading Research Quarterly* 33 (1998): 198–227.

Snyder, Katherine V. "From Novel to Essay: Gender and Revision in Florence Nightingale's 'Cassandra.'" *The Politics of the Essay: Feminist Perspectives.* Ed. Ruth-Ellen Boetcher Joeres and Elizabeth Mittman. Bloomington: Indiana UP, 1993. 23–40.

Soja, Edward W. *Postmodern Geographies: The Reassertion of Space in Critical Social Theory.* London: Verso, 1989.

Soliday, Mary. "Class Dismissed." *College English* 61.6 (1999): 731–41.

Sommers, Nancy. "Between the Drafts." *College Composition and Communication* 43 (1992): 23–31.

Spiro, Rand J. "Constructive Processes in Prose Comprehension and Recall." *Theoretical Issues in Reading Comprehension: Perspectives from Cognitive Psychology, Linguistics, Artificial Intelligence, and Education.* Ed. Rand J. Spiro, Bertram C. Bruce, and William F. Brewer. Hillsdale, NJ: Erlbaum, 1980. 245–78.

Springer, Claudia. *Electronic Eros: Bodies and Desire in the Postindustrial Age.* Austin: U of Texas P, 1996.

Stafford, Barbara Maria. *Good Looking: Essays on the Virtue of Images.* Cambridge, MA: MIT P, 1997.

Standards for the English Language Arts. International Reading Association–National Council of Teachers of English. Urbana, IL: NCTE, 1996.

Street, Brian. *Social Literacies: Critical Approaches to Literacy in Development, Ethnography and Education.* London: Longman, 1995.

Stroupe, Craig. "Visualizing English: Recognizing the Hybrid Literacy of Visual and Verbal Authorship on the Web." *CE* 62.5 (2000): 607–32.

Swearingen, C. Jan. "Women's Ways of Writing or, Images, Self-Images, and Graven Images." *College Composition and Communication* 45 (1994): 51–8.

Tannen, Deborah. *Talking from 9 to 5: Women and Men in the Workplace: Language, Sex, and Power.* New York: Avon, 1994.

———. *Talking Voices: Repetition, Dialogue, and Imagery in Conversational Discourse.* Cambridge, Eng.: Cambridge UP, 1989.

Tebeaux, Elizabeth. "Ramus, Visual Rhetoric, and the Emergence of Page Design in Medical Writing of the English Renaissance." *Written Communication* 8 (1991): 411–45.

Teich, Nathaniel. "Teaching Empathy Through Cooperative Learning." *Presence of Mind: Writing and the Domain Beyond the Cognitive.* Ed. Alice Glarden Brand and Richard L. Graves. Portsmouth, NH: Boynton, 1994. 143–54.

Todd, Dennis. *Imagining Monsters: Miscreation of the Self in Eighteenth-Century England.* Chicago: U of Chicago P, 1995.

Tyler, Lisa. "Narratives of Pain: Trauma and the Healing Power of Writing." *JAEPL: Journal of the Assembly for Expanded Perspectives on Learning* 5 (1999–2000): 14–24.

Vygotsky, Lev. *Thought and Language.* Ed. and Trans. E. Hanfmann and G. Vakar. Cambridge, MA: MIT P, 1962.

Waddell, Dave. "When a Student Ends a Wounded Silence." *JAEPL: Journal of the Assembly for Expanded Perspectives on Learning* 4 (1998–99): 61–70.

"Web Pages by Language." 21 July 01 <http://cyberatlas.internet.com/big-picture/demographics/article/0,1323,5901_408521,00.html>.

Welch, Kathleen. *Electronic Rhetoric: Classical Rhetoric, Oralism, and New Literacy.* Cambridge, MA: MIT P, 1999.

Witte, Stephen. "Context, Text, Intertext: Toward a Constructivist Semiotic of Writing." *Written Communication* 9 (1992): 237–308.

Woolf, Virginia. *A Room of One's Own.* San Diego: Harcourt, 1929.

Worthman, Christopher. "The World Through Different Eyes: Mental Imagery, Writing, and the Reconceptualization of the Self and Other." Fleckenstein, Calendrillo, and Worley 85–102.

Yaeger, Patricia. *Honey-Made Women: Emancipatory Strategies in Women's Writing.* New York: Columbia UP, 1988.

Yates, Frances A. *The Art of Memory.* London: Routledge, 1966.

Zandy, Janet. Introduction. *Calling Home: Working-Class Women's Writings.* Ed. Janet Zandy. New Brunswick, NJ: Rutgers UP, 1993. 1–13.

———, ed. *Liberating Memory: Our Work and Our Working-Class Consciousness.* New Brunswick, NJ: Rutgers UP, 1995.

Index

KRISTIE S. FLECKENSTEIN is an associate professor of English at Ball State University, where she teaches graduate and undergraduate courses in rhetoric and composition. Her essays have appeared in *College English, JAC, Rhetoric Review,* and *College Composition and Communication.* She is a coeditor of *JAEPL, Journal of the Assembly for Expanded Perspectives on Learning* and a coeditor of *Language and Image in the Reading-Writing Classroom: Teaching Vision* (2002).

Studies in Writing & Rhetoric

In 1980 the Conference on College Composition and Communication established the Studies in Writing & Rhetoric (SWR) series as a forum for monograph-length arguments or presentations that engage general compositionists. SWR encourages extended essays or research reports addressing any issue in composition and rhetoric from any theoretical or research perspective as long as the general significance to the field is clear. Previous SWR publications serve as models for prospective authors; in addition, contributors may propose alternate formats and agendas that inform or extend the field's current debates.

SWR is particularly interested in projects that connect the specific research site or theoretical framework to contemporary classroom and institutional contexts of direct concern to compositionists across the nation. Such connections may come from several approaches, including cultural, theoretical, field-based, gendered, historical, and interdisciplinary. SWR especially encourages monographs by scholars early in their careers, by established scholars who wish to share an insight or exhortation with the field, and by scholars of color.

The SWR series editor and editorial board members are committed to working closely with prospective authors and offering significant developmental advice for encouraged manuscripts and prospectuses. Editorships rotate every five years. Prospective authors intending to submit a prospectus during the 2002 to 2007 editorial appointment should obtain submission guidelines from Robert Brooke, SWR editor, University of Nebraska–Lincoln, Department of English, P.O. Box 880337, 202 Andrews Hall, Lincoln, NE 68588-0337.

General inquiries may also be addressed to Sponsoring Editor, Studies in Writing & Rhetoric, Southern Illinois University Press, P.O. Box 3697, Carbondale, IL 62902-3697.